Oracle Application Express Administration

For DBAs and Developers

Francis Mignault
Luc Demanche

⟨IOUG⟩
Independent oracle users group

Apress®

Oracle Application Express Administration: For DBAs and Developers

Francis Mignault
Insum Solutions,
Montréal, Québec, Canada

Luc Demanche
Montréal, Québec,
Canada

ISBN-13 (pbk): 978-1-4842-1957-7
DOI 10.1007/978-1-4842-1958-4

ISBN-13 (electronic): 978-1-4842-1958-4

Library of Congress Control Number: 2016955456

Managing Director: Welmoed Spahr
Lead Editor: Jonathan Gennick
Development Editor: Laura Berendson
Technical Reviewer: Alex Fatkulin
Editorial Board: Steve Anglin, Pramila Balan, Laura Berendson, Aaron Black, Louise Corrigan,
    Jonathan Gennick, Todd Green, Robert Hutchinson, Celestin Suresh John, Nikhil Karkal,
    James Markham, Susan McDermott, Matthew Moodie, Natalie Pao, Gwenan Spearing
Coordinating Editor: Jill Balzano
Copy Editor: Brendan Frost
Compositor: SPi Global
Indexer: SPi Global
Artist: SPi Global

Distributed to the book trade worldwide by Springer Science+Business Media New York, 233 Spring Street, 6th Floor, New York, NY 10013. Phone 1-800-SPRINGER, fax (201) 348-4505, e-mail orders-ny@springer-sbm.com, or visit www.springer.com. Apress Media, LLC is a California LLC and the sole member (owner) is Springer Science + Business Media Finance Inc (SSBM Finance Inc). SSBM Finance Inc is a **Delaware** corporation.

For information on translations, please e-mail rights@apress.com, or visit www.apress.com.

Apress and friends of ED books may be purchased in bulk for academic, corporate, or promotional use. eBook versions and licenses are also available for most titles. For more information, reference our Special Bulk Sales–eBook Licensing web page at www.apress.com/bulk-sales.

Any source code or other supplementary materials referenced by the author in this text are available to readers at www.apress.com. For detailed information about how to locate your book's source code, go to www.apress.com/source-code/. Readers can also access source code at SpringerLink in the Supplementary Material section for each chapter.

Printed on acid-free paper

Contents at a Glance

Contents

About IOUG Press

*IOUG Press is a joint effort by the **Independent Oracle Users Group (the IOUG)** and **Apress** to deliver some of the highest-quality content possible on Oracle Database and related topics. The IOUG is the world's leading, independent organization for professional users of Oracle products. Apress is a leading, independent technical publisher known for developing high-quality, no-fluff content for serious technology professionals. The IOUG and Apress have joined forces in IOUG Press to provide the best content and publishing opportunities to working professionals who use Oracle products.*

Our shared goals include:

- Developing content with excellence
- Helping working professionals to succeed
- Providing authoring and reviewing opportunities
- Networking and raising the profiles of authors and readers

To learn more about Apress, visit our website at **www.apress.com**. Follow the link for IOUG Press to see the great content that is now available on a wide range of topics that matter to those in Oracle's technology sphere.

Visit **www.ioug.org** to learn more about the Independent Oracle Users Group and its mission. Consider joining if you haven't already. Review the many benefits at www.ioug.org/join. Become a member. Get involved with peers. Boost your career.

www.ioug.org/join

Apress®

About the Authors

Francis Mignault has over 30 years of experience in IT and 28 using Oracle databases. In 2004, he started using Oracle Application Express and hasn't looked back since. In 2002, he cofounded Insum Solutions, where he currently holds the role of Chief Technology Officer (CTO). He has presented at several conferences in the United States, Canada, and Europe, including Oracle OpenWorld, IOUG Collaborate, ODTUG APEXposed!, Kscope, APEX World, and Ora*Gec. Francis is an Oracle ACE and coauthor of Expert Oracle Application Express.

Luc Demanche has specialized in Oracle databases since 1995, and is an Oracle 12c Certified Professional.

He has worked with major consulting companies in Canada, as well as with a major bank in France; he also had the opportunity to design Oracle infrastructures for large projects, including APEX deployment. Luc truly shows great enthusiasm in any activity he engages in, whether it is sharing his Oracle knowledge, playing hockey, or spending time with his family and friends.

About the Technical Reviewer

Alex Fatkulin is a master of the full range of Oracle technologies. His mastery has been essential in addressing some of the greatest challenges his customers have met.

Alex draws on years of experience working with some of the world's largest companies, where he has been involved with almost everything related to Oracle databases, from data modeling to architecting high-availability solutions to resolving performance issues of extremely large production sites.

Alex has a bachelor's of computer science degree from Far Eastern National University in Vladivostok, Russia. He is also an Oracle ACE and a proud OakTable member.

Acknowledgments

Many hours were invested on this project and it would not have been possible without the help of many people. First of all, we would like to thank Jonathan Gennick from Apress for giving us the opportunity of writing this book. A special thanks to Jill Balzano and all the Apress team for their great work, encouragement, and patience.

A big thank-you to Insum, and more specifically to Corina Nunez, Daniel Boudreault, and Sylvain Martel, for their input, technical help, and support.

—Luc Demanche and Francis Mignault.

Personally, I would like to thank Francis Mignault, the initiator of that project, for giving me the opportunity of writing this book with him. It has been a pleasure working with you on this project, and I hope we will have the opportunity to work on other projects like this one together again.

It is very important for me to also mention the support, patience, and understanding of my family, my kids, and my love Marie-Eve.

—Luc Demanche.

Thank you, Luc Demanche, for your hard work and willingness to participate in this project. Thanks to my colleagues Michel St-Amour, Patrick Bonneville, and Roger Leblanc for your understanding and for believing in us. A special thank-you to Viviane Latourelle, my partner in life, for your support, for your patience, and for being there for me. Without your support this would not have been possible.

—Francis Mignault.

Introduction

Oracle Application Express (APEX) is a web application development tool that enables developers to rapidly design and develop database-driven web applications by using a browser. One of the advantages of using APEX is that you can focus on the development of the application and not have to worry about availability, authentication, security, and management of the session's context as it runs as a part of the Oracle Database. Not to mention that APEX is fully supported by Oracle, and it comes with no extra cost and fully integrated with the database.

We think that database administrators (DBAs), APEX administrators, and developers would like to gain understanding of how APEX infrastructure works. Today's trend is all about DevOps and sharing the knowledge between administrators and developers.

We also noticed there was a lack of documentation covering the integration and use of database features with APEX applications.

Our objective is to show how APEX, as a database-driven application, is pretty well placed to benefit from and efficiently use all the database features. We also wanted to demystify the management of APEX and explain its integration with the database. Many clients have been asking the same questions about the administration of APEX. It is with this mindset that the book was written.

We will discuss and demonstrate how an APEX application can:

- be highly available by using Real Application Cluster (RAC) and Data Guard,
- have its data secured by using Real Application Security (RAS) and Data Redaction,
- be flexible, as APEX can be deployed using a multitenant database,
- have better response times by monitoring and tuning, by using database features like AWR, ADDM, Oracle Enterprise Manager, and SQLDeveloper,
- be controlled for resource consumption by using Oracle Resource Manager, and much more.

The book is divided into four parts:

Part I:

The first part of the book is an introduction to APEX, starting with its history, a list of its key features, and a presentation of the Application Builder interface. We explain how APEX runs entirely within the Oracle database.

Part II:

The second part of the book describes the APEX architecture, how APEX interacts with the database, and which middle-tiers are supported for either a small or an enterprise-grade deployment.

There is a chapter dedicated to data security where we explain how Real Application Security and Data Redaction can be integrated with APEX.

We will also talk about how APEX can be configured for building extensions in Oracle E-Business Suite.

These days, high availability is a very important concept, so we will demonstrate in this book how APEX applications can benefit from two of the most important features of the Oracle database: Real Application Clusters and Oracle Data Guard.

The last chapter of part II is about the deployment of APEX in an Oracle 12c multitenant database.

We describe different scenarios for moving and/or copying a pluggable database, which might or might not contain an APEX installation, into a container database that might or might not have APEX installed.

Part III:

The third part of the book covers every aspect of the installation, upgrade, patching, and setup of an optimal APEX environment.

It also includes the management of APEX in runtime mode as well as an explanation of how we should configure the backups for a database that runs APEX. It covers how to back up the APEX components, applications, and database.

The last chapter of this part explains how to use and configure the workspaces' self-provisioning feature.

Part IV:

The last part of the book presents different methods for monitoring and tuning an APEX application and how we can use the database features to help from the application performance point of view.

The first chapter of this part talks about how we can monitor an APEX application to identify queries that are abnormally consuming resources and that could benefit from a tuning process. There is also a dedicated chapter on tuning.

The last chapter of part IV is about Oracle Resource Manager. This is a very powerful database feature that can and should be used with APEX to ensure an application's optimal usage of resources and avoid database downtime caused by users' long-running DMLs.

PART I

■ ■ ■

APEX Overview

CHAPTER 1

About APEX

This book is oriented toward the administration of APEX. There is a possibility that you may be responsible for administering and managing the installation, but you do not really know what APEX is about. If you are new to APEX and wondering what it is and what it can do, this chapter is for you.

Unfortunately, many people do not know what APEX is or what it does. Oracle offers so many different tools that people sometimes mix them up.

Keep in mind that the goal of this chapter is to give an overview of the product and not document it in detail. The targeted audience is mostly administrators, but I think it is still important to understand what we are working with. First we will briefly explain what APEX is, where it is coming from, and what it can be used for. Then we will give some pointers on where to find more information, and how to get connected with the APEX community.

What Is APEX?

APEX is an abbreviation for Oracle Application Express. It was initially named Oracle HTML DB. It is a browser-based application development framework used for rapid web application development (RAD).

APEX runs on an Oracle database and is fully supported. It comes with the Oracle database at no additional cost, and works with all Oracle database editions.

It can be used to build complex enterprise web applications that will run in a web browser, and can use the latest features and functionalities available with modern web development.

History

APEX was created by Mike Hichwa and Joel Kallman based on their experience with building and using Oracle WebDB. Initially there was an internal project at Oracle called Flow that was later renamed Project Marvel, which was then officially released as HTMLDB 1.5 in 2004. HTMLDB was renamed to Oracle Application Express (APEX) in 2006.

It has been greatly improved since the first release and has always followed industry trends. As shown in Figure 1-1, APEX now supports the latest in web development. It allows the use of modern technologies like mobile, responsive design, and HTML5.

APEX 5.0 pushed it even further by creating a new page designer (PD) that is a modern and entirely web-based Integrated Development Environment (IDE). Moreover APEX 5.1 introduced a new interactive grid, declarative master detail, and Oracle Jet charts.

One of the key features, still very popular today, is the Interactive Reports released with APEX 3.1 in 2008.

F. Mignault and L. Demanche, *Oracle Application Express Administration*, DOI 10.1007/978-1-4842-1958-4_1

Figure 1-1 shows only key features for each version of APEX, but many other improvements have also been delivered each time.

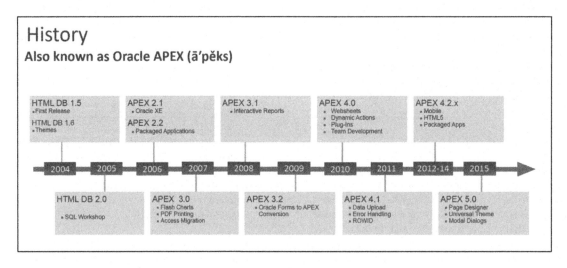

Figure 1-1. *APEX history*

The Oracle APEX team has grown over time and is now made up of a group of very talented people. They are very close to the developers' community and make sure that new releases are in line with the industry. There is also a constant effort to improve the security options available for the builder and for end-user applications.

List of Key Features for Applications

Using Oracle Application Express, it is possible to create modern web applications. Some of the key features that can be used are as follows:

- Interactive reporting
- Web forms
- Charting
- PDF printing
- Web services
- Page validations
- Multilingual applications
- Spreadsheet upload and download
- Session state management
- Modern user interface (UI)
- Upload file support
- Security and protection against SQL injection, URL tampering, and cross-site scripting

- Use of plug-ins to extend application functionalities

- Multiple item types like calendars, drop-down lists, checkboxes, passwords, text area, and so on.

- Authentication schemes

- Authorization schemes

- Mobile applications

- Responsive design themes

- Computations

- Interactive reports

- Session state management

- Conditional processing

Builder Features

APEX is a web application development tool where coding is declarative, but other features are also available in the builder. In fact, as shown in Figure 1-2, the builder includes the following features:

- Application Builder

- SQL Workshop

- Team Development

- Packaged Apps

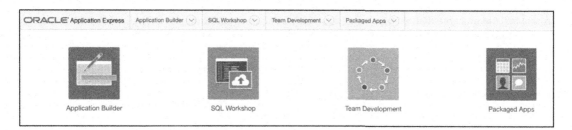

Figure 1-2. *APEX main features*

Application Builder

The Application Builder is used to build and maintain APEX applications.

It is possible to create not only desktop applications but also mobile applications. They can either be accessible on either multiple mobile devices from the browser, or use the responsive design available by default with the APEX universal theme.

The builder PD allows RAD by using drag-and-drop features and multiple object property modifications.

For UI, there is a tool called the theme roller that allows a developer to apply visual changes to the CSS of the application in real time.

It is also possible to create websheet applications. Websheets are APEX applications that can be created by superusers or nondevelopers with minimal knowledge of PLSQL. It uses a Wiki approach and makes it easy to rapidly and declaratively create applications to exploit data in the database. For more detail on websheets, see *http://www.oracle.com/technetwork/developer-tools/apex/application-express/more-websheets-154798.html*.

SQL Workshop

Creating applications often requires manipulating database objects. In the SQL Workshop section, different tools are available to manage database objects in the schemas associated with the workspace, as shown in Figure 1-3.

Figure 1-3. SQL Workshop tools

The object browser can be used to generate queries using a graphical interface, or it can also be used to browse all the objects of the schemas associated to the workspace and manage them.

SQL Commands is a SQL*Plus-like web interface to access the database.

One can manage SQL scripts, run, and store them in the database using the SQL Scripts tool. There is a SQL editor available in the browser that allows auto complete, undo, redo, and code highlighting.

In the Utilities section, there are different tools to manipulate data in the schema, like uploading data from a text file or a spreadsheet using the Data Workshop, and generating the DDL of database objects. See Figure 1-4 for a complete list.

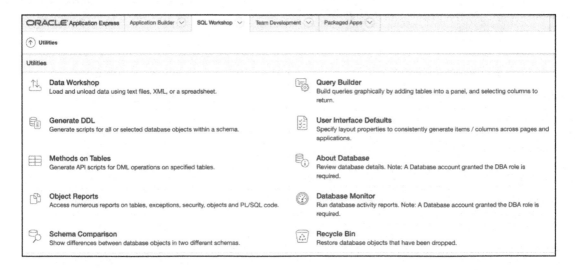

Figure 1-4. SQL Workshop utilities

SQL Workshop is also where you can create and manage web services using the RESTful services option served via Oracle Rest Data Services (ORDS).

Team Development

This section can be used to help a team of APEX developers manage application development. It is possible to link this section with applications so that end users can provide feedback directly from a running application. The team can then set milestones; define change requests as features, to-dos, or bugs; and manage the end-user feedbacks. See Figure 1-5.

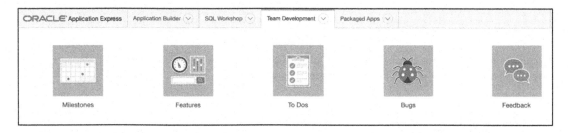

Figure 1-5. *Team Development*

Packaged Apps

APEX comes with a set of 36 packaged applications. Some are sample applications while some are real productive applications that can be used in real-life situations. They are supported by Oracle, and if they are not unlocked they will be automatically upgraded with every release of APEX.

For example, you could use the Survey Builder packaged application to create surveys for your company, or use the project tracking application to manage your projects.

They can also be used to learn and understand how certain options and features work. It is possible to unlock them and have access to the code of every component in the packaged application.

Specific Characteristics

What makes APEX different from other web application development tools is that it is a 100% browser-based tool. There is no client software required at all. The only requirement is to have a browser installed.

Everything is stored in the database. The applications' definitions are stored in the database as metadata, and there is no compilation required when an application is created or modified.

Because of this database-centric architecture, it is easy to manage and deploy. This makes it ideal for data-driven applications, since applications literally sit right next to the data.

Development / Deployment Options

APEX applications can run in any Oracle database edition (XE, SE, EE), and there are export and import options to deploy applications.

As mentioned before, because of the database-centric architecture, APEX applications can seamlessly be run locally, on enterprise servers, or on the cloud. It is also very simple to move from one to the other. For example, an application developed locally could then be imported directly to the cloud.

Locally

It is possible to run APEX on a desktop or laptop using Oracle Express (XE) or any other edition of the database.

On-Premise Enterprise Servers

The IT department can install APEX on the enterprise servers and allow self-service for workspaces to employees and use it as a private cloud. Or it could be managed by the IT department and offer the multitude of capabilities that APEX can offer to end users in the company.

Cloud

Of course, the cloud can also be used to leverage fast application development, prototyping, user acceptance test, or training without the need for new hardware at low cost.

APEX Administration

Once again, one of APEX's main advantages is the fact that it is part of the database and it uses the Oracle database functionalities.

Administering a database that has APEX installed is the same as administering any other Oracle database. APEX is installed in a schema that uses tablespaces, and contains standard database objects like tables, indexes, triggers, sequences, and packages.

As you will see throughout this book, because of its simple architecture, APEX is easy to maintain, install, and upgrade.

Why APEX?

There are many good reasons to use APEX. Here is a list of the ones that we think are the most important:

- It improves delivery time of fully functional applications.
- It is the perfect development tool for developers with SQL skills.
- It is secure and scalable, because it uses the Oracle database's strength.
- It is aligned with industry trends, and that is true for every releases of APEX.
- It is a no-cost option of the database.
- It is cloud-enabled and ready.
- The community is great, and there is a lot of documentation, books, and blogs available.

What Is It For?

Although APEX is often seen as a departmental application development tool, and as a replacement to Microsoft Access and Excel, it is now also commonly used for major enterprise mission-critical applications. Oracle even uses it for its own public applications, mainly for the cloud, but also for selling their products at *shop.oracle.com.*

It is the perfect tool for Oracle Forms modernization, especially with the declarative master detail feature, and the interactive grid features of APEX 5.1

APEX is an official and supported tool for extending Oracle E-Business Suite. Because of its ability to easily manage database data, it can also be used to extend any ERP like SAP, Peoplesoft, JD Edwards, and others.

It can also be a great complement to BI applications by using the charting and interactive report functionalities.

The APEX Community

The APEX community is very active and is there to help others in their day-to-day usage of the tool.

APEX.ORACLE.COM

The best place to start with is *APEX.ORACLE.COM/community*. It is where you will find information about the APEX community, including hosting companies, books, and more, as shown in Figure 1-6. The links section contains a nice list of APEX-related blogs. This is another good place to start learning as well as meeting the APEX community.

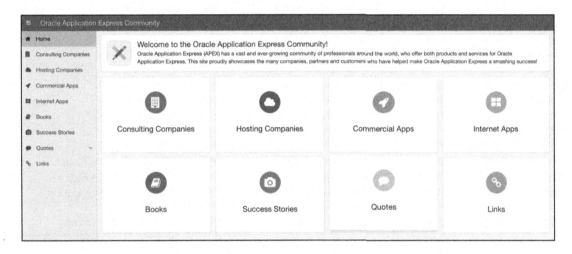

Figure 1-6. *APEX.ORACLE.COM/community*

OTN

There is an APEX section on the Oracle Technology Network (OTN) at *OTN.ORACLE.COM/APEX*. This is where you will find the Oracle APEX forum under the community tab, among other things. The Oracle APEX forum is one of the most active forums at Oracle, and it is common for the APEX development team to provide answers directly to the developers.

APEX.WORLD

To exchange with the community, go to *APEX.WORLD*; there you can download application plug-ins, get news from the community, and discuss with other APEX developers in a dedicated Slack account.

Oracle User Groups

Another great way of getting connected with the community is by joining an Oracle user group. There are many user groups across the world. One user group very active with the APEX community is the Oracle Development Tool User Group (*ODTUG*). Some of their sections on their site are dedicated to APEX, and they also host a yearly conference called KScope where there is a dedicated track for APEX sessions.

LinkedIn

The LinkedIn community is a good place to exchange and start a conversation on APEX topics. There are many LinkedIn groups for APEX, but there is only one official group, called Oracle Application Express (APEX) – The Official Group, *https://www.linkedin.com/groups/8263065*.

Meetups

To meet other people that are part of the APEX community, check your local APEX meetup. This is a nice place to network and learn about APEX. There a many APEX meetups around the world. To see all the existing meetups and to register go to *apexmeetups.com* or www.meetup.com and search for *orclapex*. If there is no APEX meetup group in your area, you are more than welcome to start one.

Twitter

Finally, you can go on Twitter and follow the hashtag *#orclapex* for live interactions with the APEX community.

Summary

APEX is a database-centric development tool; the applications, workspaces, and other APEX-related information are stored in the database as metadata. It makes it easy to use and deploy. Not only is it a great tool for small departmental desktop applications, but it is also good for enterprise mission-critical applications since it is using the Oracle database features and capabilities.

Above all, there is a wealth of information available on the Internet and a very active community.

In the next chapter, we will cover in detail how APEX interacts with the database.

PART II

■ ■ ■

Architecture

CHAPTER 2

APEX in the Database

Installing APEX is essentially creating database schemas and creating database objects like packages, views, tables, trigger, sequences, and indexes. APEX is a database-driven application that is built using the PL/SQL Oracle web toolkit; in fact, APEX is built using APEX.

From an administrator point of view, it is interesting to see what schemas are required for APEX to work. It is also interesting to understand how applications execute, connect to, and use the database. Like any other tool that uses an Oracle database, there is a database schema used to store the application data and to store business logic using database packages.

Because APEX is essentially made of database objects and packages, it runs in all the different editions of the database: Enterprise Edition (EE), Standard Edition (SE, SE1, SE2), and Oracle Express (XE). It is also easy to maintain since it does not require any new knowledge as far as the database is concerned.

In the first sections of this chapter, we will talk about the APEX database schemas and also explain how the connection to the database works.

We will talk about the notion of workspaces in APEX and how database schemas are assigned to applications. There is a section on scheduled database jobs that are created when APEX is installed and a section on Oracle support explaining how support works for APEX.

Finally, we will talk about the different cloud offerings that are supported by Oracle for running Oracle Application Express.

Database Schemas

APEX requires three database schemas to work. They are created during the installation process as explained in Chapter 8.

Those database schemas are as follows:

- APEX_PUBLIC_USER

- FLOWS_FILES

- APEX_050000

APEX_PUBLIC_USER

The APEX_PUBLIC_USER database user is used for the connections to the database and to execute APEX applications. For security reasons, the minimal database privileges given automatically at creation should be the only ones granted to this user at all times. In APEX 5.0 these are as follows: Create Session and Select, Insert, Update, delete on WWV_FLOW_FILE_OBJECTS$. Of course, everything granted to PUBLIC is also available to this user.

© Francis Mignault and Luc Demanche 2016
F. Mignault and L. Demanche, *Oracle Application Express Administration*, DOI 10.1007/978-1-4842-1958-4_2

APEX_PUBLIC_USER needs to be unlocked at all times for APEX and applications to be able to run. As explained in the "**APEX Database Sessions**" section later in this chapter, the database connections are made using this user and then the application is executed dynamically using dynamic sql in the application schema.

Make sure that if you change the password of this user that you also change the ORDS configuration accordingly.

FLOWS_FILES

This schema is the owner of a table called WWV_FLOW_FILE_OBJECTS$. This table is used when there is a file upload in APEX or in an application. When files are uploaded, they get temporarily stored in that table before being copied to its appropriate table. The rows in WWV_FLOW_FILE_OBJECT$ are marked as temporary when a file is uploaded and it gets deleted later.

There is a database-scheduled job called ORACLE_APEX_PURGE_SESSIONS that will clean this table for sessions that need to be purged. If you have been using APEX for a while, some old APEX applications might still be using this table to store files. Be careful if you delete rows in that table. It is possible to link the files to a session of a workspace using the SESSION_ID column or the SECURITY_ID column.

An APEX view called APEX_APPLICATION_TEMP_FILE can be used to see the different files that are stored in WWV_FLOW_FILE_OBJECTS$ contextually to a workspace. It replaces the WWV_FLOW_FILES view.

This schema is locked at creation and should stay locked at all times. The password of this schema can be changed at any time and does not have any impact on the APEX engine. It is possible to use a specific tablespace for this owner and table when running the installation script. See Chapters 8 and 9 for more detail on this.

APEX_050000

This schema is where the APEX engine and metadata are stored. As mentioned in the introduction of this chapter, APEX is a collection of database objects in the database. The APEX engine and application pages are being generated dynamically each time they are requested. To execute APEX, a specific URL has to be used and will be in the form of http://<hostname>/ords/f?p=<appid>:<pageid>. The APEX database function "f" called in this URL reads the metadata and dynamically generates the required HTML page with all the necessary components.

The name of the schema contains the APEX version number and is unique per APEX main versions. For example APEX_040200 is for storing the engine and metadata of APEX 4.2 and APEX_050000 is for APEX 5.0. As mentioned in Chapter 9, the first two position of the version of APEX are the major release and the minor release. For example, 5.1.2.03.04 means it is the major release 5 and minor release 1. The other last numbers, 03 and 04, refers to patches and fixes.

When an Oracle database instance is created, it is possible that the APEX schema gets created automatically. Starting from Oracle 10G up to 12C APEX is automatically included with the database binaries. The APEX version that comes with the database binaries is not the latest since the releases of APEX are more frequent than the database releases. See the chapter 8 on installation and the chapter 9 on upgrades for more information on how to install the latest version of APEX.

This schema is locked at creation and should stay locked at all times. The password of this schema can be changed at any time and does not have any impact on the APEX engine.

APEX Views

Since all the information regarding APEX workspaces, applications, users, and so on are stored in a metadata, it is also possible to access a wealth of information via the APEX views. Those views can be queried to gather all kinds of information about workspaces, users, applications, and more.

This can be useful for many different things such as impact analysis, performance tuning, and quality control.

We use those views a lot during the testing phase when APEX is upgraded, for identifying all the applications that need to be modified if a specific piece of code is causing an issue. The APEX views are very useful in a runtime-only installation as well.

They can be used within your APEX applications and interactive reports make it even easier to retrieve and search information from them.

APEX views are accessible in the database using sqlplus, sqldeveloper, sqlcl, or any other database tools. They are also available in the APEX builder. Go to Application Builder, Workspace Utilities, Application Express Views to have access to a built-in interactive report that lists all the APEX views and a description, as shown in Figure 2-1. Using the "Tree View" tab as demonstrated in Figure 2-2, they will be listed in a tree view based on their dependencies.

Figure 2-1. *APEX views in workspace utilities*

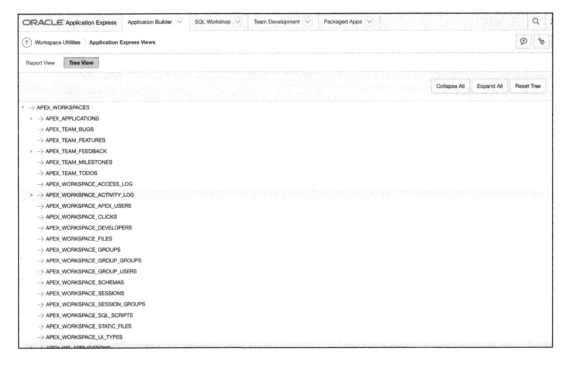

Figure 2-2. *APEX views listed in a tree view*

To see all the APEX views available, there is a view called `APEX_DICTIONARY`.

For example, in APEX 5.0, to see all the 130 available views you can run the following query:

```
select distinct apex_view_name from APEX_DICTIONARY order by 1;
```

Queries on the APEX Views Examples

Let's say that you are wondering what all the locked pages of all the applications in all the workspaces for a particular user are. The following query would answer this question:

```
select workspace_display_name
     ,application_id
     ,page_id
     ,locked_by
     ,locked_on
from apex_application_locked_pages
```

WORKSPACE_	APPLICATION_ID	PAGE_ID	LOCKED_BY	LOCKED_ON
DEMO	100	1	ADMIN	08-JUN-16
DEMO	100	2	ADMIN	08-JUN-16

Here are some other examples of APEX view queries:

Select all the shared List Of Values that does not have an "order by" clause:

```
select application_id
      ,list_of_values_name
      ,list_of_values_query
from APEX_APPLICATION_LOVS
where upper(lov_type) = 'DYNAMIC'
 and  instr(upper(list_of_values_query),'ORDER BY') = 0
 and  application_id = 100 ;
```

```
APPLICATION_ID LIST_OF_VALUES_NAME      LIST_OF_VALUES_QUERY
-------------- ------------------------ ------------------------------------
           100 PRODUCTS                 select product_name d, product_id r
                                        from demo_product_info
```

Select all the applications and show their workspace name, application ID, application name and current authentication scheme:

```
select workspace
      ,application_id appid
      ,application_name name
      ,authentication_scheme auth
from APEX_APPLICATIONS
order by 1,2 ;
```

```
WORKSPACE  APPID NAME                          AUTH
---------- ------ ----------------------------- -------------------------------
DEMO         100  Sample Database Application   Application Express Accounts
DEMO         111  Sample Charts                 Application Express Accounts
DEMO         112  File Upload Demo              Application Express Authentication
DEMO         121  Data Reporter                 Application Express
DEMO         124  test1                         Application Express Authentication
DEMO         125  TEST2                         Application Express Authentication
DEMO         129  demo1                         Application Express Authentication
FM           128  Sample Database Application   Application Express Accounts
FM           130  My Sample Application         Application Express Accounts
FM2          136  Universal Theme Sample App    Application Express Accounts
FM4          131  Sample Database Application   Application Express Accounts
```

Select the workspace ID and the number or associated schemas:

```
select workspace
      ,workspace_id
      ,schemas
from APEX_WORKSPACES
```

```
WORKSPACE                                  WORKSPACE_ID         SCHEMAS
------------------------------------------ -------------------  -------
DEMO                                       3201226568081376     1
FM                                         4751176150785001     1
FM2                                        8411926900287889     3
FM4                                        8413503886353821     1
```

Select the workspace name, the name of the associated schemas and the date and time it was created:

```
select workspace_name
    ,schema
    ,to_char(schema_created,'YYYY/MM/DD HH24:MI:SS') schema_created
from APEX_WORKSPACE_SCHEMAS
order by 1,2;
```

```
WORKSPACE_NAME                      SCHEMA       SCHEMA_CREATED
----------------------------------- ----------   -------------------
DEMO                                DEMO         2014/01/22 16:05:41
FM                                  FM           2016/01/24 14:08:47
FM2                                 FM           2016/01/24 14:08:47
                                    FM2          2016/01/28 11:55:44
                                    TEST         2016/02/16 07:12:38
FM4                                 FM4          2016/01/28 12:06:43
```

Application Schemas

As with most Oracle database applications, an application schema has to be created to store the application data and business logic using tables, packages, and so on.

Each APEX application is associated to one and only one database schema defined in the application properties.

The application schema is never accessed directly so it can be locked at all times. Changing the password on the application schema does not impact the APEX engine.

If the application has to execute or access other database objects in other schemas, simply use database grants to give it the required privileges. Since the application runs inside the database and is accessing the application schema, it is possible to use any database options and functionalities in the database like database links, DBMS packages, Oracle Text, and Advanced Security. In the next section about APEX database sessions, there is more information about the relation between the APEX schema, the application schema, and the database sessions.

APEX Database Sessions

This section explains how an APEX application is executed. Having the database accessed for running applications concerns many people. This is done in a very secure manner and the connection is never made directly using the application schema.

Application Execution

The web listener, in this example ORDS, will connect to the database via the database user APEX_PUBLIC_USER and use one of the database connections from the connection pool initiated when ORDS is started.

The f function called from the URL of the browser will then be executed in the database and will call APEX packages in the APEX schema APEX_050000. The metadata will be read to generate the application page. Then, the SYS.DBMS_SYS_SQL internal Oracle package will be used to dynamically execute the application SQL calls in the application schema. Once the page is generated, it will then be sent back to the browser. See the graphical representation of this in Figure 2-3.

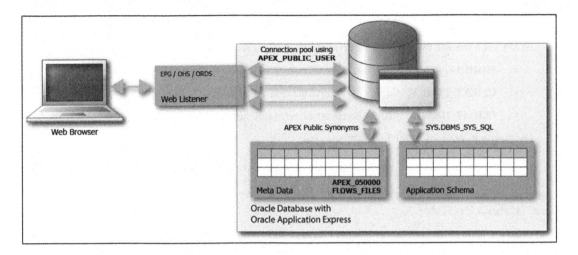

Figure 2-3. *APEX schemas and application execution*

All of these steps have been carefully designed by Oracle so that the access to the database schemas is secured. Performance has also been taken into account, and the overhead of these calls is very minimal on the execution of the application.

Connection Pool

When the ORDS web listener is started, a set of database connections is made, depending on the ORDS configuration, and creates a connection pool to the database as shown in Figure 2-3. Those database sessions are by default inactive. When an APEX page is requested, then one of the database connections from the connection pool is used to generate the page. Once the page has been rendered, the database session is not used anymore and becomes inactive.

This means that the same application user can use different Oracle database sessions for the same APEX application even within the same APEX session.

In order to keep track of an application session and to store the session information, Oracle Application Express saves the session state in database tables. This is what we call stateless sessions. These tables are stored in the APEX_050000 schema. This method is more secure because the session state is stored on the server side instead of the client. It is possible to encrypt the APEX session state in the database by setting the attribute "store value encrypted in session state" to yes at the item level in the application. This can be done by the developer in the page item properties.

Since the database connection is only used for the rendering of the page, this means that even if someone leaves a page open for a long time, there will be no activity generated in the database. This allows other pages to access the database sessions and at the same time allows more application users to run the application. This is one of the reasons why APEX can scale so much and allows a large number of application users.

v$session

When we look at v$session in the database we see a lot of sessions for the APEX_PUBLIC_USER user. Those are the database sessions used by the connection pool.

19

In order to facilitate the monitoring of its sessions, APEX has been instrumented to set the module, client_info, and client_identifier with information related to the APEX application using the database session.

In APEX 5.0 you will find the following information in those columns:

- **MODULE**: Parsing database user /APEX:APP Application ID:Page ID

- **CLIENT_INFO**: Workspace ID : authenticated username :

- **CLIENT_IDENTIFIER**: Authenticated username : session ID

For example, let's look at the following query:

```
select sid, module, client_info, client_identifier, status
from   v$session
where username = 'APEX_PUBLIC_USER'
 and   status = 'ACTIVE';
```

```
SID MODULE                          CLIENT_INFO            CLIENT_IDENTIFIER
--- ------------------------------  ---------------------  --------------------
53  APEX_050000/APEX:APP 4500:1204  3201226568081376:ADMIN ADMIN:27135994032614
```

Here we can see that there is an active APEX session running in the database.

The MODULE indicates that the schema APEX_050000 using the application 4500 in page 1204 is being accessed.

The CLIENT_INFO shows that the workspace ID for that specific application is 3201226568081376. By querying the APEX_WORKSPACES view, it is possible to find out more information about this workspace.

The CLIENT_IDENTIFIER indicates that the APEX session id is 27135994032614.

For more information on monitoring APEX sessions, see Chapter 14.

APEX Workspaces

APEX applications are developed in an area called a workspace. Each workspace has an administrator user and can have developer users and runtime users.

A developer from one workspace cannot access the applications from another workspace. This allows grouping of applications for development. We could have a dedicated workspace for each business units. For example we could have one for human resources applications and another one for sales. This way, all the applications related to HR will be in the same workspace and will make it easier to maintain.

A workspace will have one primary database schema assigned and can have many secondary database schemas assigned. The developers of one workspace will only see and have access to the schemas assigned to that workspace.

Applications can only be assigned one database schema, which has to be part of the assigned workspace schemas. An application ID is unique to an APEX instance, that is, for the entire APEX installation in a database instance. For example and as shown in Figure 2-4, application App 1 is unique across all workspaces and cannot exist anywhere else. It is possible to have a copy of an application but it must have a different application ID.

Figure 2-4 shows the relationships between APEX users, applications, and database schemas assigned to the workspaces.

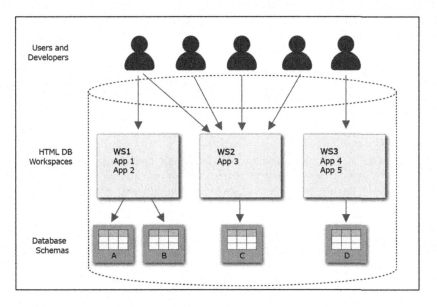

Figure 2-4. *APEX workspaces*

There is a special workspace called "internal." This workspace is used for configuring the APEX installation. The ADMIN user of that workspace is created during the installation and the password is also configured during the post-installation steps.

For more information about the "internal" workspace and to learn more on managing workspaces, see Chapter 10.

APEX Users

What we call APEX users are in fact workspace users. As mentioned before, each workspace has at least one admin user and can have many developer users and runtime user accounts.

Admin users can create other accounts and have access to more utilities to manage the workspace.

Developer users can create and maintain applications and access the other tools of the builder.

Runtime users are user accounts that are not administrator and are not developers. These users are usually created to access end-user applications.

By default, when an application is created, the authentication scheme will be based on APEX users and will allow logging in using APEX user credentials of that application's workspace. This can later be changed in the shared components of the application.

See Chapter 10 for more information on how to manage APEX users.

Application Users

When people are first introduced to APEX, they often mix up database users and application users. In Oracle Forms, the user used to connect to an application is usually an Oracle database user. With Oracle Application Express, the application user is not a database user. It is however possible to authenticate application users in different ways. Authentication is the process by which the username and password is validated. The authentication process can be configured to use an LDAP repository, the Oracle database users, APEX users, or any other solutions. For more information on authentication, see the APEX documentation development guide.

21

As explained earlier, the database connection is not using the application user. APEX is working in the same way as any other three-tier web application.

Scheduled Jobs

During the installation process, some Oracle database scheduled jobs are created.

Here is the list of those database scheduled jobs related to APEX:

ORACLE APEX PURGE SESSIONS

This job purges sessions from the session state internal tables. By default it will purge sessions older than 12 hours. It runs every hour by default. Session state is created even for public sessions. On a highly accessed public application, it may be required to purge sessions more frequently. See Chapter 10 for more details.

ORACLE APEX MAIL QUEUE

This job sends mail that is in the mail queue and runs every 5 minutes by default.

ORACLE APEX WS NOTIFICATIONS

This job is used for websheet notifications and runs every 30 minutes.

ORACLE APEX DAILY MAINTENANCE

This job runs every night at 1:00 AM and summarizes the APEX_WORKSPACE_ACTIVITY_LOG. It also runs the workspace purge process explained in Chapter 10.

It is possible to see the APEX-scheduled job in APEX when connected as the instance administrator using the internal workspace.

There is a list of all the database-scheduled jobs available in the Monitor Activity tab, using the jobs option in the Logs section: see Figure 2-5. Clicking each job will give a history of the last times it ran and the status.

Job Name	Enabled	State	Run Count	Failure Count	Retry Count	Last Start Date	Last Run Duration	Next Run Date
ORACLE_APEX_DAILY_MAINTENANCE	TRUE	SCHEDULED	91	0	0	5/31/2016 7:0:2 -05:00	+000000000 00:00:00.475824	6/1/2016 1:0:0 -05:00
ORACLE_APEX_MAIL_QUEUE	TRUE	SCHEDULED	7,159	0	0	5/31/2016 7:0:2 -05:00	+000000000 00:00:00.003526	5/31/2016 7:5:0 -05:00
ORACLE_APEX_PURGE_SESSIONS	TRUE	SCHEDULED	679	0	0	5/31/2016 7:0:54 -05:00	+000000000 00:00:00.010470	5/31/2016 8:0:51 -05:00
ORACLE_APEX_WS_NOTIFICATIONS	TRUE	SCHEDULED	1,179	0	0	5/31/2016 7:0:1 -05:00	+000000000 00:00:00.611396	5/31/2016 7:30:0 -05:00

Figure 2-5. *APEX scheduled jobs report*

Oracle Support

How to Get Support

In order for APEX to be fully supported by Oracle, a valid database license is required and it must include database support even if APEX is a no-cost option of the database. Having a valid database license allows using APEX, upgrading, and patching. Patches are only available from Oracle support. All releases of APEX are available for download from OTN.

With a valid license, it is possible to open Service Requests (SR) on the Oracle support portal available at support.oracle.com and get full APEX support. You will also find support documents for APEX in the Oracle support portal.

The Oracle OTN APEX forum is also very popular, and the APEX team is constantly monitoring it. It is accessible from APEX.ORACLE.COM and can be a good addition to the official Oracle support.

APEX Oracle Lifetime Support

Usually ORDS is fully supported for a period of 5 years after it is released, and APEX is fully supported by Oracle for 3 years after it is released. But that can change, so it is always better to confirm whether or not you are fully supported by contacting your Oracle sales representative.

■ **Caution**   Always check with your Oracle sales representative before taking any business decisions related to licensing and to whether you are fully supported.

Here is some information about ORDS and APEX lifetime support. Figures 2-6 and 2-7 were taken from the official Oracle document called *Lifetime Support Policy: Oracle Technology Products* available at www.oracle.com/us/support/lifetime-support/index.html.

Oracle REST Data Services (formerly Application Express Listener)

Release	GA Date	Premier Support Ends	Extended Support Ends	Sustaining Support Ends
1.0	Jul 2010	Jul 2015	Not Available	Indefinite
1.1	Mar 2011	Mar 2016	Not Available	Indefinite
2	Dec 2012	Dec 2017	Not Available	Indefinite
3.0	Jun 2015	Jun 2020	Not Available	Indefinite

Figure 2-6. ORDS lifetime support policy

Oracle Application Express (Formerly HTML DB)

Release	GA Date	Premier Support Ends	Extended Support Ends	Sustaining Support Ends
1.6	Jul 2005	Dec 2008	Not Available	Indefinite
2.0	Sep 2005	Dec 2008	Not Available	Indefinite
2.2	Aug 2006	Aug 2009	Not Available	Indefinite
3.0	Mar 2007	Mar 2010	Not Available	Indefinite
3.1	Feb 2008	Feb 2011	Not Available	Indefinite
3.2	Feb 2009	Feb 2012	Not Available	Indefinite
4.0	Jun 2010	Jun 2015	Not Available	Indefinite
4.1	Aug 2011	Aug 2016	Not Available	Indefinite
4.2	Oct 2012	Oct 2017	Not Available	Indefinite
5.0	Apr 2015	Apr 2020	Not Available	Indefinite

Figure 2-7. *APEX lifetime support policy*

APEX in the Cloud

We cannot talk about APEX in the database without having a specific section about the cloud. Since APEX fully resides in an Oracle database, it is very easy to deploy on a cloud instance.

Basically, all that is required is an ORDS listener and an Oracle database. Both can be deployed on the cloud.

When installing Oracle on the cloud, be aware that, besides the Oracle Cloud, there are two others approved vendors that are certified for database licensing: Amazon Web Services (AWS) and Microsoft Azure. See www.oracle.com/us/corporate/pricing/cloud-licensing-070579.pdf for more information on this.

■ **Important** Always validate with your Oracle sales representative before taking any business decisions related to licensing and to validate if you are fully supported.

Microsoft Azure

On the Microsoft Azure cloud service, it is possible to create a virtual machine with the Oracle software or install Oracle using your own licenses. See https://azure.microsoft.com/en-us/campaigns/oracle/ for more detail.

Amazon Web Services

On the Amazon cloud called Amazon Web Services (AWS), it is possible to use the Elastic Cloud (EC2) to create a virtual machine and install Oracle. There are different solutions available. See `https://aws.amazon.com/oracle/` for more details. Be aware that there is also a cloud service called Amazon Relation Database Services (AWS RDS) available but it has limited capabilities regarding APEX. RDS is a database service and gives you access to an Oracle database without any access to the server operating system.

At the time of writing of this section, APEX within Amazon's RDS is limited to version 4.1 if running the 11g version of the database and version 4.2.6 if running the 12c version of the database. For APEX upgrades under RDS, Amazon has to provide the upgrade scripts and they may not be available for any recent APEX releases.

Oracle Cloud

It is interesting to note that the Oracle cloud makes great use of APEX. For example, the Oracle Cloud Database Schema Service in the Database as a Service (DBAAS) allows you to have an APEX workspace in the cloud. A lot of other Oracle cloud offerings are also using APEX, like for example the Oracle business intelligenge cloud services (BICS). See `https://cloud.oracle.com/business_intelligence` for more information.

Using the Oracle Database Cloud Database as a Service, you can deploy Oracle APEX in a virtual image and even use the Oracle cloud tools to monitor the database. For more information, go to `https://cloud.oracle.com/database`.

At Oracle Openworld 2016, Oracle annouced a new database cloud service using APEX. It is called Oracle Database Exadata Express Cloud Service. With this new Oracle database cloud offering it is possible to provision a database instance and start to develop APEX applications on the cloud within minutes. For more information see `https://cloud.oracle.com/en_US/opc/database/exadata-express/features`.

There is also the free APEX cloud that has been available for quite some time now. It is possible to ask for a free workspace and try APEX simply by signing in at `apex.oracle.com`. This is a free cloud and is intended only for customer evaluation. At the moment of writing these lines, there was a rumor that Oracle had plans to offer a free public APEX cloud where production applications would be allowed and supported. The Oracle cloud is still being developed and is evolving rapidly.

Summary

First of all, keep in mind that APEX is simply PL/SQL packages. It is installed in a standard schema in the database and fully uses the database functionalities to generate web applications.

It has been instrumented so that it is easy to monitor and make the link between Oracle database sessions and APEX sessions.

APEX is really a three-tier web application development tool that has the application tier in the database stored as metadata. That is what makes it more secured and more efficient since the data of the applications is stored in the database with the applications. This way, it is easy for the Oracle optimizer to optimize the generation of the applications since it can analyze the application and the data being retrieved at the same time. There are limited network calls that are required to go from the application server to the database server.

One other thing to keep in mind is that an APEX application user is not a database user. Connections to the database are made to be secured and fast.

Finally, APEX has been a multitenant cloud tool since day one, even before cloud was such a big thing. APEX is great for the cloud and, as you will see in the next chapters, it is easy to maintain only using a web browser.

In the next chapter we will talk about the different middle-tier architectures that can be used with APEX.

CHAPTER 3

■ ■ ■

Middle-Tier

This chapter is about the different configurations possible in the middle-tier for Oracle Application Express. The general purpose here is to demystify the different components that can be installed on the middle-tier and the reasons why.

Depending on company policies or on the level of knowledge of the APEX administrators, there are some configurations that are more appropriate than others.

Like what we explained in Chapter 1, APEX requires a web listener to be able to make the communication between the client browser and the database as shown in Figure 3-1.

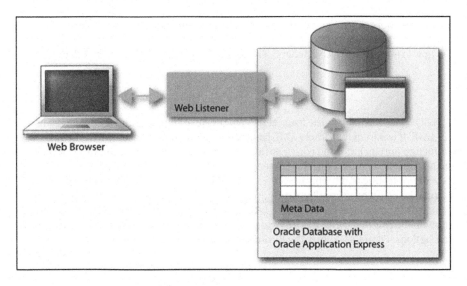

Figure 3-1. APEX architecture: web listener

The last section of this chapter is about reverse proxies. We normally use a reverse proxy configuration to allow a secure access to APEX applications for clients outside of the company network.

Web Listeners

In the middle-tier, a web listener has to be installed. This web listener will be the one making the calls to the APEX engine in the database in order to be able to generate the pages of the application.

F. Mignault and L. Demanche, *Oracle Application Express Administration*, DOI 10.1007/978-1-4842-1958-4_3

Three different web listeners are available for APEX: EPG, OHS, and ORDS, as shown in Figure 3-2.

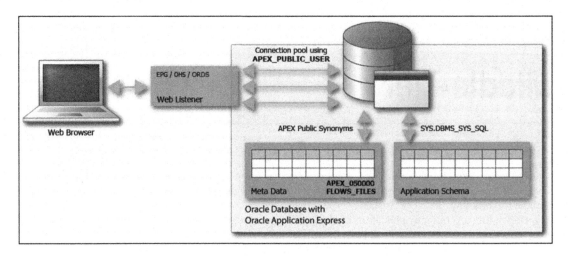

Figure 3-2. *Web listeners*

Note that all three web listeners can be configured and used simultaneously, as long as they are configured on different network ports, of course.

For instructions on how to install those web listeners, see the Oracle Application Express Installation Guide.

EPG

EPG is for Embedded PLSQL Gateway. This is the listener used in the default installation for Oracle Database Express Edition ORACLE XE. It is part of the Oracle XML Database configuration. It uses the Database SQLNet listener infrastructure and includes the core features of mod_plsql. It does not require a separate web server and it is usually installed on the database server.

Generally, EPG is great for testing and trying an APEX installation. But for a production configuration, it is not recommended. It can be complex to configure properly on larger and more active installations. It does not scale as efficiently as the other listeners in enterprise-level architecture. It can also be difficult to find support and information on the Internet, since it is not widely used, and EPG can also present security issues not present in the other options. Figure 3-3 shows the EPG configuration.

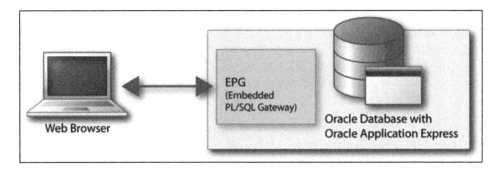

Figure 3-3. *EPG*

OHS / mod_plsql (Deprecated)

OHS stands for Oracle HTTP Server. It used to be the norm for running Oracle web applications. OHS is using an APACHE HTTP Server as its base, and Oracle added different modules to it. One of those modules is called mod_plsql, and it is used to call database procedures that generate web applications. See Figure 3-4.

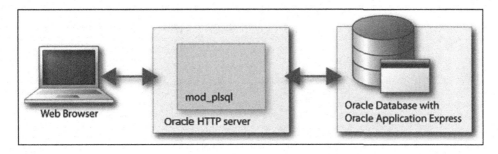

Figure 3-4. *OHS and mod_plsql*

When APEX first came out, this was the recommended configuration. But mod_plsql has now been deprecated. It has been removed from the Oracle HTTP Server 12c (12.2.1) release. For more information, see the Oracle document Future Direction for Application Express (APEX) and the Oracle HTTP Server (OHS) / Mod_plsql (Doc ID 1945619.1)

If you are currently using OHS and mod_plsql with your APEX installations, Oracle recommends migrating to ORDS.

ORDS

ORDS is for Oracle Rest Data Services. This is the recommended web listener for Oracle Application Express. It was formerly known as the "APEX listener" but it is now also widely used for other things. ORDS is the APEX web listener used on the Oracle Cloud.

ORDS is downloadable for free from the OTN web site at `http://www.oracle.com/technetwork/developer-tools/rest-data-services`. You will also find the installation documentation, a forum, and a lot of other pertinent information on ORDS at this address.

Starting with APEX 4.0, ORDS is required for some features like the use of RESTFul web services. New features for APEX will be developed only for installations using ORDS, like for example, the new static file-handling feature in APEX 5.0. So again, make sure that you are using this configuration.

ORDS is very lightweight and it contains a lot of useful features. The fact that it is java based makes it compatible with existing architecture commonly used in enterprises. In order to be able to use it for production, it has to be installed on the middle-tier and deployed in an application server. (ORDS can be deployed in a stand-alone mode. Where no application server is needed, however, this comes with significant performance loss and security issues as well and thus is not for production use.) See Figure 3-5 for the representation of an ORDS configuration.

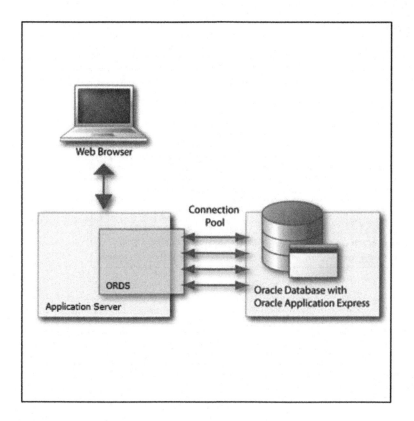

Figure 3-5. ORDS

Application Servers

In order to be able to run ORDS, a JAVA EE application server has to be installed on the middle-tier. There are currently three options supported by Oracle: GlassFish, Tomcat, and WebLogic, as shown in Figure 3-6.

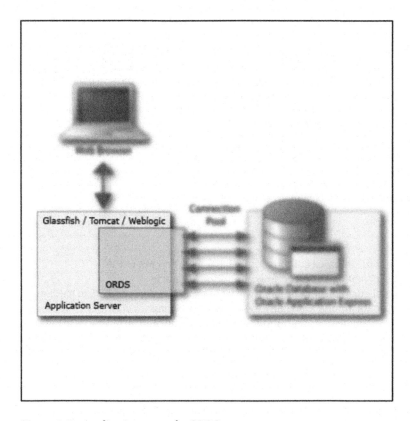

Figure 3-6. *Application server for ORDS*

GlassFish

GlassFish is an open-source application server sponsored by Oracle. This is what we use most with our customers. We like to keep our technology stack within Oracle products.

The GlassFish application server can be installed on the middle-tier and ORDS will be deployed in it. The port number and web server security is managed in GlassFish. There are log files that can be monitored for errors, and configurations can be changed for performance tuning. See the GlassFish documentation for more information on this. ORDS will also write any log information in the GlassFish logs.

Since November 2013, there is no more commercial support available from Oracle. The open-source project is still active and new features and patches are being released and developed. Due to the simplicity of use with ORDS, stability, and popularity, and because it is free, we still recommend it for APEX enterprise installations when official support is not required.

For documentation and a lot more information or to download GlassFish, go to `https://glassfish.java.net/`.

For information on how to deploy ORDS on a GlassFish server, see the Oracle REST Data Services Installation and Configuration Guide, section Deploying to GlassFish Server.

Tomcat

Apache Tomcat is also an open-source application server sponsored by the Apache Software Foundation (ASF). It is widely used and a lot of information can be found on the Internet, which can be very useful. It is probably better known than GlassFish and WebLogic, especially for administrators outside of the Oracle community. This is certainly why it is a supported solution for APEX and Oracle REST Data Services (ORDS).

Tomcat has to be installed on the middle-tier in order to be able to deploy ORDS in it. Like GlassFish, there are error logs and there are different configurations options available for performance tuning. The documentation and download are available at `http://tomcat.apache.org/`.

Apache Tomcat is an open-source product, so is no official product support available, but there are some companies offering support.

For information on how to deploy ORDS on an Apache Tomcat server, see the Oracle REST Data Services Installation and Configuration Guide, Deploying to Apache Tomcat.

WebLogic

WebLogic Server Standard Edition is the minimal edition required to deploy and run ORDS.

When properly licensed, Oracle WebLogic Server is fully supported by Oracle.

WebLogic Server has to be installed on the middle-tier in order to be able to deploy ORDS in it. Like GlassFish, there are error logs and configuration available for performance tuning.

WebLogic is probably the most complicated application server to configure and install because of the multiple features and options that are available. It is also probably the most robust and flexible. Depending on the administrator knowledge, it may require research, learning, and effort to master and fully understand its configuration.

Oracle WebLogic Standard Edition can be downloaded at `https://www.oracle.com/middleware/weblogic/standard-edition.html`.

For information on how to deploy ORDS on a WebLogic server, see the Oracle REST Data Services Installation and Configuration Guide, section Deploying to Oracle WebLogic Server.

Reverse Proxy

In some cases we want to give access to APEX applications to clients outside of our internal network. For example: mobile applications, web services, partner companies' applications, or public-facing applications.

To do so, we only want to open the access to a specific application ID and not the entire APEX application install or all the applications in that environment.

Giving access to a specific application ID is really about giving the ability to access a specific URL. We can restrict the access to a specific URL using the reverse proxy configuration.

Architecture

The concept of the reverse proxy is to put a web server in a demilitarized zone (DMZ) that will accept and filter the requests from the internet. Then, the valid requests will go through a firewall and to the web listener used for APEX as shown in Figure 3-7.

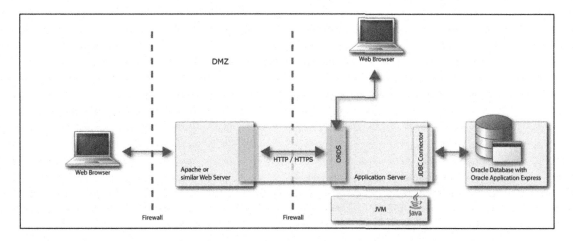

Figure 3-7. *Reverse proxy architecture*

This configuration will avoid opening the web listener to the public. The web server in the DMZ first filters the requests before sending them to the web listener. This reverse proxy server has to have the latest security patches at all times and must have minimal functionality and applications installed on it to avoid any security holes. This also allows only calls from the proxy server through the firewall.

Using Apache as an example for the reverse proxy, it is possible to use mod_rewrite, mod_ssl, and mod_proxy modules to filter the calling URL, encrypt all communications, and allow only specific requests or queries to go through. If the request source is known, like a partner company that wants to call an application inside the secured network, it is possible to secure this access via a firewall in front of the reverse proxy server. This way, only specific IP addresses could call specific APEX applications. See the following example of an Apache configuration.

Example of a Reverse Proxy Apache Configuration

Here is an example of an Apache configuration as a reverse proxy.

First, we change the `httpd.conf` configuration file as described in the following. This is to force HTTPS usage while allowing end users to still find the site when using standard HTTP. This example is using the NameVirtualHost option. All required modules that are not loaded by default are also added in the appropriate section of the configuration file.

```
<VirtualHost *:80>
        ServerName      mydomain.com
        Redirect permanent / https://mydomain.com/
</VirtualHost>
```

Then, we change the `ssl.conf` configuration file. In this example, all requests to mydomain.com are rewritten to access application ID 123. Those requests are then redirected to the middle-tier server at `https://hostname:8181` located in the internal private network.

```
NameVirtualHost *:443

<VirtualHost *:443>
ServerName mydomain.com
```

```
#Allows proxying to Secure Socket Layer (SSL)-enabled servers
SSLProxyEngine On

    RewriteEngine on
    RewriteCond %{REQUEST_URI} !^/i/
    RewriteCond %{REQUEST_URI} !^/ords
    RewriteCond %{REQUEST_URI} !^/robots.txt
    RewriteRule ^/$ /ords/f?p=123:1:0 [R]

    <Location /ords/>
          RewriteEngine on
          RewriteCond %{QUERY_STRING} !^p=123:*
          RewriteCond %{REQUEST_URI} !^/ords/wwv_flow.accept*
          RewriteCond %{REQUEST_URI} !^/ords/apex_authentication.logout*
          RewriteCond %{REQUEST_URI} !^/ords/wwv_flow.show*
          RewriteCond %{REQUEST_URI} !^/ords/wwv_flow_file_mgr*
          RewriteCond %{REQUEST_URI} !^/ords/wwv_flow_utilities*
          RewriteCond %{REQUEST_URI} !^/ords/APEX_050000.wwv_flow_utilities*
          RewriteCond %{REQUEST_URI} !^/ords/apex_util.*
          RewriteRule /ords/.* [F]
          ProxyPass https://hostname:8181/ords/
          ProxyPassReverse https://caesar.insum.intranet:8181/ords/
    </Location>

    # Proxy the apex images directory
    <Location /i/>
          ProxyPass https://hostname:8181/i/
          ProxyPassReverse https://hostname:8181/i/
    </Location>
</VirtualHost>
```

SSL / HTTPS

To make everything even more secure, it is recommended to use SSL configuration (HTTPS).
There are basically three steps to setup HTTPS and install a secure certificate:

1. Generate a private key, a public key, and a certificate request on your server
    which will hold/contain the certificate such as the Apache web server. This can
    be done with tools such as OpenSSL. Instructions are also generally available on
    certificate authority websites such as Verisign.

2. Buy a signed certificate from a certificate authority such as Verisign, Comodo,
    Digicert, or others. You will need the certificate request file and possibly the
    public key to do so. Once approved, the certificate authority will send you a
    certificate chain file and the signed certificate itself.

3. Configure the server to use the certificate. For example, in an Apache setup,
    change the ssl.conf file. To do so, two (possibly three) files are required; the
    signed certificate, the private key, and in some cases a certificate chain file
    (depending on the vendor). The file must be dropped into the appropriate
    locations and then the configuration file must be changed to point to these
    files as well.

In order to maintain a high level of security and robust encryption, the private and public key generation must use a recommended key size and algorithm. It is important to research what is the current recommendation when any new certificate is to be purchased/generated. As of the writing of this document, SHA-2 is the go-to, and previous algorithms, while available, are slowly being deprecated. It is very important because SSL is the front-line defense and it is constantly evolving.

As shown in Figure 3-8, a signed certificate is required on the proxy server to use HTTPS for the public-facing requests. It is also possible to have a self-signed certificate on the application server to serve the request from the proxy to ORDS with HTTPS.

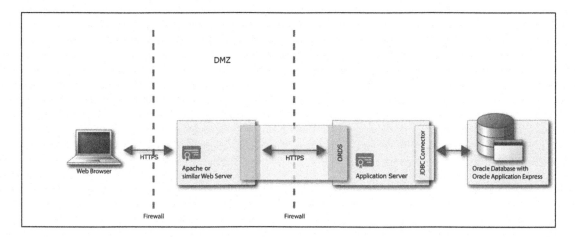

Figure 3-8. *SSL in a reverse proxy architecture*

For detailed information on how to configure HTTPS and install a certificate, see the following documentation based on the web server used:

- Tomcat Apache: `https://tomcat.apache.org/tomcat-6.0-doc/ssl-howto.html`.

- Oracle GlassFish: `https://docs.oracle.com/cd/E19798-01/821-1794/aeogl/index.html`.

- Oracle WebLogic: `http://docs.oracle.com/cd/E24329_01/web.1211/e24422/ssl.htm#SECMG384`.

Summary

There are currently three different web listeners that can be used for APEX: EPG, OHS, and ORDS. It is strongly recommended to use ORDS because of all the functionalities that it provides. ORDS is a java component that can be deployed on three supported application servers: WebLogic, GlassFish, and Tomcat.

In an APEX installation, the middle-tier is used to make the connection between the client browser and the database where applications are executed in a secure way. This does not mean that external users can access the database directly. See Chapter 2 for more information on how the connection is made to the database.

Using standard reverse proxy methods, APEX can be secured for external access like, for example, mobile applications. It is also possible to configure HTTPS and SSL to make it even more secure.

In the next chapter, we will cover advanced database security features and show how it integrates with Oracle Application Express.

CHAPTER 4

■ ■ ■

Database Advanced Security

The need to secure data is driven by an expending privacy and a dangerous world of hackers, inside threats, and people intent on stealing valuable data. Information targeted for attack has included citizen data, intellectual property, credit card data, financial information, government data, and competitive bids. Attack methodologies include hacking of privileged user accounts, exploitation of application vulnerabilities, and so on.

Oracle 12c provides tools and options to ease the deployment of an advanced data security. The first tool we will discuss is the Real Application Security (RAS), which is the next generation of Virtual Private Database (VPD). We will also discuss the Data Redaction, a feature in the Oracle Advanced Security option that provides selective, on-the-fly redaction of sensitive data. Then, we will also discuss the Database Vault, which provides the most comprehensive access control capabilities for the Oracle Database. We will not explain how to deploy Database Vault, but the impact on APEX when running in a database with Database Vault enabled.

Real Application Security

Real Application Security is the next generation of VPD. Using the access control framework, you can create policy-based authorization models that recognize application-level users, privileges, and roles within the database, as well as control access to created collections that are seen as business objects. This chapter will demonstrate how to deploy these controls to secure the access of the data made by the APEX applications.

What Is Real Application Security

Traditional data security was usually built within the application. The developers were creating their own set of tables to manage the application users and were using application roles to determine if that user has access to the specific data or not. Deploying this kind of security is working well within the application, but because the security is encoded in the application level rather than in the database, application users and roles were typically known only in the application, which could lead to having unprotected data if a user is connected directly to the database.

Here are the advantages of using RAS:

- Enforce access control at the database layer.

- Database provides uniform security model across all tiers and can be used by every application to access the secured data.

- Database natively supports the usage of application context. Information will be exchanged between the application and RAS to enforce the security policies.

© Francis Mignault and Luc Demanche 2016

F. Mignault and L. Demanche, *Oracle Application Express Administration*, DOI 10.1007/978-1-4842-1958-4_4

Architecture of RAS

We need to explain different concepts before configuring RAS. To properly define the security policies with RAS, we have to define and use three components:

- Application users (principals)

- Which operation is allowed (application privileges)

- On which data (data realms)

Once these three components are defined, we are creating an Access Control List (ACL) to relate the principal and the application privilege. These ACLs are then related to the data by defining the Data Security policy that protects rows and columns of table data. Here is an example of the three components and the ACLs that relate these three components together. Figure 4-1 shows the three main components.

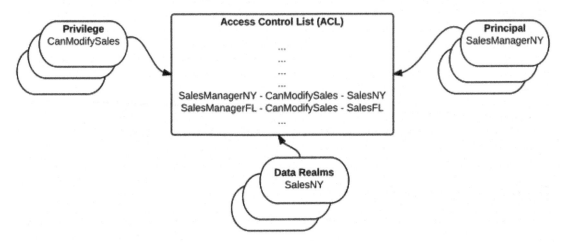

Figure 4-1. *Main components of RAS*

Definition of a Few Concepts

A **principal** is either a user or a role. User could be a database user or an application user; as for the role, it could be a database role or an application role. Here are some details about principals:

- Database user and role

A database user is related to a schema or a database account. If you are connecting to the database, you are using a database user. A database role corresponds to a set of database privileges that are granted to a database user or a database role.

- Application user and role

RAS refers to the creation of an application user and application role. An application user or role is not tied to an Oracle schema; these components are known by RAS but can be used for a direct connection to the database using SQL*Plus for example.

Unlike a database role that we grant to a database user, with application role and user we have to use ACL to relate them together.

The **privileges** control application-level operations on components. For example, an application user can have the privilege called "ViewSSN" which will give him access to see the Social Security Number (SSN). Another application user, the manager for example, could have the privilege to update the salary information of his employees.

The **data realms** represent the securable business object as a logical collection of data rows in an application. This collection or dataset is specified using a SQL predicate, where each row of the collection satisfies the predicate. For example, a data realm could be all employee records that report to a specific manager.

All of these components will be put together in an example later in the chapter.

Real Application Security Administration Application (RASADM)

The Oracle Real Application Security Administration Application (RASADM) simplifies management of Oracle Database 12c Real Application Security (RAS). Application developers and security administrators can easily create and manage RAS security policies, application users, and roles. RASADM complements the comprehensive RAS PL/SQL API available with Oracle Database 12c.

Once RASADM is installed, you can log to the home page as shown in Figure 4-2.

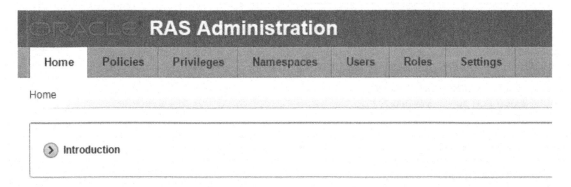

Figure 4-2. *Selecting Manage Instance*

We are not covering the tool in this chapter, as the example of the deployment of RAS will be performed using SQL*Plus.

Example of a RAS Deployment

We are now ready to demonstrate how RAS works with a simple example using SQL*Plus. We will also explain how to integrate RAS in an APEX application and demonstrate the RAS policy from the APEX application.

Here is the context of the example. We have developed an APEX application that manages car sales in the United States. We are following three different vendors. One of the vendors is also the manager of the team and another one is responsible for the Ford Focus model.

Let's first define the different application roles:

- Vendor_role

    The vendor that has the vendor_role has permission to see his own sales information, the number of cars, commissions, and so on.

- Focus_role

  The vendor that has the focus_role has permission to see the sales information for the model Focus only. He can't see the commission of the vendor that made the sale.

- Manager_role

  The vendor that has the manager_role has permission to see all the sales information including the commissions. He can also update any information.

Here are the vendors and the associated roles:

Name of the vendor	RAS username	Associated roles
Paul Smith	PSMITH	vendor_role
Bill Brown	BBROWN	vendor_role manager_role
Jack Williams	JWILLIAMS	vendor_role focus_role

The table that contains the sales data must be owned by the workspace's parsing schema. Here is the create statement for the creation of the table "FORD_SALES":

```
CREATE TABLE "SCH_BOOK"."FORD_SALES"
("VENDOR_LAST_NAME" VARCHAR2(20),
 "VENDOR_FIRST_NAME" VARCHAR2(20),
 "VEHICLE" VARCHAR2(20),
 "STATE" VARCHAR2(20),
 "NB_VEHICLE" NUMBER,
 "VENDOR_USERNAME" VARCHAR2(20),
 "COMMISSION" NUMBER
);
```

■ **Note** To ease the data manipulation, I have not created any primary key.

We will create another table, "VENDOR_INFO", which will be used in the next section, "Data Redaction." We will not apply any RAS rule on this table.

```
CREATE TABLE "SCH_BOOK"."VENDOR_INFO"
("USERNAME" VARCHAR2(20),
"FIRST_NAME" VARCHAR2(20),
"LAST_NAME" VARCHAR2(20),
"SSN" VARCHAR2(11), CONSTRAINT "PK_VENDOR_INFO" PRIMARY KEY ("USERNAME") VALIDATE
);
```

We have to link the database privileges (using a database role) to the application role. Let's create the database role first and grant the object's privileges:

```
SQL> create role db_ford_sales;

Role created.

SQL> grant select, insert, update, delete on ford_sales to db_ford_sales;

Grant succeeded.
```

We can now start the deployment of the security using RAS. All the following SQL commands will be performed while connected to the RAS administrator previously created on the installation of Real Application Security Administration Application.

- Connect to the RAS administrator

```
SQL> connect rasadm/password@pdb001;
Connected.
```

■ **Note** If you are using a multitenant database, make sure you are connected to the proper PDB.

- Create the application roles, and grant the database role to the new application roles

  ```
  SQL> exec sys.xs_principal.create_role(name => 'vendor_role', enabled =>
  true);

  PL/SQL procedure successfully completed.

  SQL> exec sys.xs_principal.create_role(name => 'focus_role', enabled =>
  true);

  PL/SQL procedure successfully completed.

  SQL> exec sys.xs_principal.create_role(name => 'manager_role', enabled
  => true);

  PL/SQL procedure successfully completed.

  SQL> grant db_ford_sales to vendor_role;

  Grant succeeded.

  SQL> grant db_ford_sales to focus_role;

  Grant succeeded.

  SQL> grant db_ford_sales to manager_role;

  Grant succeeded.
  ```

  The application roles have now all the privileges on the table FORD_SALES.

- Create the application users, and provide the password and the appropriate roles (I have removed the output of SQL*Plus after every execution)

  Creation of the user PSMITH with the vendor_role

  ```
  SQL> exec  sys.xs_principal.create_user(name => 'psmith', schema =>
  'sch_book');
  SQL> exec  sys.xs_principal.set_password('psmith', 'password');
  SQL> exec  sys.xs_principal.grant_roles('psmith', 'vendor_role');
  ```

  Creation of the user BBROWN with the vendor_role and manager_role

  ```
  SQL> exec  sys.xs_principal.create_user(name => 'bbrown', schema =>
  'sch_book');
  SQL> exec  sys.xs_principal.set_password('bbrown', 'password');
  SQL> exec  sys.xs_principal.grant_roles('bbrown', 'vendor_role');
  SQL> exec  sys.xs_principal.grant_roles('bbrown', 'manager_role');
  ```

  Creation of the user JWILLIAMS with the vendor_role and focus_role

  ```
  SQL> exec  sys.xs_principal.create_user(name => 'jwilliams', schema =>
  'sch_book');
  SQL> exec  sys.xs_principal.set_password('jwilliams', 'password');
  SQL> exec  sys.xs_principal.grant_roles('jwilliams', 'vendor_role');
  SQL> exec  sys.xs_principal.grant_roles('jwilliams', 'focus_role');
  ```

■ **Note** By giving a password to the user, the user becomes a direct login application account user. We can now use that user to connect directly to the database using SQL*Plus.

- We are now at the step to create security class to control the access to the commission column.

  ```
  SQL> declare
  begin
    sys.xs_security_class.create_security_class(
      name         => 'managerprivs',
      parent_list => xs$name_list('sys.dml'),
      priv_list    => xs$privilege_list(xs$privilege('view_commission')));
  end;

  PL/SQL procedure successfully completed.
  ```

- We are now creating the ACLs that relate the principals to the privileges.

  ```
  declare
    aces xs$ace_list := xs$ace_list();
  begin
    aces.extend(1);
  ```

```
-- VENDOR_ACL: This ACL grants VENDOR_ROLE the privileges to view an
   vendor's own record including COMMISSION column.
aces(1) := xs$ace_type(privilege_list => xs$name_list('select','view_
commission'),
                       principal_name => 'vendor_role');

sys.xs_acl.create_acl(name     => 'vendor_acl',
                ace_list => aces,
                sec_class => 'managerprivs');

-- FOCUS_ACL:  This ACL grants FOCUS_ROLE the privilege to view the
   sales records for Focus model, but it does not grant the VIEW_
   COMMISSION privilege
-- that is required for access to COMMISSION column.
aces(1) := xs$ace_type(privilege_list => xs$name_list('select'),
                       principal_name => 'focus_role');

sys.xs_acl.create_acl(name     => 'focus_acl',
                ace_list => aces,
                sec_class => 'managerprivs');

-- MANAGER_ACL:  This ACL grants MANAGER_ROLE the privileges to view
   and update all sales' records including COMMISSION column.
aces(1):= xs$ace_type(privilege_list => xs$name_list('all'),
                      principal_name => 'manager_role');

sys.xs_acl.create_acl(name     => 'manager_acl',
                ace_list => aces,
                sec_class => 'managerprivs');
end;
/

PL/SQL procedure successfully completed.
```

As you can see, the VENDOR_ACL as for privileges, "select" and "view_commission." FOCUS_ACL as only "select", whereas MANAGER_ACL has the privileges "all."

- Now we are ready to create the Data Security Policy. We will then create data realms, one for every role saying which data we want to have access to.

  For the vendor_role, the data realm condition is where column "vendor_username" equal to the username of the user connected to the application.

  For the focus_role, the data realm condition is where column "vehicle" equals "FOCUS".

  For the manager_role, the data realm condition is where 1 = 1, that is, every line of the table.

  We will also create a column constraint named "view_commission" to control the access on the commission column.

```
declare
  realms  xs$realm_constraint_list := xs$realm_constraint_list();
  cols    xs$column_constraint_list := xs$column_constraint_list();
begin
  realms.extend(3);

  -- Realm #1: Only the vendor's own record.
  --           VENDOR_ROLE can view the realm including COMMISSION
    column.
  realms(1) := xs$realm_constraint_type(
    realm    => 'vendor_username = xs_sys_context(''xs$session'',''user
    name'')',
    acl_list => xs$name_list('vendor_acl'));

  -- Realm #2: The records for Focus model.
  --           FOCUS_ROLE can view the realm excluding COMMISSION
    column.
  realms(2) := xs$realm_constraint_type(
    realm    => 'vehicle = ''Focus''',
    acl_list => xs$name_list('focus_acl'));

  -- Realm #3: All the records.
  --           MANAGER_ROLE can view and update the realm including
    COMMISION column.
  realms(3) := xs$realm_constraint_type(
    realm    => '1 = 1',
    acl_list => xs$name_list('manager_acl'));

  -- Column constraint protects COMMISSION column by requiring VIEW_
    COMMISSION
  -- privilege.
  cols.extend(1);
  cols(1) := xs$column_constraint_type(
    column_list => xs$list('commission'),
    privilege   => 'view_commission');

  sys.xs_data_security.create_policy(
    name                  => 'ford_sales_ds',
    realm_constraint_list => realms,
    column_constraint_list => cols);
end;
/

PL/SQL procedure successfully completed.
```

- Now that the Data Security Policy is created, we will apply it to the table.

```
begin
  sys.xs_data_security.apply_object_policy(
    policy => 'ford_sales_ds',
    schema => 'sch_book',
```

```
      object =>'ford_sales');
  end;
  /

  PL/SQL procedure successfully completed.
```

- Validation of the objects

```
  set serveroutput on;
  begin
    if (sys.xs_diag.validate_workspace()) then
      dbms_output.put_line('All configurations are correct.');
    else
      dbms_output.put_line('Some configurations are incorrect.');
    end if;
  end;
  /

  All configurations are correct.

  PL/SQL procedure successfully completed.
```

- XS$VALIDATION_TABLE contains validation errors if any

  -- Expect no rows selected.

```
  select * from xs$validation_table order by 1, 2, 3, 4;
```

Demonstration Using SQL*Plus

We can now use SQL*Plus with the application users and see the results of the queries against the FORD_SALES table. First let's connect with the user PSMITH.

```
SQL> connect psmith/password@pdb001
Connected.
SQL> select vendor_first_name, vendor_last_name, vehicle, state, nb_vehicle, commission from
ford_sales;

VENDOR_FIRST_NA VENDOR_LAST_NAM VEHICLE     STATE      NB_VEHICLE COMMISSION
--------------- --------------- ----------  ---------- ---------- ----------
Paul            Smith           Escape      TX               5000        500
Paul            Smith           Escape      TX               5000        500
Paul            Smith           Escape      NY               2501        100
Paul            Smith           Focus       NY               3000        300

4 rows selected.
```

As you remember, PSMITH has the vendor_role, which gives access to his sales information. He also has the "select" and the "view_commission" privileges, which give him access to his commission information. Now let's connect with the user JWILLIAMS.

```
SQL> connect jwilliams/password@pdb001
Connected.
SQL> select vendor_first_name, vendor_last_name, vehicle, state, nb_vehicle, commission from
ford_sales;

VENDOR_FIRST_NA VENDOR_LAST_NAM VEHICLE     STATE      NB_VEHICLE COMMISSION
--------------- --------------- ----------  ---------- ---------- ----------
Jack            Williams        Escape      FL               2000        200
Bill            Brown           Focus       CA               5500 *****
Paul            Smith           Focus       NY               3000 *****
Jack            Williams        Mustang     FL               5000        500

4 rows selected.
```

As you remember, JWILLIAMS has the vendor_role and focus_role. That gives him access to his own sales information as well as the sales information for the model Focus. Because he doesn't have "view_commission" privileges, he can't see the commission information of the other vendors, and these are displayed with "*****." Now let's connect with the user BBROWN.

```
SQL> connect bbrown/password@pdb001
Connected.
SQL> select vendor_first_name, vendor_last_name, vehicle, state, nb_vehicle, commission from
ford_sales;

VENDOR_FIRST_NA VENDOR_LAST_NAM VEHICLE     STATE      NB_VEHICLE COMMISSION
--------------- --------------- ----------  ---------- ---------- ----------
Paul            Smith           Escape      TX               5000        500
Paul            Smith           Escape      TX               5000        500
Paul            Smith           Escape      NY               2501        100
Jack            Williams        Escape      FL               2000        200
Bill            Brown           Focus       CA               5500        550
Paul            Smith           Focus       NY               3000        300
Jack            Williams        Mustang     FL               5000        500

7 rows selected.
```

As you remember, BBROWN has the vendor_role and manager_role. That gives him access to his own sales information as well as all of the other sales information. Additionally, he has "all" for privilege, which is giving him access to modify any information.

Let's test the update of the information using SQL*Plus. The first test will be done using PSMITH and the other one with BBROWN. We are expecting that only BBROWN can modify the data in the table.

```
SQL> connect psmith/password@pdb001
Connected.
SQL> select vendor_first_name, vendor_last_name, vehicle, state, nb_vehicle, commission from
ford_sales;

VENDOR_FIRST_NA VENDOR_LAST_NAM VEHICLE     STATE      NB_VEHICLE COMMISSION
--------------- --------------- ----------  ---------- ---------- ----------
Paul            Smith           Escape      TX               5000        500
Paul            Smith           Escape      TX               5000        500
Paul            Smith           Escape      NY               2501        100
Paul            Smith           Focus       NY               3000        300
```

4 rows selected.

Let's try to update the number of cars sold in New York State by Paul Smith.

```
SQL> update ford_sales set nb_vehicle = nb_vehicle + 500 where vendor_first_name='Paul' and
vehicle='Escape' and state = 'NY';

0 rows updated.
```

As you can see, no rows were updated. Let's connect with BBROWN and run the same update statement.

```
SQL> connect bbrown/password@pdb001
Connected.
SQL> update ford_sales set nb_vehicle = nb_vehicle + 500 where vendor_first_name='Paul' and
vehicle='Escape' and state = 'NY';

1 row updated.
```

One row was updated while we are connected with the manager. Now we will connect with PSMITH and see the result of the update.

```
SQL>  connect psmith/password@pdb001
Connected.
SQL> select vendor_first_name, vendor_last_name, vehicle, state, nb_vehicle, commission from
ford_sales;
```

VENDOR_FIRST_NA	VENDOR_LAST_NAM	VEHICLE	STATE	NB_VEHICLE	COMMISSION
Paul	Smith	Escape	TX	5000	500
Paul	Smith	Escape	TX	5000	500
Paul	Smith	Escape	NY	3001	100
Paul	Smith	Focus	NY	3000	300

4 rows selected.

Now, we can see that the number of cars sold by Paul Smith increased by 500 in New York State.

In this example, we have explained how to create the application roles and application users. We have shown how to relate the different components together by creating the ACLs and by creating the data realms.

Using SQL*Plus, we have demonstrated how the RAS works in a real example and now we are ready to deploy an APEX application and explain how to integrate RAS with APEX.

Demonstration Using an APEX Application

We have developed a little APEX application that is querying the table FORD_SALES. We will demonstrate the integration and how easy it is to use RAS with an APEX application. The first page of the application is used for the login, and once we are connected, we are having the second page that queries the table with a simple "select * from ford_sales;". The display of that query will depend on the user that we are connected with.

First of all, we need to perform a few configuration steps for the integration of RAS with APEX. You have to log into the INTERNAL workspace with the admin user and click "Manage Instance," as you can see in Figure 4-3.

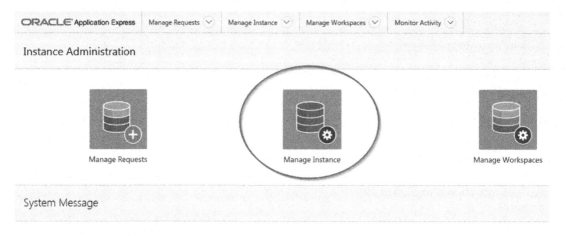

Figure 4-3. *Selecting Manage Instance*

Under "Instance Settings," click "Security," as shown in Figure 4-4.

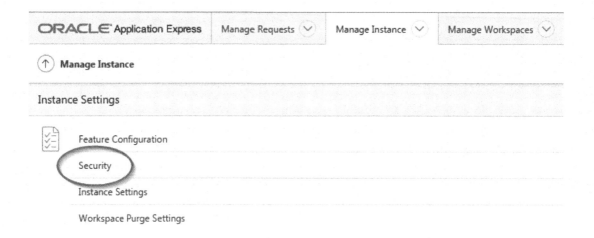

Figure 4-4. *Selecting Security*

From the Security page, scroll down until you find the section "Real Application Security." As shown in Figure 4-5, select "Yes" for "Allow Real Application Security" and click "Apply Changes."

Figure 4-5. Allow Real Application Security to "Yes"

The INTERNAL workspace is now configured to permit the usage of RAS. You can now log into the workspace of your application and select the application that you want to use RAS with. As shown in Figure 4-6, click "Shared Components."

Figure 4-6. Select Shared Components

Under "Security," click "Authentication Scheme" and select the current authentication scheme. You will be on the main page of the Authentication Scheme and you have to scroll down to find the section "Real Application Security." As shown in Figure 4-7, change the "RAS Mode" for "Internal Users."

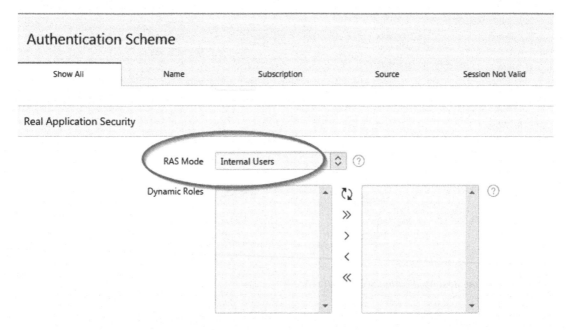

Figure 4-7. *Change the RAS Mode to Internal Users*

The integration of RAS is now done for the workspace as well as for that APEX application. Before continuing with the example, it is important to understand how the relation between the user used for the authentication and the application user defined in RAS is done. The authentication in the application is done through the usual method, as we can see the list in Figure 4-8.

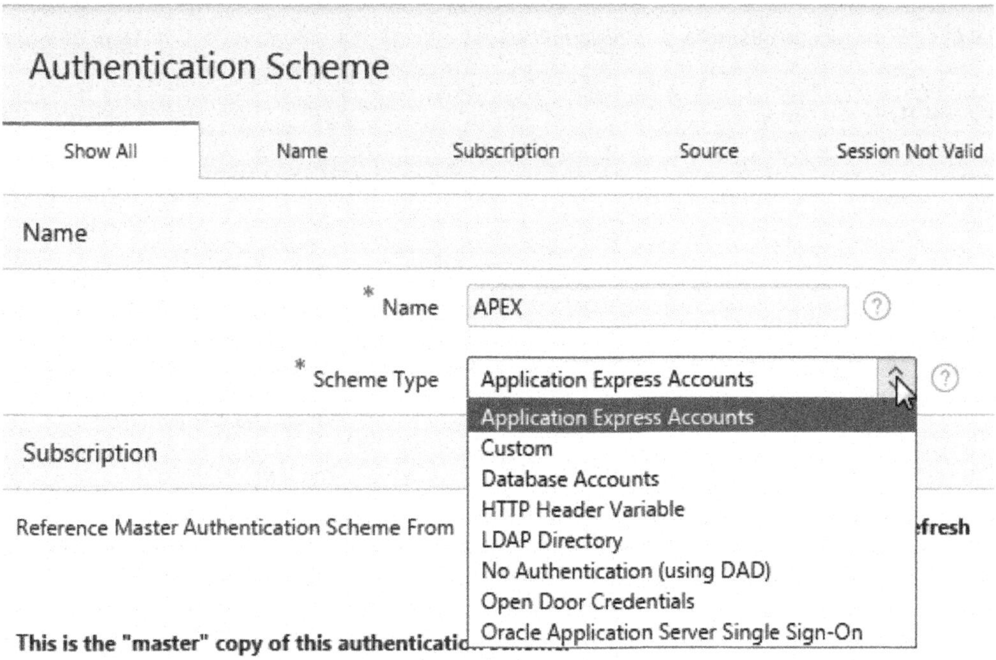

Authentication Scheme

Show All	Name	Subscription	Source	Session Not Valid

Name

* Name   APEX   ⑦

* Scheme Type   Application Express Accounts   ⑦

> Application Express Accounts
> Custom
> Database Accounts
> HTTP Header Variable
> LDAP Directory
> No Authentication (using DAD)
> Open Door Credentials
> Oracle Application Server Single Sign-On

Subscription

Reference Master Authentication Scheme From   efresh

This is the "master" copy of this authentication scheme.

Figure 4-8. *Authentication Scheme type list*

Once the authentication is done in the application, APEX will try to match that user with any application users defined in RAS. If a user is found, APEX will attach the RAS context associated to this account to the APEX session. In my example, I'm using the "Application Express Accounts" authentication schema, so my accounts "PSMITH", "BBROWN", and "JWILLIAMS" exist in APEX. Figure 4-9 shows that my three application accounts exist in the definition of the workspace.

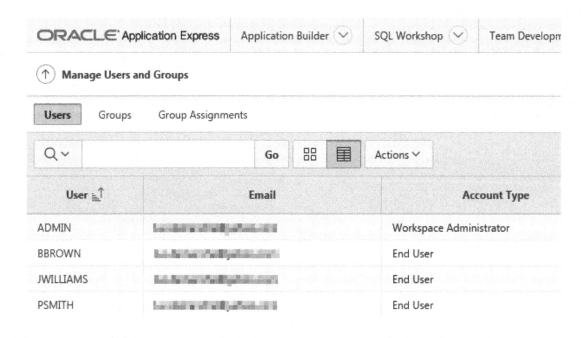

Figure 4-9. List of application users defined

Let's compare with the users already created in RAS.

```
SQL> select name,status,account_status,direct_logon_user from dba_xs_users;
NAME                STATUS    ACCOUNT_STATUS             DIR
------------------- --------- -------------------------- ---
XSGUEST             ACTIVE    OPEN                       NO
ADMIN               ACTIVE    OPEN                       YES
PSMITH              ACTIVE    OPEN                       NO
BBROWN              ACTIVE    OPEN                       YES
JWILLIAMS           ACTIVE    OPEN                       YES
```

We recognize the application users PSMITH, BBROWN, and JWILLIAMS, which we have used earlier in the example using SQL*Plus. We can see that DIRECT_LOGON_USER (DIR) for PSMITH is now set to NO. This means that PSMITH can't log directly to the database using SQL*Plus, but it is not necessary for APEX to relate his user to the RAS application user, as long as the both usernames are the same.

Let's demonstrate the integration of RAS in APEX with an example. We will long into the application using the user PSMITH. The authentication will be done using the APEX Express Accounts and if a RAS account exists with the same name, RAS policies will be used for that user. Figure 4-10 shows the authentication in the APEX application using PSMITH.

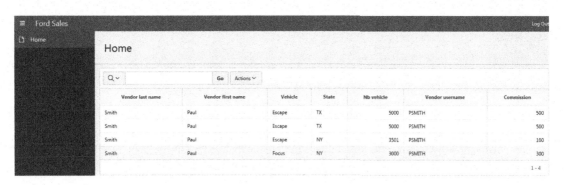

Figure 4-10. *Authentication into the application using the APEX Express Account*

■ **Note** The RAS user PSMITH doesn't have to be created with DIRECT LOGON USER option to "YES".

Figure 4-11 is showing the result of the SQL statement against the FORD_SALES table using the RAS context for the application user PSMITH.

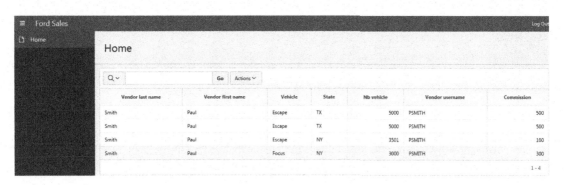

Figure 4-11. *Display of the SQL statement using the RAS context of PSMITH*

As a reminder, PSMITH has the vendor_role only. Let's execute the exact same steps but authenticated with JWILLIAMS. Figure 4-12 displays the result of the SQL statement using the RAS context of JWILLIAMS.

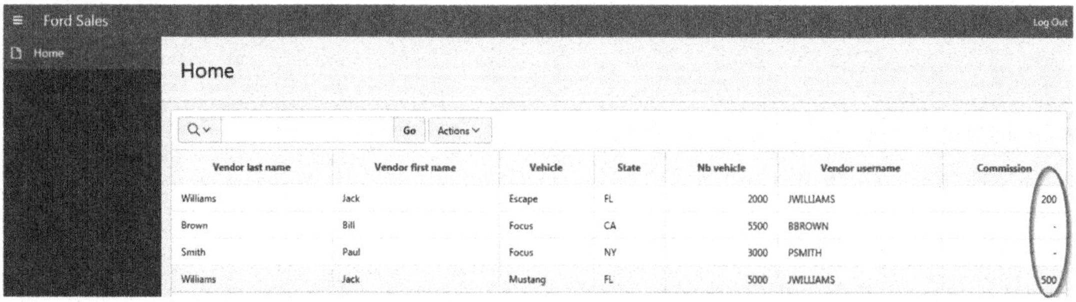

Figure 4-12. *Display of the SQL statement using the RAS context of JWILLIAMS*

As a reminder, JWILLIAMS has the vendor_role and the focus_role. He can't see the commissions of the other vendors. Let's execute the exact same steps but authenticated with BBROWN, who has the vendor_role and the manager_role. Figure 4-13 displays the result of the SQL statement.

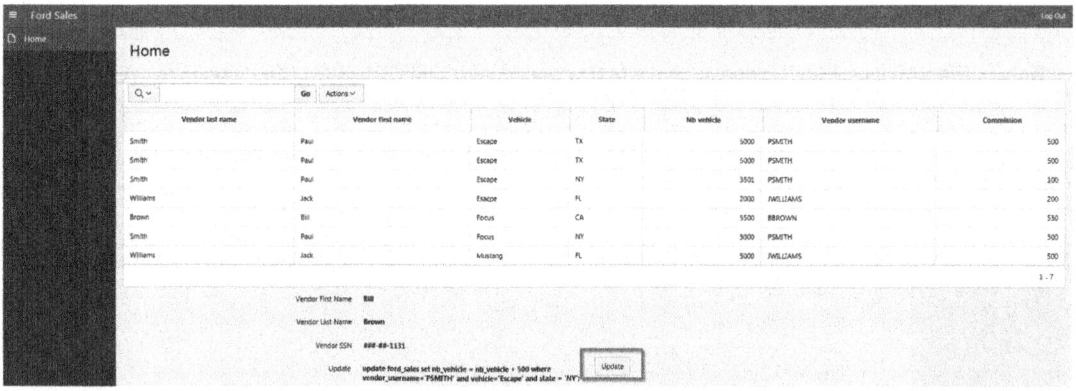

Figure 4-13. *Display of the SQL statement using the RAS context of BBROWN*

As a manager, BBROWN has the possibility to update the data as well. If you click the "Update" button, as we can see in Figure 4-14, after the execution of the SQL statement by the manager, the vendor PSMITH will have his number of cars sold in NY increased by 500.

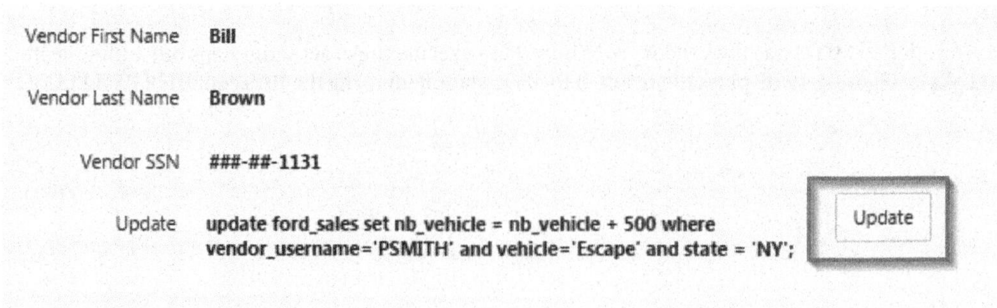

Figure 4-14

Figure 4-15 shows that BBROWN has the capability of updating the data, and you can see the results.

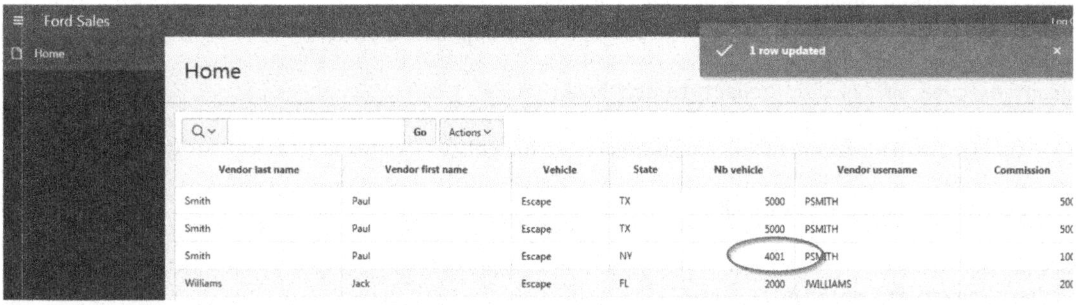

Figure 4-15. *New display of the SQL statement using the RAS context of BBROWN*

As in the example using SQL*Plus, we can see that BBROWN is able to update the data of the table FORD_SALES. You can perform the same operation while you are connected with either PSMITH or JWILLIAMS and you will see that the data will not change.

In that section, we have demonstrated the usage of Real Application Security. With the creation of application roles, application users, privileges, and data realms, we can control the access of data depending of the application user you are using. In the example, we were using three different application users, and we were always using the SQL statement "select * from ford_sales." Depending on which user we were connected with, the results and the permission on data are not the same. All of that is managed internally by RAS.

Data Redaction

Data Redaction provides on-the-fly redaction of sensitive data in SQL query results prior to display by applications so that unauthorized users cannot view the sensitive data. It gives consistent redaction of database columns across application modules accessing the same database information. This solution doesn't have any impact on operational activities such as backup and restore, upgrade, and patch, and high-availability deployment. From a performance point of view, Data Redaction is so far the faster approach, as the policies are enforced directly in the database kernel, resulting in tighter security and better performance.

Data Redaction policies can apply different transformations such as partial, random, and full redaction. Data Redaction can be applied conditionally, based on different factors that are tracked by the database or passed to the database by applications such as user identifiers, application identifiers, or client IP addresses.

Data Redaction fully supports Oracle Multitenant. When moving a pluggable database (PDB) that has redaction policies, the policies transfer directly to the new multitenant container database as part of the PDB. Redaction resumes its normal operation after the PDB has been plugged in and configured.

Example of a Data Redaction Deployment

We have a column in the "VENDOR_INFO" table that contains the Social Security Number (SSN) of the vendor. We need to store this information in our system, but we don't want to display it all in the application. For that reason, we will modify only the display of that information using Data Redaction policy.

The objective is to modify the output of the SSN. We will create a policy where it will replace the first five numbers with "#". Instead of having "546-78-1123" displayed, we will see "###-##-1123." Here are the commands to create the Data Redaction policy needed:

First, grant the execute on the PL/SQL package to the application owner

```
grant execute on sys.dbms_redact to sch_book;
```

Connect with the owner of the objects and create the policy:

```
connect sch_book/password@pdb001

begin
  dbms_redact.add_policy(
    object_schema => 'SCH_BOOK',
    object_name   => 'VENDOR_INFO',
    policy_name   => 'SSN_INFO',
    column_name   => 'SSN',
    function_type => dbms_redact.partial,
    function_parameters => 'VVVFVVFVVVV,VVV-VV-VVVV,#,1,5',
    expression    => '1=1'
  );
end;
/
```

Let's connect with the user BBROWN through SQL*Plus and query the table VENDOR_INFO.

```
SQL> connect bbrown/password@pdb001
Connected.
SQL> select * from vendor_info;

USERNAME             FIRST_NAME           LAST_NAME            SSN
-------------------- -------------------- -------------------- -----------
BBROWN               Bill                 Brown                ###-##-1131
```

The integration of Data Redaction in APEX is pretty simple as there is nothing to configure. Figure 4-16 shows an example of the output of a column with the Data Redaction on it.

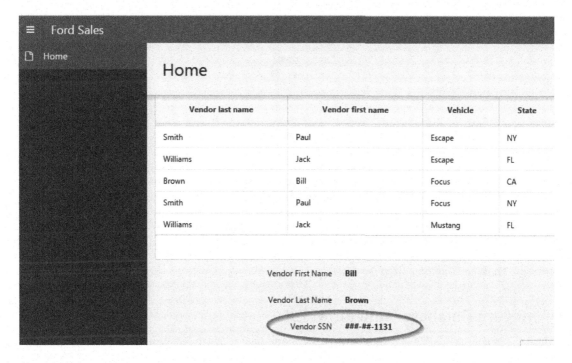

Figure 4-16. *Output of a column with a Data Redaction policy*

We have demonstrated how Data Redaction could be used to mask sensitive data. As we have seen in our example using SQL*Plus and the APEX application, Data Redaction policy protects sensitive data against any kind of application of data access.

Database Vault

Oracle Database Vault provides powerful security controls. Data breaches in the last few years are the result of unauthorized data access or abuse of privileged accounts. Database Vault secures existing data in the database and also controls sensitive commands made by DBA or high-privilege users. This section will not describe the usage of Database Vault but the impact on APEX.

What is the impact of having Database Vault enabled in a conjunction with APEX application? As you know, in the process of workspace creation, a new Oracle schema will be created. That is the issue while we have Database Vault enabled. APEX engine will not be able to create the Oracle schema associated to the new workspace. Figure 4-17 is showing the error when you want to create a new schema in a database with Database Vault enabled.

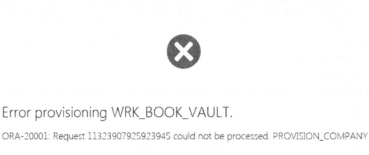

Figure 4-17. *When Database Vault is enabled*

Configure Database Vault for APEX

The APEX engine user "APEX_0*" must be given the appropriate access to Database Vault default realms and command rules. This user should be able to create new Oracle schemas within the workspace creation process. Oracle provided a script that gives the appropriate access so APEX engine will be able to create the necessary Oracle schema without errors. (See www.oracle.com/technetwork/database/options/database-vault/twp-security-database-vault-apex-2213126.pdf). In my example, APEX engine and Database Vault are installed in a PDB called "PDB001." Make sure the connection is properly done to the PDB.

■ **Note**   The following piece of code is coming from the Oracle documentation mentioned previously.

```
--###########################################################
--# Grant dv_acctmgr, ODD and Account manager for APEX_0XXXXX;
--# Update command rules
--# Please note that if the database has multiple APEX_0* schema, please replace
--# APEX_0% with APEX_ schema name that is relevant to your environment if right APEX_
--# schema is not selected.
--###########################################################
ACCEPT DVOWNER PROMPT "DV OWNER USERNAME: "
ACCEPT DVOWNERPWD hide PROMPT "DV OWNER USER PASSWORD: "
ACCEPT DVACCTMGR PROMPT "DV ACCOUNTMGR USERNAME: "
ACCEPT DVACCTMGRPWD hide PROMPT "DV ACCOUNTMGR USER PASSWORD: "

connect &DVOWNER/&DVOWNERPWD@PDB001

whenever sqlerror exit sql.sqlcode

connect &DVACCTMGR/&DVACCTMGRPWD@PDB001

connect &DVOWNER/&DVOWNERPWD@PDB001;
```

```
column max(username) new_val apex_user
select max (username) from all_users where username like 'APEX_0%';

whenever sqlerror continue

--###########################################################
-- If already granted, delete authorizations to the default realms for Oracle
Application Express schema user.
-- Ignore ORA-47261 error if authorizations are not granted before
--###########################################################
begin
 dbms_macadm.delete_auth_from_realm(realm_name => 'Oracle Default Schema Protection Realm',
grantee => '&apex_user');
end;
/
begin
 dbms_macadm.delete_auth_from_realm(realm_name => 'Oracle System Privilege and Role
Management Realm', grantee => '&apex_user');
end;
/
begin
 dbms_macadm.delete_auth_from_realm(realm_name => 'Oracle Default Component Protection
Realm', grantee => '&apex_user');
end;
/
begin
 dbms_macadm.delete_auth_from_realm(realm_name => 'Database Vault Account Management',
grantee => '&apex_user');
end;
/

whenever sqlerror exit sql.sqlcode

begin
 dbms_macadm.add_auth_to_realm(realm_name => 'Oracle Default Schema Protection Realm',
grantee => '&apex_user', rule_set_name => null, auth_options => dbms_macutl.g_realm_auth_
owner);
end;
/
begin
 dbms_macadm.add_auth_to_realm(realm_name => 'Oracle System Privilege and Role Management
Realm', grantee => '&apex_user', rule_set_name => null, auth_options => dbms_macutl.g_realm_
auth_owner);
end;
/

begin
 dbms_macadm.add_auth_to_realm(realm_name => 'Oracle Default Component Protection Realm',
grantee => '&apex_user', rule_set_name => null, auth_options => dbms_macutl.g_realm_auth_
owner);
end;
/
```

```
begin
 dbms_macadm.add_auth_to_realm(realm_name => 'Database Vault Account Management', grantee =>
'&apex_user', rule_set_name => null, auth_options => dbms_macutl.g_realm_auth_owner);
end;
/
```

```
exec dbms_macadm.update_rule('Is User Manager','DVSYS.DBMS_MACUTL.USER_HAS_ROLE_
VARCHAR(''DV_ACCTMGR'',SYS_CONTEXT(''userenv'',''current_user'')) = ''Y''')
exec dbms_macadm.update_rule('Is Alter DVSYS Allowed','DVSYS.DBMS_MACADM.IS_ALTER_USER_
ALLOW_VARCHAR(SYS_CONTEXT(''userenv'',''current_user'')) = ''Y''')
```

```
connect &DVACCTMGR/&DVACCTMGRPWD
alter session set container=PDB001;
```

```
grant dv_acctmgr to &apex_user;
```

Now that APEX engine has the privileges to create schema, let's perform the workspace creation again. Make sure the Database Vault is enabled with this SQL statement while connected to the DV_OWNER.

```
SQL> connect c##dbv_owner_root/password@PDB001
Connected.
```

```
SQL> select parameter, value from v$option where parameter = 'Oracle Database Vault';
```

```
PARAMETER                       VALUE
----------------------          ---------------------------------------
Oracle Database Vault           TRUE
```

Now that we know the Database Vault is enabled and we have permitted APEX to create a new schema, let's try to create a new APEX workspace. Figure 4-18 shows the creation of the APEX workspace.

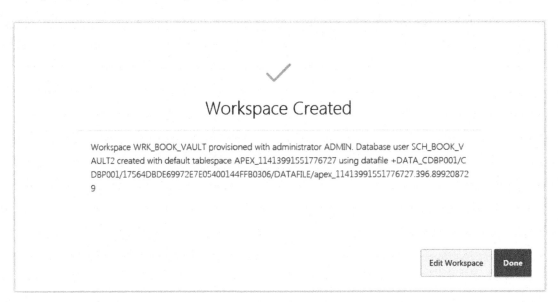

✓

Workspace Created

Workspace WRK_BOOK_VAULT provisioned with administrator ADMIN. Database user SCH_BOOK_V
AULT2 created with default tablespace APEX_11413991551776727 using datafile +DATA_CDBP001/C
DBP001/17564DBDE69972E7E05400144FFB0306/DATAFILE/apex_11413991551776727.396.89920872
9

Edit Workspace   Done

Figure 4-18. *APEX workspace creation with Database Vault enabled*

We have seen in this section that when Database Vault is enabled in a database, APEX is not able to process with the workspace creation. Oracle provides a script for the configuration of Database Vault to give access to APEX engine user to create the necessary objects for the workspace creation.

Summary

The objective of this chapter was to demonstrate the usage of database's advanced data security features within an APEX application.

The first feature called Real Application Security enforces data security by creating policy-based authorization models to secure the data access using application-level users, privileges, and roles. Once we have built the data security model, we have tested the functionally of RAS through SQL*Plus as well as through an APEX application.

We have also demonstrated how to use the Data Redaction feature. The usage of this feature is totally transparent to the APEX application.

We concluded by talking about the Database Vault feature and the way you must deploy it in a context of APEX environments.

CHAPTER 5

∎ ∎ ∎

APEX and Oracle E-Business Suite

Sometimes in Oracle E-Business Suite (EBS) there are some functionalities that are not tailored or are missing to satisfy specific business domains or requirements. In order to accommodate those specific requirements, it is possible to build custom applications that extend the original functionalities of EBS while still being totally integrated with it. These types of applications are called **extensions**.

Having these extensions created properly increases the organization value by removing manual processes done in Excel spreadsheets or any other external systems.

APEX is a supported and recommended tool to build EBS extensions. In order to use APEX in an EBS environment, it has to be properly configured and installed following the best practices for an EBS environment. This will make it easier to maintain, upgrade, patch, and support the EBS software. We all know how complex keeping the infrastructure at the right patch level can be, especially in an EBS environment. This chapter covers the architecture required to ease this patching process of EBS installs having extensions.

Architecture

Installing APEX in an EBS architecture is somewhat simple. As mentioned in Chapter 3, APEX requires the Oracle Rest Data Services (ORDS) to be installed on an application server in the middle-tier. In order to keep things well organized and easily maintainable, it is recommended to install ORDS on a separate application server. ORDS is very lightweight and can be deployed on Oracle WebLogic, Apache Tomcat, or Oracle GlassFish. See Chapter 3 for more information.

With EBS 11i, 12.0, and 12.1, the middle-tier uses the Oracle HTTP Server (OHS). So it may be an option to install an Oracle WebLogic server on the same physical server. Ideally, it is recommended to use a separate server to avoid any conflicts when EBS is being patched or upgraded.

With EBS 12.2, the middle-tier already uses an Oracle WebLogic server, as shown in Figure 5-1. In that case, it is also recommended to deploy ORDS on a separate Oracle WebLogic server or one of the other supported application servers like Apache or GlassFish. Again, this is to avoid any issues when patching or upgrading EBS. See the section on patching EBS vs. patching APEX later in this chapter.

© Francis Mignault and Luc Demanche 2016

F. Mignault and L. Demanche, *Oracle Application Express Administration*, DOI 10.1007/978-1-4842-1958-4_5

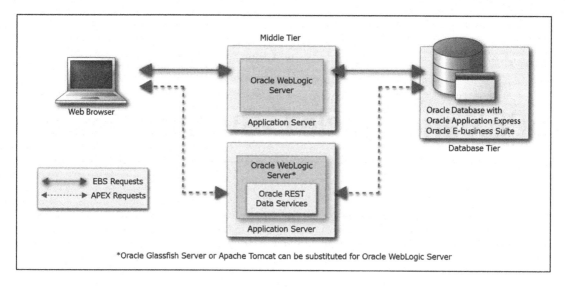

Figure 5-1. *APEX architecture in EBS*

■ **Note** For more information on using and building APEX extensions, see the Oracle White Paper written by the Oracle APEX team in conjunction with the Oracle EBS team: Extending Oracle E-Business Suite Release 12.1 and Above with Oracle Application Express (Revision 2, Note 1306563.1).

APEX Schema vs. APPS Schema

As mentioned in Chapter 2, APEX requires specific database schemas to work. The main APEX schema is APEX_050000 where the engine and the applications are stored. As shown in Figure 5-2, APEX can be installed directly in the EBS database. Application requests will connect to the database using the APEX_PUBLIC_USER schema. This is the recommended architecture.

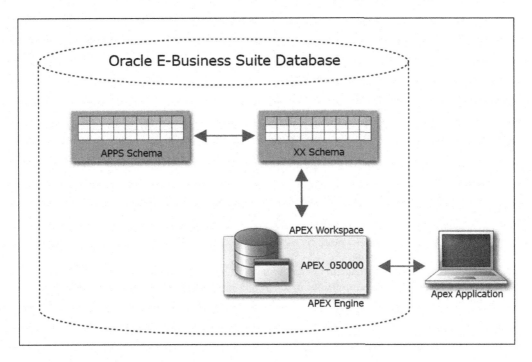

Figure 5-2. *APEX in the EBS database*

If, for some reason, it is not possible to install APEX in the same database as EBS, a database link can be used for applications to connect to the *XX Schema* as shown in Figure 5-3. Be aware that using this configuration will impact performance since all the transactions in the application will have to go through the database link. It is possible to gain some performance by using different methods like using Oracle Materialized views on the remote database.

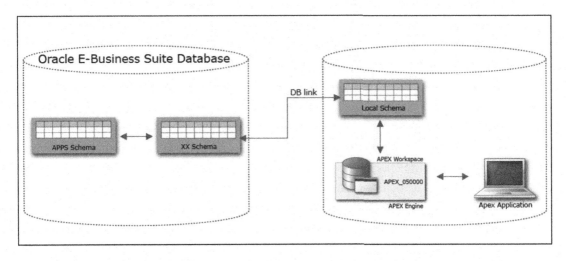

Figure 5-3. *APEX in a separate database and using a DBLink to the EBS database*

In Oracle EBS, one of the most important schemas is called APPS. This is the main schema for EBS where views, PL/SQL code (procedure, functions, and packages) and synonyms reside. Each EBS module's schema grants full privileges to the APPS schema. It has synonyms to all base module tables and sequences. It is the only schema that has universal access to all the modules in EBS.

As explained in Chapter 2, each APEX application is associated to one database schema. In EBS, this schema should be your custom *XX Schema*.

The *XX Schema* should be used to store your specific database objects for extensions. It is prefixed by *XX* to differentiate it from the standard EBS objects. Some organizations are creating an *XX schema* for each EBS modules, while others prefer to only have one *XX schema* for all custom objects created to satisfy the execution of each extension. It all depends on your organization's standards and preferences. There may be one or multiple *XX schemas* in your EBS database for other types of extension already in place. It is perfectly fine to reuse them for building APEX extensions.

When building extensions, you might need to access database packages, functions, procedures, or views that are located in the APPS schema. Tables from different modules (GL, AP, PO, etc.) can be accessed through synonyms in the APPS schema. Unless there is no other way to get to these tables, you should never access them directly but instead use views pointing to these tables. For additional security, it is also possible to use "read only" views when applicable.

In order to keep things clean and to facilitate maintenance, it is recommended to create the custom database objects required for the APEX extensions in the proper schema. See Figure 5-4 to see where the custom XX database objects should be created.

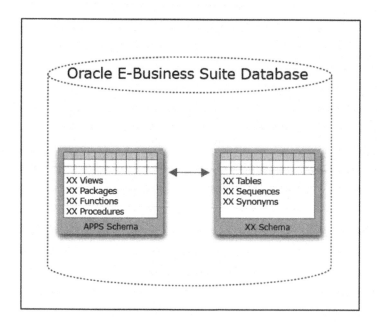

Figure 5-4. *XX database objects*

Custom database packages, functions, procedures, and views should be created directly in the APPS schema. Synonyms, tables, sequences, triggers, and indexes should be created in the *XX Schema*.

For the *XX Schema* to be able to execute the packages, functions, and procedures in the APPS schema, created for the APEX extensions, the proper database privileges have to be given on those objects to the *XX Schema*. Grants may have to be granted from the *XX Schema* to the APPS schema also, in order for the custom packages to be able to access the custom tables.

In the *XX Schema*, you may have to create another set of *XX* views based on the *XX* synonyms to fully use the declarative and rapid development features of the APEX wizards. The APEX wizards can only see tables or views, not synonyms or granted objects.

The objective of these recommendations is to keep the APEX extensions and their related database objects as decoupled as possible from the EBS database objects. This will prevent problems that may arise after patching or upgrading EBS.

For example, a very popular functionality in most EBS process is the use of profile options. FND_PROFILE is the package used to read or save profile values, which is defined in the APPS schema. In order to keep everything as decoupled as possible, it is recommended to create a custom database package called XX_FND_ PROFILE in the APPS schema, which becomes a wrapper package to make calls to the proper procedures in the standard PL/SQL package.

You need to grant execute on APPS.XX_FND_PROFILE to the *XX Schema* and create a synonym in the XX schema that points to this procedure. This way, if ever the FND_PROFILE package is changed during an EBS patch, only the XX_FND_PROFILE has to be changed for the APEX applications to continue working. Nothing has to be changed in the APEX applications used for the extensions.

EBS Patching vs. APEX Patching

The biggest advantage of using Oracle Application Express to create EBS extensions is the fact that patching EBS gets a lot easier. As explained before, APEX uses the same recommended structures for the database objects as any other technologies used for building extensions. This is to make the work of the database administrator the same as if other technologies were used, from a database schema perspective.

The biggest difference, from Oracle Forms for example, is that the APEX technology stack is not integrated with the EBS technology stack as shown in the architecture section of this chapter. Patching EBS will not affect APEX in the database or on the middle tier. On the other hand, patching EBS when Oracle Forms is used might have an impact on the Oracle Forms binaries since it is embedded in the EBS configuration. It might also force a recompile of all the Oracle Forms application source files (.fmb) to comply with the new release.

When patching or upgrading the Oracle database or EBS, there is no impact on the APEX install. The only possible problem can come from the *XX* packages, functions, or procedures if the signature of an EBS database object has changed. If the recommended structure explained in the previous sections is used, then the only adjustments will have to be made at the database level on the *XX* objects. There will be no changes required in the APEX applications.

The same applies for patching or upgrading APEX. It is possible to patch and upgrade APEX without having to patch EBS. That means that if a new release of APEX comes out, it will be possible to upgrade to that new release without having to apply an EBS patch. New features of APEX will be available much more rapidly and at different times than the required EBS patch cycle. This way, extensions can use the latest in web technologies and at the same time make end users much more productive, and happier.

Security

Security in the context of EBS APEX extensions can be leveraged at multiple levels (authentication, function security, operating unit access, GL segments, etc.). In this section, we will concentrate on two specific elements:

- User authentication for the integration of the EBS session with the APEX applications

- Authorization security allowing restriction of access to functions based on the menu definition of a responsibility.

Authentication

User authentication is the validation of the username and password against the EBS credentials already defined. Since APEX requires an authentication in order to execute the defined applications, the issue is to share the secured EBS authentication with APEX.

For authenticating users when accessing an APEX application in an EBS context, it is possible to use EBS functions, which will make sure the EBS user exists and is still active.

There are two ways you can access an APEX application as an EBS extension.

1. Standalone: an APEX application offers a login screen where the EBS credentials are expected

2. Full integration access from the EBS navigator: the user is navigating to an APEX application the same way it would navigate to a forms screen or an Oracle Application Framework (OAF) page

We will not go in the detail on how to install or use these functionalities since this book is more oriented toward the general concepts of integrating EBS with APEX from an administrator point of view.

There is a prepackaged library available which helps in creating the bridge between EBS and APEX and provides instructions on how to configure an EBS-enabled APEX extension. This integration package can be found at the following address: `http://www.insum.ca/services/` in the *Oracle EBS Extensions* section. It is a well-documented, open-source project that can be used free of charge.

Single Sign-on

In order to prevent users from having to provide credentials and reconnect every time they access an APEX extension, there are different ways to implement a single sign-on process.

There are different single sign-on solutions available for EBS extensions. When using APEX as a tool for building extensions, it is possible to link the authentication to any single sign-on process already in place.

If OAM is used, then the APEX HTTP Header built-in authentication should be used. For detailed information on how to use APEX with Oracle Access Manages OAM see the following white paper from Oracle: Oracle Application Express and Integration with Oracle Access Manager (OAM)(Doc ID 1323373.1).

If there is not any single sign-on process already in place and the usage of other commercial single sign-on tools is not an option, it is possible to implement a custom single sign-on solution.

There is an open-source single sign-on solution, available in the same place and same zip file as the authentication package mentioned previously, that can be used in multiple different combinations.

This single sign-on solution can be used when the APEX database is remote using either a database link or web services to connect to the EBS database, as well as in a standard installation. It is surely the most secured and up-to-date option available as an open-source solution. At the moment of writing these lines, a new open-source project is being built for offering an updated SSO for EBS that will be made available at the same address as the current package.

Authorization

Once the user is authenticated, the APEX extensions have to give access to functionalities specific to the user privileges within the EBS responsibility used to access the APEX application. This is called authorization. Responsibilities assigned to users are the vehicle by which users can have access to an APEX application defined as a function in a custom EBS menu. Functions can also be used to give access to specific functionalities within an application in a more granular way.

For authorization, the APEX application used for the extension has to go and read the profile of the connected user. Reading the profile will give different information about the user like, for example, the language used, the responsibilities that this user has access to, and the organization he is part of. Those utilities are part of the open-source package mentioned in the "Authentication" section.

Summary

APEX is a supported and easy solution for extending and accessing Oracle EBS. Using APEX for extensions will simplify the upgrade and patching process of EBS compared to the other solutions available. It is easy to integrate the management of sessions, user logins, security, and user interface for a better user experience. By doing so, end users will gain various new modern capabilities that will make their work more productive.

CHAPTER 6

High Availability

The availability of an application is measured by how it's perceived by the users. They can get frustrated when they expect the application and data to be available, when it is not. The user who wants the application to be always up and running needs high availability. Oracle offers different strategies to deploy high availability environments. Real Application Cluster (RAC) and Data Guard are the main technologies and are designed to provide uninterrupted computing service during the essential period of time. It is important to note that whichever high availability strategies you deploy, it will be totally transparent for APEX. We will demonstrate how to deploy these strategies so APEX can benefit of these high availability features.

This chapter is divided into two main sections, the overview of RAC and an example of deployment and we will also describe how Data Guard can be a complement of a RAC deployment to maintain a disaster recovery site.

Overview of a High Availability Solution Using RAC

As mentioned earlier, high availability refers to systems that are durable and likely to operate continuously without failure for a long time. This means that we have to deploy redundancy in every layer of the application, such as network infrastructure, storage, server, database, application, and so on.

As we know, APEX keeps its session's context stored in the database using a unique identifier which we can see in the APEX URL. This unique identifier is used to retrieve the session's information of the corresponding session in the database. Keeping the session's information in the database actually makes high availability easier as the browser can use any application server in the cluster as well as any database instance in the RAC, as long as the URL contains the unique identifier to retrieve the session's information in the database. We will see the importance of this later in the scenarios.

High Availability Solution for the Database

Oracle RAC is a shared clustered database infrastructure that provides database performance, scalability, and reliability without any changes on the application side. This technology is also complimentary with any other Oracle technology such as Multitenant, Oracle Data Guard, Active Data Guard, Golden Gate, and so on.

Oracle RAC provides the customer with complete flexibility for scaling database workloads. Customers build servers and storage pools that they can easily scale out by simply adding servers to the cluster and as demand requires.

Oracle RAC is a key component of Oracle's Maximum Availability Architecture (MAA). RAC is not only enabling the customer to continue processing database workloads in the event of a server failure, it also helps the customer by minimizing the downtime for server maintenance.

© Francis Mignault and Luc Demanche 2016
F. Mignault and L. Demanche, *Oracle Application Express Administration*, DOI 10.1007/978-1-4842-1958-4_6

Oracle Database Quality of Service (QoS) makes sure the user's performance and service level expectations for specific workloads are respected. Using logical pools of servers, QoS can either recommend or automatically move servers between pools to maintain the performance objectives. We can imagine having a customer deploying Oracle RAC and Oracle Database QoS to consolidate all of the database workloads on one RAC infrastructure.

High Availability Solution for the Application Server

When we want to design a high availability infrastructure for the application side, we are thinking of having multiple application servers. As we know with APEX, the application resides in the database, so it means that we don't have to deploy the application code on every application server, which simplifies the deployment, as well as the maintenances of the code. In regards to the APEX listener, we have decided to use ORDS deployed in Tomcat in our example. Chapter 3 discusses using WebLogic or GlassFish as alternative web containers instead of Tomcat.

Usage of a Load Balancer

In front of the application servers, we will deploy a web server, in this case Apache, using a load balancer module and a proxy module that will redirect incoming requests to one of the available application servers. In real-world production environments, an SSL module would also be used to serve the application(s) over HTTPS. In the next section we will see a basic deployment of Apache with the load balancer and proxy module.

Deploying a High Availability Solution

This section presents an example of the high availability solution for the database, Oracle RAC, as well as the deployment of multiple application servers that will serve an APEX application. We will also see the configuration of the web server, using the load balancer and proxy modules in front of the application servers.

Deployment and Configuration of RAC

The objective of this section is not to demonstrate the deployment of a RAC database. We will instead use Oracle Cloud to easily create and host our RAC database. We have created a database using two nodes that use Oracle Single Client Access Name (SCAN) for the management of the virtual IPs.

■ **Note** To ease the deployment of that solution in regards to the networking and the security, all nodes created in Oracle Cloud are part of the same Identity Domain.

Here is the information about the RAC database:

CDB Name	cdb1.xxx.oraclecloud.internal
PDB Name	pdb1.xxx.oraclecloud.internal
Apex version	5.0 installed in the PDB
Service name for OLTP	appserv.xxx.oraclecloud.internal
Service name for report	reportserv.xxx.oraclecloud.internal

Here is the information about the SCAN listener:

SCAN name	ora-ext-db2-scan-int
SCAN 0 IPv4 VIP	10.106.50.162
SCAN 1 IPv4 VIP	10.106.50.166

As we have seen in Chapter 7, when a new Oracle 12c (12.1.0.2) is created, the APEX version by default is 4.2, and the installation is done in the CDB. The first thing we need to do is to uninstall that version of APEX and install APEX 5.0 in the PDB.

Creation of Dynamic Database Services

The usage of the dynamic database services allows us to use multiple database features. The most interesting features are as follows:

- Usage of multiple instances of the RAC
- Load Balancing Advisor
- Run-Time Connection Load Balancing
- Database Resource Manager
- Failover capabilities

After the configuration of the RAC database, we will then create two database services that will be used by the application for OLTP or Reporting, depending on the type of work that needs to be done. The first database service called "appserv" will be used by the web application, and the service "reportserv" will be used by any reporting tools. Here is the definition we want for both database services:

Database Service Name	APPSERV	REPORTSERV
Container Database Name	CDB1	CDB1
Pluggable Database Name	PDB1	PDB1
Preferred Instances	CDB11,CDB12	CDB12
Database Resource Manager Consumer Group	OLTP PLAN	DSS PLAN
Management Policy	AUTOMATIC	AUTOMATIC
Connection Load Balancing Goal	SHORT	LONG
Runtime Load Balancing Goal	SERVICE_TIME	SERVICE_TIME

■ **Note** The service "reportserv" is a noncritical service and will be assigned only to CDB12. We don't want the service to failover to CDB11 and having a negative performance impact on that instance.

In addition to defining which instances the database service will be assigned to, it also allows us to use server-side load balancing by communicating with the Load Balancing Advisor. As discussed in Chapter 16, database service also allows us to use the Resource Manager feature. Two different Resource Manager Consumer Groups will be used in this example.

■ **Note**   We are creating the database service "reportserv" even though it will not be used in our demonstration. I wanted to highlight the best practice of using multiple database services depending on the needs.

Here are the commands to create and start both services:

```
srvctl add service -db cdb1 -service appserv -pdb pdb1 -preferred cdb11,cdb12 -policy
automatic -clbgoal short -rblgoal service_time

srvctl start service -db cdb1 -service appserv

srvctl add service -db cdb1 -service reportserv -pdb pdb1 -preferred cdb12 -policy automatic
-clbgoal long -rblgoal service_time

srvctl start service -db cdb1 -service reportserv
```

As mentioned, the service "reportserv" is assigned only to the instance cdb12 as we don't want any negative impact on cdb11.

■ **Note**   We could have included the concept of Transparent Application Failover by using the options for "Failover type" and "Failover method" at the database services creation.

Figure 6-1 shows the configuration of the RAC database, the database services, as well as the installation of APEX.

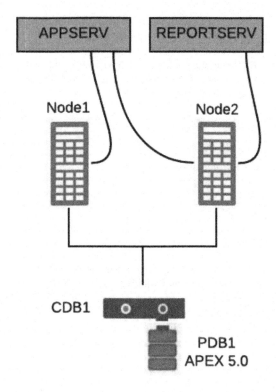

Figure 6-1. *RAC, database services, and APEX configuration*

Deployment and Configuration of ORDS

Once the database side is up and running with the latest version of APEX and the database services, we will be ready to configure the application side. We have once again used the Oracle Cloud to easily create and host the application servers. As we would like to have a high availability environment, we have created two application servers that are running ORDS in Tomcat as the web container. Here is the information:

Application Server	IP	Server Name	Web container	APEX Listener and port	Database Service
Application Server #1	129.191.14.54	b70c7d	Tomcat	ORDS – 8080	appserv
Application Server #2	129.152.159.71	e228b8	Tomcat	ORDS – 8080	appserv

Before starting the configuration and deployment of ORDS, we will need to transfer the APEX source folder onto both application servers since the configuration of the APEX listener requires having the APEX images on the same server.

Refer to Chapter 8 for the installation of ORDS on the first application server. ORDS will be configured using port 8080 and the connection to the database will be done using the database service "appserv". Please note that we are using the SCAN listener IP for the connectivity to the database.

```
Enter the name of the database server [localhost]:10.106.50.162
Enter the database listen port [1521]:
Enter 1 to specify the database service name, or 2 to specify the database SID [1]:
Enter the database service name:appserv.xxx.oraclecloud.internal
.... (output lines have been removed for simplicity)
Enter 1 if you wish to start in standalone mode or 2 to exit [1]:
Enter the APEX static resources location:/app/apex/images
Enter 1 if using HTTP or 2 if using HTTPS [1]:
Enter the HTTP port [8080]:
```

If ORDS doesn't want to start, the connectivity between the application server and the database server might be blocked. Make sure the connectivity using port 1521 (default port on Oracle Cloud) is allowed. You can install the Oracle Instant Client on the application server to validate the network configuration. Once the connectivity to the database is confirmed using Oracle Instant Client, there is no reason ORDS can't connect to the database. When you complete the configuration of ORDS, stop the APEX listener before performing the next step.

Deployment of ORDS into Tomcat

Assuming that Tomcat is already up and running on the application server. Two steps are required for the deployment of ORDS to Tomcat. First, create a folder that stores the APEX images.

```
$ mkdir $CATALINA_HOME/webapps/i/
$ cp -R $APEX_HOME/images/* $CATALINA_HOME/webapps/i/
```

Next, copy the "ords.war" file to Tomcat's "webapps" folder

```
$ cp ords.war $CATALINA_HOME/webapps/
```

A quick way to validate if ORDS and Tomcat are fully functional is to use a web browser and try this URL using the IP of the application server; http://129.191.14.54:8080/ords/f?p=4550.

You should see the APEX Home Page from the application server as we can see in Figure 6-2.

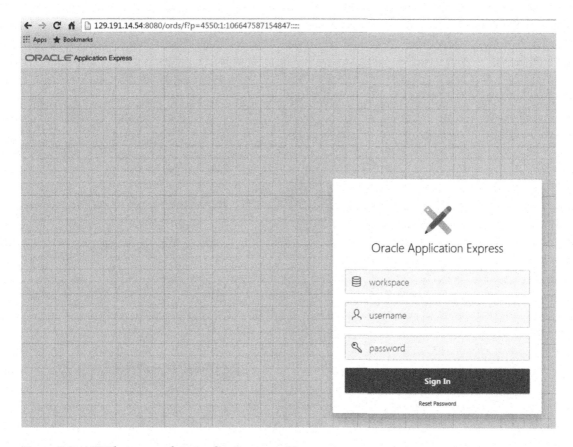

Figure 6-2. *APEX home page from application server #1*

Once the first application server is functional, perform the same steps to deploy and configure ORDS and Tomcat on the second application server. Again, use the following URL, `http://129.152.159.71:8080/ords/f?p=4550,` using the IP address of the application server to validate if the second application server is functional as we can see in Figure 6-3.

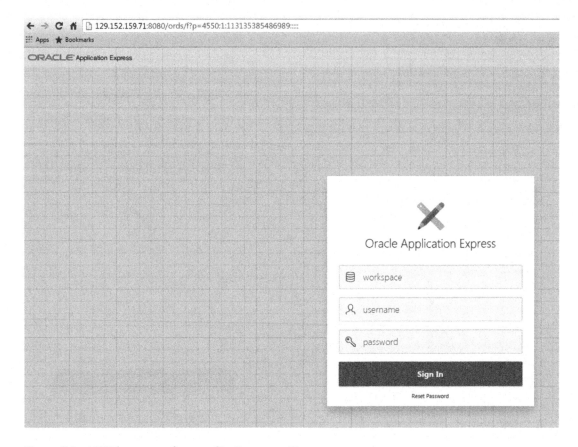

Figure 6-3. *APEX home page from application server #2*

Deployment of the Load Balancer

Once the database level and the application level are deployed, both with a certain level of high availability, we are now ready to deploy the load balancer in front of the application servers. We will use Apache as the web server with the module "mod_proxy_balancer". Simply add this section to the end of the httpd.conf file:

```
ProxyPreserveHost On
<Proxy balancer://mycluster>
                BalancerMember http://129.191.14.54:8080
                BalancerMember http://129.152.159.71:8080
</Proxy>
ProxyPass "/ords" "balancer://mycluster/ords"
ProxyPassReverse "/ords" "balancer://mycluster/ords"
ProxyPass "/i" "balancer://mycluster/i"
ProxyPassReverse "/i" "balancer://mycluster/i"
```

We can recognize the two IP addresses belonging to the application servers deployed in the previous section. The balancer tag encloses the list of machines which will be used by the balancer to forward requests. The ProxyPreserveHost directive is used to avoid any issues with CORS (Cross Origin Resource

Sharing) by telling the back-end application server (ORDS) the necessary information for it to correctly serve the APEX application. The ProxyPass and ProxyPassReverse directives are used for both root paths used by APEX, namely, ords and i (i being for the images and static files). This allows for all traffic corresponding to these two paths to be correctly forwarded on the way in and the way out.

■ **Note** If you want to add another application server in the cluster, simply add its IP address as a new BalancerMember.

It is not necessary for your front-end web server to listen on the same port(s) as the application server tier. In fact it is often even necessary to have Apache listening on the standard HTTP and HTTPS ports, 80 and 443, to not confuse end users. The proxy and reverse proxy directives translate from one port to another and can also translate from HTTPS to HTTP as well. For example, the incoming request could be on port 443 and thus in HTTPS and Apache can proxy that request to the application tier which is listening on port 8080 and using standard HTTP. Once configured, the web server will redirect the request to one available member of the cluster. The URL to be used is the IP of the web server.

In our example, we are using this URL, using the IP of the Apache server, http://129.152.159.118:8080/ords/f?p=4550. Apache is listening on port 8080 and proxying the request onto port 8080 as well (for simplicity's sake), and Figure 6-4 is showing the APEX home page, coming from one of the application servers.

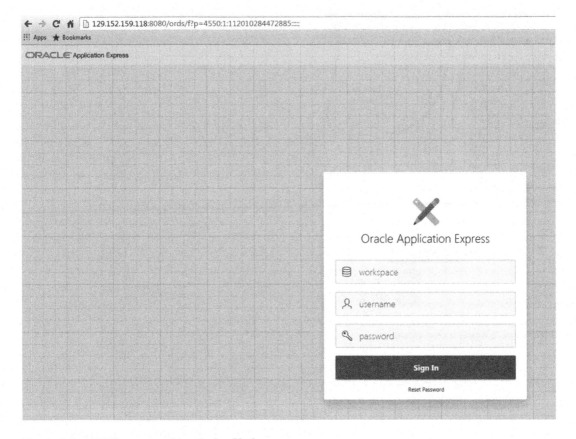

Figure 6-4. APEX home page from the load balancer

We have seen in this section how to deploy, using Oracle Cloud, the different layers of the application, including the database using RAC, multiple application servers, and the web server in front of them. Figure 6-5 shows the entire configuration.

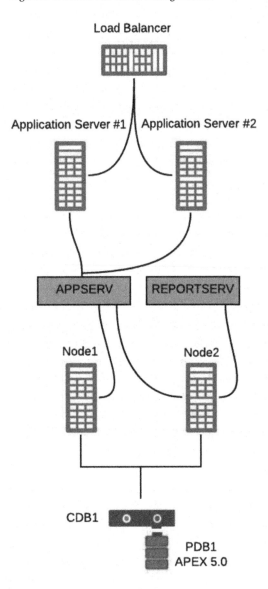

Figure 6-5. *Complete configuration*

High Availability Scenarios

In this section we would like to cover a few scenarios of planned and unplanned downtime. The first scenario will present a situation where we lost one node of the database cluster. The second scenario will demonstrate what happens if we lost one of the application servers. In both cases, we will focus on the impact the users will experience from the application point of view.

Loss of a Database Node

To demonstrate the functionalities of RAC, database services, and the impact on the application front end, we will be accessing the application through application server #1 directly, not through the load balancer.

For the demonstration, we will use the application called "Incident Tracking." Figure 6-6 shows the home page of this application.

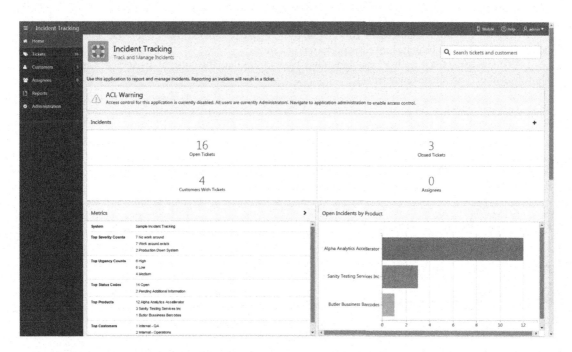

Figure 6-6. *Home page of the application Incident Tracking*

Here is the status of the connectivity between application server #1 (server name is b70c7d) and the database RAC. From the Oracle instance, cdb11 running on node #1, we have the following connections:

```
USERNAME                         MACHINE
-------------------------------- ----------------------------------------
APEX_PUBLIC_USER                 b70c7d
APEX_PUBLIC_USER                 b70c7d
```

From the Oracle instance, cdb12 running on node #2, we have the following connection:

```
USERNAME                      MACHINE
----------------------------  ---------------------------------------
APEX_PUBLIC_USER              b70c7d
```

We can see that application server #1 is using both instances. Let's also validate the status of the instances as well as the database service.

```
$ srvctl status instance -db cdb1 -instance cdb11,cdb12
Instance cdb11 is running on node ora-ext-db21
Instance cdb12 is running on node ora-ext-db22

$ srvctl status service -db cdb1 -service appserv
Service appserv is running on instance(s) cdb11,cdb12
```

We can see that both instances are running on their respective nodes, and the service "appserv", used by the application, is using both instances as preferred instances.

Let's imagine database node #1 is going down. We will simulate the crash of the server by issuing a "shutdown abort" on the instance cdb11.

```
SQL> shutdown abort
ORACLE instance shut down.
```

Let's rerun the select statement on both instances to have the status of the connections between the application server and the instances. From the Oracle instance, cdb11 running on node #1, we have an error because of the crash.

```
SQL> select username,machine from v$session where username = 'APEX_PUBLIC_USER';
select username,machine from v$session where username = 'APEX_PUBLIC_USER'
*
ERROR at line 1:
ORA-01034: ORACLE not available
Process ID: 0
Session ID: 0 Serial number: 0
```

From the Oracle instance, cdb12 running on node #2, we have the following connections:

```
USERNAME                      MACHINE
----------------------------  ---------------------------------------
APEX_PUBLIC_USER              b70c7d
```

Let's also validate the status of the instances as well as the database server.

```
$ srvctl status instance -db cdb1 -instance cdb11,cdb12
Instance cdb11 is not running on node ora-ext-db21
Instance cdb12 is running on node ora-ext-db22

$ srvctl status service -db cdb1 -service appserv
Service appserv is running on instance(s) cdb12
```

We can confirm that the instance cdb11, which was running on node #1, is down. Also, the database service "appserv" is using the instance cdb12 only.

Here is the impact on the front-end application, let's click the "Tickets" menu on the left side. Figure 6-7 shows the result.

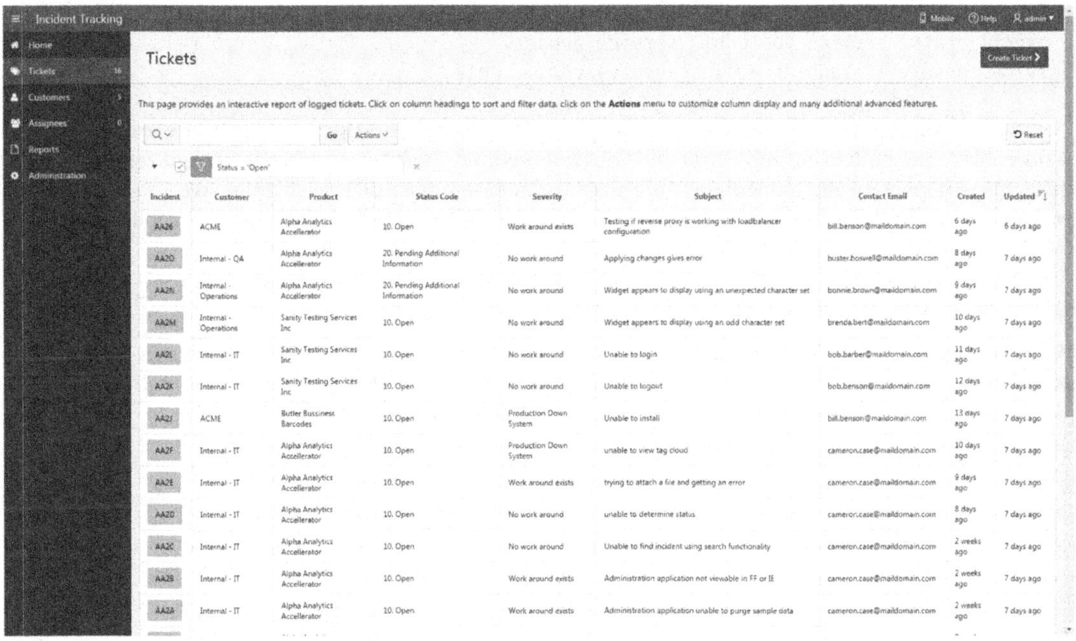

Figure 6-7. *Selection on the "Ticket" menu*

There is no error in the application front end; that means APEX was able to complete the request by using the context information that was stored in the database. The application server, using the database service "appserver" (now using cdb12 only), was able to complete the request, even though the last request might have been executed using the instance cdb11, and now the database instance cdb11 is down. APEX can use any of the available database instances in the cluster totally transparently.

To complete the demonstration, we will restart the failed instance and see how the database service will handle this. Let's start the failed instance cdb11.

```
SQL> startup
ORACLE instance started.

Total System Global Area 8053063680 bytes
Fixed Size                  2943408 bytes
Variable Size            1325401680 bytes
Database Buffers         5083496448 bytes
Redo Buffers               30609408 bytes
In-Memory Area           1610612736 bytes
Database mounted.
Database opened.
```

Let's also validate the status of the instances as well as the database service.

```
$ srvctl status instance -db cdb1 -instance cdb11,cdb12
Instance cdb11 is running on node ora-ext-db21
Instance cdb12 is running on node ora-ext-db22

$ srvctl status service -db cdb1 -service appserv
Service appserv is running on instance(s) cdb11,cdb12
```

We can confirm that the instance cdb11 is up and running now, and also the database service "appserv" is now able to use both instances, cdb11 and cdb12, if required. Oracle automatically recognized that the instance cdb11 was up and immediately informs the database service of its availability. We know now that we can lose any node in the database cluster and there is no impact at all on the front-end application.

Loss of an Application Server Node

We would like to demonstrate the impact of the loss of one application server. Figure 6-8 shows that scenario.

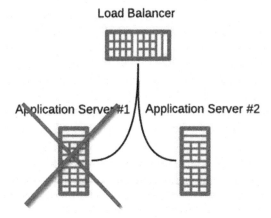

Figure 6-8. *Loss of one application server*

As we were mentioning in the section "Deployment of the Load Balancer," we have configured the load balancer with the two IP addresses of the application servers in the "BalancerMember" section. The load balancer is redirecting the request to one of the available application servers. If the application server #1 becomes not available, the load balancer will redirect the request to the next available one.

Once the failed application server is back online, it will be back in the list of available application servers and the load balancer will start redirecting requests to it. Let's demonstrate the impact when an application server goes down.

We will be using three different URLs:

- URL of the application through application server #1

- URL of the application through application server #2

- URL of the application through load balancer

Using a browser with three tabs, let's see the output of the three URLs; first Figure 6-9 shows the page from applications server #1.

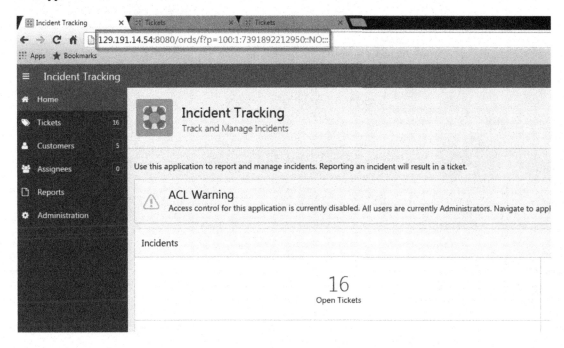

Figure 6-9. *Page request through the application server #1*

Now, we will see Figure 6-10 showing the page from application server #2.

Figure 6-10. *Page request through application server #2*

Now, we will see Figure 6-11 showing the page when we are requesting from the load balancer.

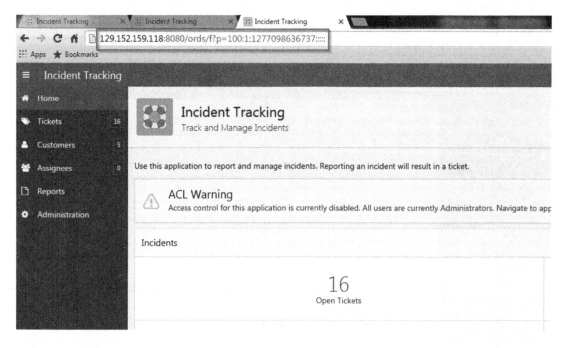

Figure 6-11. *Page request through the load balancer*

Now we will see what the impact would be when the application server #1 goes down. We will now shut down Tomcat on application server #1.

```
# $CATALINA_HOME/bin/shutdown.sh
Using CATALINA_BASE:   /app/apache-tomcat-7.0.70
Using CATALINA_HOME:   /app/apache-tomcat-7.0.70
Using CATALINA_TMPDIR: /app/apache-tomcat-7.0.70/temp
Using JRE_HOME:        /app/jdk1.8.0_101
Using CLASSPATH:       /app/apache-tomcat-7.0.70/bin/bootstrap.jar:/app/apache-
                       tomcat-7.0.70/bin/tomcat-juli.jar
```

Now that application server #1 is down, let's click the "Tickets" menu on the left side to see the impact on the front-end application. Figure 6-12 shows the page from application server #1.

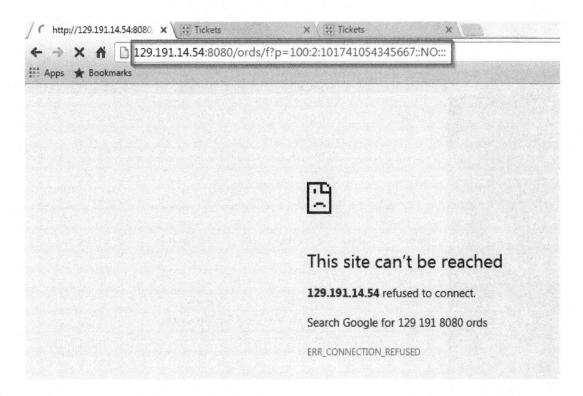

Figure 6-12. *Page request through application server #1*

As expected, application server #1 is not responding. Let's see the impact on application server #2; Figure 6-13 shows that page.

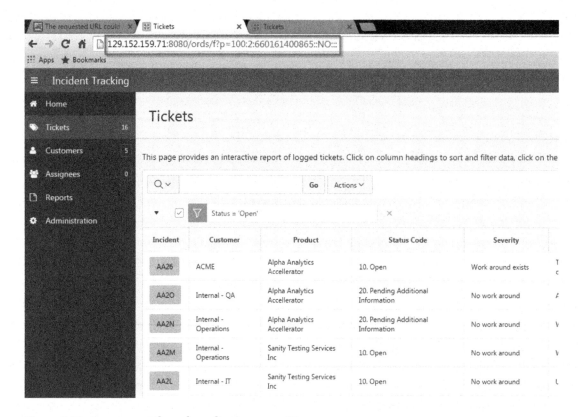

Figure 6-13. *Page request through application server #2*

Application server #2 still responds to new page requests, as expected. Now, let's see when we are requesting a new page from the load balancer. Figure 6-14 shows the results.

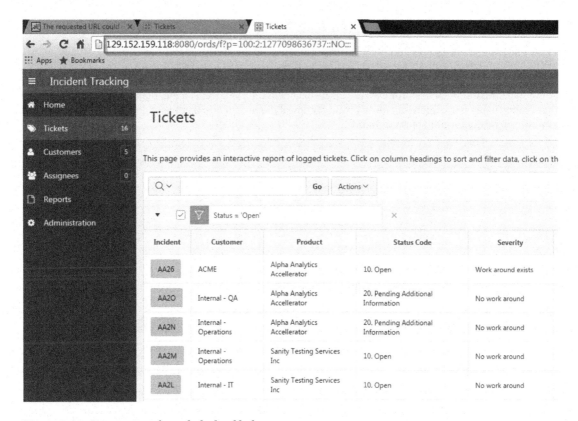

Figure 6-14. *Page request through the load balancer*

This demonstrates that the load balancer is sending the request to the available application server. If one of the application servers is not available, the load balancer will not send it any requests. Once it is back online, it will become available for the load balancer to send page requests. In this example, when application server #1 was down, the load balancer was sending page requests to application server #2.

In this section we have seen the impact when we lost one of the database nodes as well as when we lost an application server. Because of the deployment of the RAC, the usage of the load balancer, and the deployment of multiple application servers, we haven't seen any impact on the front-end application at all.

Overview of a Solution Using Data Guard

Oracle Data Guard provides a set of tools to create, maintain, and monitor one or multiple standby databases, usually in a different data center, and provide a solution in case of a server-side disaster. Data Guard will ease the role switching between the production databases with any of the standby databases. This section will not cover every feature of Data Guard but will give a high-level view of how Data Guard can help having a more complete solution for high availability.

Data Guard as a Complement to RAC

As we have seen in the last section, RAC builds a cluster of database servers and this cluster is usually within the same data center. Most of the companies these days need to have a disaster recovery site that, by definition, is at a certain distance from the primary site. The deployment of a RAC cluster comes with additional limitations. Oracle proposes the usage of Oracle Data Guard to create, maintain, and monitor the standby databases, which is in fact a physical copy of the production databases. Figure 6-15 shows an example of the deployment of Data Guard.

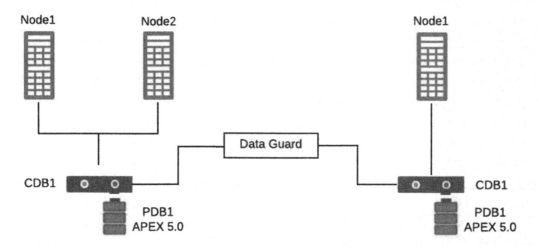

Figure 6-15. *Example of Data Guard deployment between two sites*

In this example, Data Guard is responsible for keeping the standby database in sync with the production database. In this example, we have decided that the standby database is not in a RAC cluster. If we have a major failure on the production site, we know that we do have an exact copy of the database ready to be used. We know as well that the database contains the APEX session information, so any application servers that can connect to this database will retrieve all the necessary information to continue the APEX session.

As for the application servers, we recommend having application servers on the disaster recovery site as well. Having the application code reside in the database means that any modification to the code will be replicated by Data Guard. Figure 6-16 shows what would be the ideal configuration using Data Guard.

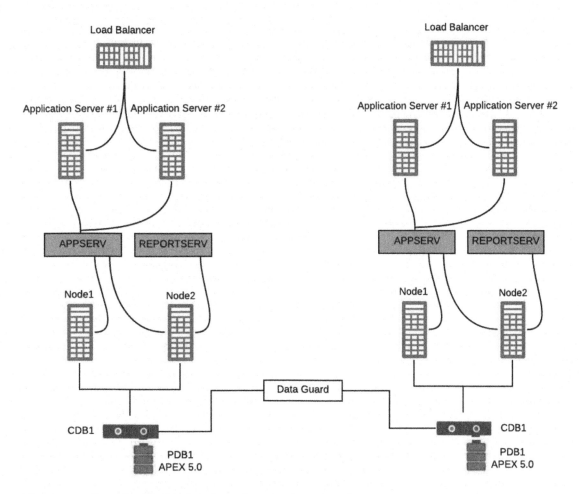

Figure 6-16. *Example of the ideal configuration using Data Guard*

As mentioned, this is the ideal configuration as we have the exact same configuration on the primary and the disaster recovery site. Data Guard is responsible to keep the standby database in sync with the production database which includes the APEX engine, the APEX application, and the business data. The application team would have to maintain the application servers in sync as well and we would have a ready-to-use disaster recovery site for every APEX applications.

Summary

In this chapter we explained the importance of having a high availability environment. We covered how we can deploy a high availability solution for the database and application server layers. As mentioned, Oracle RAC is the solution to guarantee redundancy at the database level. For the application servers, a mix of multiple application servers and a load balancer in front guarantee redundancy at the application server layer.

We have tested and demonstrated that with the deployment of a solution like Oracle RAC and multiple application servers, even though we lose a database or an application node, there is no impact on the front-end application. Having the context session information stored in the database, APEX is able to retrieve that information and continue to process the page request without any interruptions.

Unfortunately, Oracle RAC was designed to be deployed within the same data center. If we have to consider having a disaster recovery site, we have seen that the usage of Oracle Data Guard will be necessary. Data Guard is responsible to maintain the standby databases, running on the disaster recovery site, in sync with the production databases. In that case, any major disaster in the primary data center will be recovered by using the disaster recovery site with a very low risk of data loss.

CHAPTER 7

APEX in a Multitenant Database

Oracle 12c introduces the multitenant architecture. This architecture has a multitenant container database that includes the root container (CDB$ROOT), a seed container (PDB$SEED), and multiple pluggable database (PDB). The root container holds the common objects that are accessible to every PDB through METADATA LINK. As we discuss in Chapter 8, APEX could be installed locally in the PDB, which APEX is totally independent of the other PDBs or we can have APEX installed in the root container.

This chapter will explain how APEX is installed by default in a multitenant database, version 12.1, and the operations of deinstallation and reinstallation you could perform. We will also give some examples of PDBs moving or cloning through other root containers and the impact on the APEX installation.

Note Starting with Oracle database 12.2, APEX will not be installed by default anymore.

Default Installation of APEX in a Multitenant Database

When configuring a new multitenant database, version 12.1, APEX is installed by default as common objects in the root container, CDB$ROOT. The installation process also creates necessary objects and METADATA LINK in the PDB$SEED. When we create new PDB, these objects and METADATA LINK will be then created and will point to the object in the root container.

Note The version of APEX installed by default is 4.2.

Here is the representation, Figure 7-1, of APEX after the creation of the database release 12.1.

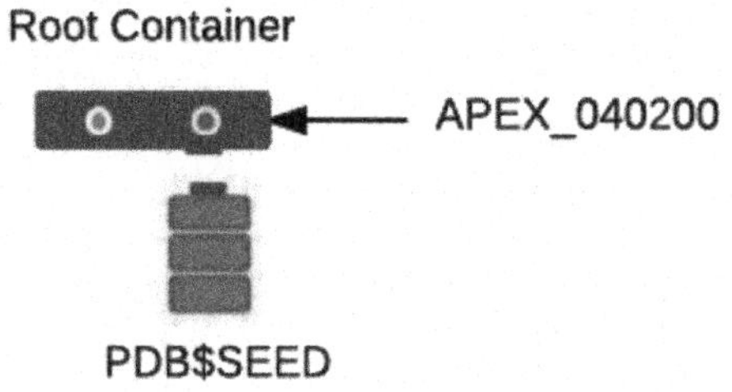

Root Container

APEX_040200

PDB$SEED

Figure 7-1. *Representation of the installation of APEX*

© Francis Mignault and Luc Demanche 2016

F. Mignault and L. Demanche, *Oracle Application Express Administration*, DOI 10.1007/978-1-4842-1958-4_7

This section will talk about the operation you can perform on the installation of APEX after the creation of the database in a multitenant architecture. You can decide to do one of the following:

- Upgrade the version of APEX

- Deinstall APEX from the root container (CDB)

- Install APEX in the PDB

If you decide to upgrade this version of APEX, please read Chapter 9. If you want to install APEX in every PDB, you have to first deinstall it from the root container. It is important to understand that running the deinstall script will completely remove the common APEX objects in the root container and also all the application definitions stored in the PDBs. The deinstallation of APEX is covered in Chapter 8.

■ **Note** We are recommending upgrading to APEX 5.

Different Scenarios of APEX Deinstallation and Installation

As mentioned earlier, from the installation of APEX in the root container, we may want to perform one of the following:

Upgrade APEX in the CDB

As you know, the default version of APEX is 4.2. We recommend upgrading the version of APEX to the latest version 5.0. We are covering new features of APEX 5.0 in this book. Follow Chapter 9 for the upgrades of APEX.

Deinstallation of the Common APEX from the CDB

You may decide to deinstall the common APEX 4.2 from the CDB from the root container; run the script "apxremov_con.sql". If the version of APEX is 5.0, run the script "apxremov.sql". It is important to use the proper version of scripts depending of the current version of APEX installed.

■ **Note** Deinstalling APEX from the root container will also delete the metadata (application definitions) in every PDB. Be careful when you run this script.

Here is the way to find the exact version of APEX, and then we will run the appropriate script to deinstall that component from the root container.

```
SQL> select r.COMP_NAME, r.VERSION, c.NAME from CDB_REGISTRY r, V$CONTAINERS c where r.CON_
ID=c.CON_ID and r.COMP_ID='APEX' order by c.CON_ID;
```

```
COMP_NAME                    VERSION       NAME
-----------                  ----------    ----------------
Oracle Application Express   4.2.5.00.08   CDB$ROOT

SQL> @apxremov_con.sql
```

```
PL/SQL procedure successfully completed.

Performing installation in multitenant container database in the background.
The installation progress is spooled into apxremov*_con*.log files.

Please wait...

catcon: ALL catcon-related output will be written to apxremov1_con_catcon_27432.lst
catcon: See apxremov1_con*.log files for output generated by scripts
catcon: See apxremov1_con_*.lst files for spool files, if any
catcon.pl: completed successfully

catcon: ALL catcon-related output will be written to apxremov2_con_catcon_27741.lst
catcon: See apxremov2_con*.log files for output generated by scripts
catcon: See apxremov2_con_*.lst files for spool files, if any

catcon.pl: completed successfully

Installation completed. Log files for each container can be found in:

apxremov*_con*.log

You can quickly scan for ORA errors or compilation errors by using a utility
like grep:

grep ORA- *.log
grep PLS- *.log

SQL>
```

Review the log files to validate the deinstallation process.

Installation of the Common APEX in the CDB

After deinstalling APEX from the root container, you may decide to install a new version, or to install the runtime version. Please read Chapters 8 and 11 to have the details of the installation of APEX in the root container. You can imagine having a common APEX installation of the runtime version in the root container, which ensures that every PDB is running the same version of APEX. This will ease the administration, upgrades, and patches of the centralized installation of APEX.

We can imagine the configuration of the preprod, UAT, and production environments running APEX, runtime mode, directly in the root container. Figure 7-2 shows this configuration.

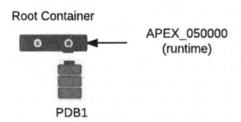

Figure 7-2. Installation of the runtime version of APEX in the root container

Installation of a Dedicated APEX in the PDB

After deinstalling APEX from the root container, you may decide to install dedicated APEX into PDB. The advantage of having local APEX in PDBs is that you can run different version of APEX in each PDB. The disadvantage is that you have to manage separately each APEX in respect of upgrades and patches. Follow Chapter 8 for the installation of APEX in PDB.

■ **Note**   Oracle recommends removing APEX from the root container and installing it into the PDBs.

Figure 7-3 represents the APEX installation in the PDBs, using two different versions. We have installed APEX 5.0 in the PDB1 and we have installed APEX 4.2 in the PDB2.

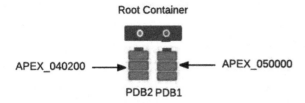

Figure 7-3. *Installation of different version of APEX locally in PDBs*

■ **Note**   For the installation and upgrade processes, we are inviting you to read Chapters 8 and 9 as we are presenting best practices for APEX. For this chapter, I'm using the default tablespace SYSAUX to ease the demonstration.

Different Scenarios of Moving/Cloning a PDB

With the multitenant architecture, we have to understand the concept of metadata links to the common objects in the root container and the impact of moving or copying a PDB between CDBs. As we have said, by default APEX is installed in the root container. Every PDB has metadata links to the common objects in the root container. What will be the impact of moving the PDB (that has pointers on common objects in the CDB) to another CDB?

Depending of your decision of having APEX installed in the CDB or in every PDB, here are different scenarios when we are moving or copying PDB from the source CDB to the destination CDB. The strategy to handled APEX will defer depending where APEX is installed.

Source PDB Has APEX in the CDB

- Destination has APEX in CDB

Even though it's not recommended, we could have APEX installed in CDB on both sides. The PDB contains the metadata links to the root container, same as in the destination CDB. If the version of APEX is identical on both CDB, we only have to move/copy the PDB from the source CDB to the destination CDB. We also have to configure the Web listener to point to the new PDB. Figure 7-4 shows what we want to perform.

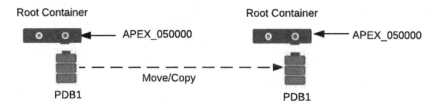

Figure 7-4. *Move/copy PDB between CDBs*

First, validate the version of APEX in both CDB.

```
SQL> select r.COMP_NAME, r.VERSION, c.NAME from CDB_REGISTRY r, V$CONTAINERS c where r.CON_
ID=c.CON_ID and r.COMP_ID='APEX' order by c.CON_ID;

COMP_NAME                    VERSION      NAME
-----------                  -----------  ----------------
Oracle Application Express   5.0.1.00.06  CDB$ROOT
```

Then, use any PDB unplug and plug procedure to transfer the PDB from the source to the destination root container. From the source root container, do the following:

```
SQL> alter pluggable database pdbbook close immediate;
SQL> alter pluggable database pdbbook unplug into '/tmp/pdbbook.xml';
SQL> drop pluggable database pdbbook keep datafiles;
```

Now we are going to the destination root container. First we will validate if the PDB can be plugged into the root container. If everything is ok, we will plug it.

```
set serveroutput on
DECLARE
    compatible BOOLEAN := FALSE;
BEGIN
    compatible := DBMS_PDB.CHECK_PLUG_COMPATIBILITY(
        pdb_descr_file => '/tmp/pdbbook.xml');
    if compatible then
      DBMS_OUTPUT.PUT_LINE('Is pluggable PDBBOOK compatible? YES');
    else DBMS_OUTPUT.PUT_LINE('Is pluggable PDBBOOK compatible? NO');
    end if;
END;
/
Is pluggable PDBBOOK compatible? YES

PL/SQL procedure successfully completed.
```

We are now ready to plug the PDB into the destination root container.

```
SQL> create pluggable database pdbbook using '/tmp/pdbbook.xml' nocopy;

Pluggable database created.
```

```
SQL> alter pluggable database pdbbook open;

Pluggable database altered.
```

Here is the excerpt from the alert log file of the CDB.

```
Successfully created internal service pdbbook at open
ALTER SYSTEM: Flushing buffer cache inst=0 container=3 local
****************************************************************
Post plug operations are now complete.
Pluggable database PDBBOOK with pdb id - 3 is now marked as NEW.
****************************************************************
Completed: create pluggable database pdbbook using '/tmp/pdbbook.xml nocopy'
...
...
Pluggable database PDBBOOK opened read write
Completed: alter pluggable database pdbbook open
```

- Destination doesn't have APEX in CDB

The complexity of this situation is that the destination CDB doesn't have APEX installed in the root container. You will get errors on the opening of the new PDB due to the originating PDB contains metadata links to objects in the originating root container. The destination CDB doesn't have APEX installed so the objects can't be recompiled. You will not be able to open the PDB unless you deinstall APEX from it or you install APEX in the root container. Oracle doesn't support installing APEX in the root container, unless there is not PDB. Oracle support is then required and they will probably ask you to run the script "apex_to_local.sql". Figure 7-5 shows that situation.

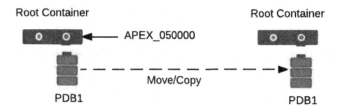

Figure 7-5. *Move/copy PDB between CDBs*

If we try to perform this transfer, let's see what would be the output of the verification that we have to do prior of the transfer.

First, let's compare the version of the common APEX component. Here is the output from the CDB that doesn't have the common APEX installed:

```
SQL> select r.COMP_NAME, r.VERSION, c.NAME from CDB_REGISTRY r, V$CONTAINERS c where r.CON_ID=c.CON_ID and r.COMP_ID='APEX' order by c.CON_ID;

no rows selected
```

If we decide to perform the PDB unplug and plug process, here is what we will get from the "CHECK_PLUG_COMPATIBILITY" procedure.

```
set serveroutput on
DECLARE
   compatible BOOLEAN := FALSE;
BEGIN
   compatible := DBMS_PDB.CHECK_PLUG_COMPATIBILITY(
        pdb_descr_file => '/tmp/pdbbook.xml');
   if compatible then
     DBMS_OUTPUT.PUT_LINE('Is pluggable PDBBOOK compatible? YES');
   else DBMS_OUTPUT.PUT_LINE('Is pluggable PDBBOOK compatible? NO');
   end if;
END;
/
Is pluggable PDBBOOK compatible? NO

PL/SQL procedure successfully completed.

SQL> select message,action from pdb_plug_in_violations;

MESSAGE
--------------------------------------------------------------------------------
ACTION
--------------------------------------------------------------------------------
APEX mismatch: PDB installed version NULL CDB installed version 5.0.1.00.06
Install or upgrade APEX in the PDB or the CDB

APEX mismatch: PDB has installed common APEX. CDB has not installed APEX.
Please contact Oracle Support.

APEX mismatch: PDB has installed common APEX. CDB has not installed APEX.
Please contact Oracle Support.
```

As we can see, the destination CDB doesn't have a common APEX installed. As the output of the view "pdb_plug_in_violations" mentioned, the only option you have is to install APEX in the root container prior to continuing with the PDB plugging process.

Before proceeding with the plug operation of the PDB into the destination root container, we need to install APEX in the destination CDB.

Make sure APEX 5 is installed under the ORACLE_HOME/apex folder. Remember by default we have APEX 4.2 under ORACLE_HOME/apex.

Make sure you are located into ORACLE_HOME/apex folder.

```
SQL> @apexins.sql sysaux sysaux temp /i/
```

▪ **Note** This is an example of the installation of APEX 5.0. Please refer to Chapter 8.

We are now ready to plug the PDB into the destination root.

```
SQL> create pluggable database pdbbook using '/tmp/pdbbook.xml' nocopy;

Pluggable database created.
```

```
SQL> alter pluggable database pdbbook open;
```

Here is the excerpt from the alert log file of the CDB.

```
Completed: create pluggable database pdbbook using '/tmp/pdbbook.xml' nocopy
alter pluggable database pdbbook open
Mon Jul 18 09:00:28 2016
Pluggable database PDBBOOK dictionary check beginning
Pluggable Database PDBBOOK Dictionary check complete
Database Characterset for PDBBOOK is AL32UTF8
Mon Jul 18 09:00:46 2016
Opening pdb PDBBOOK (3) with no Resource Manager plan active
Pluggable database PDBBOOK opened read write
Completed: alter pluggable database pdbbook open
```

Source PDB Has APEX in the PDB

- Destination has APEX in CDB

In this situation, APEX is installed differently in source and destination CDB. We have to move/copy the PDB to the destination and we have to run the script "apex_to_common.sql". The script will remove local APEX objects and will create metadata links to the common installation of APEX in the root container. The next step is to configure the Web listener to the new PDB. Figure 7-6 represents that situation.

Figure 7-6. *Move/copy PDB between CDBs*

First, we need to validate the installation of APEX in the source PDB.

```
SQL> select r.COMP_NAME, r.VERSION, c.NAME from CDB_REGISTRY r, V$CONTAINERS c where r.CON_
ID=c.CON_ID and r.COMP_ID='APEX' order by c.CON_ID;
```

```
COMP_NAME                    VERSION         NAME
-----------                  -----------     ----------------
Oracle Application Express   5.0.1.00.06     PDBBOOK
```

Also, I want to show that the objects owned by APEX_050000 are locally created in the PDB and are not using METADATA LINK from the root container. Column SHARING = NONE confirms this.

```
SQL> select owner,object_name,object_type,sharing from cdb_objects where owner =
'APEX_050000' and object_name = 'WWV_FLOWS';
```

```
OWNER                OBJECT_NAME      OBJECT_TYPE       SHARING
---------------      -------------    ---------------   -------------
APEX_050000          WWV_FLOWS        TABLE             NONE
```

We also need to validate the installation of common APEX in the destination root container.

```
SQL> select r.COMP_NAME, r.VERSION, c.NAME from CDB_REGISTRY r, V$CONTAINERS c where r.CON_
ID=c.CON_ID and r.COMP_ID='APEX' order by c.CON_ID;
```

```
COMP_NAME                   VERSION        NAME
-----------                 ----------     ----------------
Oracle Application Express  5.0.1.00.06    CDB$ROOT
```

We are now ready to proceed with the PDB unplug and plug procedure from the source root container to the destination root container.

```
SQL> alter pluggable database pdbbook close immediate;
SQL> alter pluggable database pdbbook unplug into '/tmp/pdbbook.xml';
SQL> drop pluggable database pdbbook keep datafiles;
```

Now we are going to the destination root container. First we will validate if the PDB can be plugged into the root container. If everything is ok, we will plug it.

```
set serveroutput on
DECLARE
   compatible BOOLEAN := FALSE;
BEGIN
   compatible := DBMS_PDB.CHECK_PLUG_COMPATIBILITY(
       pdb_descr_file => '/tmp/pdbbook.xml');
   if compatible then
     DBMS_OUTPUT.PUT_LINE('Is pluggable PDBBOOK compatible? YES');
   else DBMS_OUTPUT.PUT_LINE('Is pluggable PDBBOOK compatible? NO');
   end if;
END;
/
Is pluggable PDBBOOK compatible? NO

PL/SQL procedure successfully completed.

SQL> select message,action from pdb_plug_in_violations;

MESSAGE
---------------------------------
APEX mismatch: the PDB has installed local APEX.

ACTION
---------------------------------
Run apex_to_common.sql.
```

As we can see, if we open the PDB once plugged into the destination root container we will get warnings. The issue is due to the conflict between the installation of APEX locally into the PDB and the installation of APEX in the destination root container. The strategy is to run "apex_to_common.sql" to modify the installation of the local APEX to create METADATA LINK that will point to the common APEX installation in the root container.

We are now ready to plug the PDB into the destination root container.

```
SQL> create pluggable database pdbbook using '/tmp/pdbbook.xml' nocopy;

Pluggable database created.

SQL> alter pluggable database pdbbook open;

Warning: PDB altered with errors.

SQL> alter session set container=PDBBOOK;

Session altered.
```

Let's run the script and compare the object property SHARING of WWV_FLOWS with the previous situation.

```
SQL> @?/rdbms/admin/apex_to_common.sql

SQL> select owner,object_name,object_type,sharing from cdb_objects where owner =
'APEX_050000' and object_name = 'WWV_FLOWS';

OWNER             OBJECT_NAME      OBJECT_TYPE       SHARING
---------------   -------------    ---------------   -------------
APEX_050000       WWV_FLOWS        TABLE             METADATA LINK
```

We can see that now, the object WWV_FLOWS in the PDB is using METADATA LINK to point to the object in the root container.

The PDB is now properly plugged into the root container by modifying the local installation of APEX to use METADATA LINK instead and point to the common installation.

- Destination doesn't have APEX in CDB

In this scenario, APEX is installed in the PDB at the source and no installation of APEX is done in the destination CDB. We have then to move/copy the PDB to the destination CDB and configure the Web listener to the new PDB. Figure 7-7 shows this simple configuration.

Figure 7-7. Move/copy PDB between CDBs

First, we need to validate the installation of APEX in the source PDB.

```
SQL> select r.COMP_NAME, r.VERSION, c.NAME from CDB_REGISTRY r, V$CONTAINERS c where r.CON_
ID=c.CON_ID and r.COMP_ID='APEX' order by c.CON_ID;


COMP_NAME                     VERSION      NAME
-----------                   ----------   ----------------
Oracle Application Express    5.0.1.00.06  PDBBOOK
```

Now verification if APEX is installed in the destination root container:

```
SQL> select r.COMP_NAME, r.VERSION, c.NAME from CDB_REGISTRY r, V$CONTAINERS c where r.CON_
ID=c.CON_ID and r.COMP_ID='APEX' order by c.CON_ID;

no rows selected
```

Then, use any PDB unplug and plug procedure to transfer the PDB from the source to the destination root container. From the source root container, do the following:

```
SQL> alter pluggable database pdbbook close immediate;
SQL> alter pluggable database pdbbook unplug into '/tmp/pdbbook.xml';
SQL> drop pluggable database pdbbook keep datafiles;
```

Now we are going to the destination root container. First we will validate if the PDB can be plugged into the root container. If everything is ok, we will plug it.

```
set serveroutput on
DECLARE
   compatible BOOLEAN := FALSE;
BEGIN
   compatible := DBMS_PDB.CHECK_PLUG_COMPATIBILITY(
       pdb_descr_file => '/tmp/pdbbook.xml');
   if compatible then
     DBMS_OUTPUT.PUT_LINE('Is pluggable PDBBOOK compatible? YES');
   else DBMS_OUTPUT.PUT_LINE('Is pluggable PDBBOOK compatible? NO');
   end if;
END;
/
Is pluggable PDBBOOK compatible? YES

PL/SQL procedure successfully completed.
```

We are now ready to plug the PDB into the destination root container.

```
SQL> create pluggable database pdbbook using '/tmp/pdbbook.xml' nocopy;

Pluggable database created.

SQL> alter pluggable database pdbbook open;

Pluggable database altered.
```

Here is the excerpt from the alert log file of the CDB.

```
create pluggable database pdbbook using '/tmp/pdbbook.xml' nocopy
Sun Jan 10 12:17:22 2016
****************************************************************
Pluggable Database PDBBOOK with pdb id - 3 is created as UNUSABLE.
If any errors are encountered before the pdb is marked as NEW,
then the pdb must be dropped
****************************************************************
Database Characterset for PDBBOOK is AL32UTF8
Deleting old file#49 from file$
Deleting old file#50 from file$
Deleting old file#51 from file$
Adding new file#28 to file$(old file#49)
Adding new file#29 to file$(old file#50)
Adding new file#30 to file$(old file#51)
Successfully created internal service pdbbook at open
ALTER SYSTEM: Flushing buffer cache inst=0 container=3 local
****************************************************************
Post plug operations are now complete.
Pluggable database PDBBOOK with pdb id - 3 is now marked as NEW.
****************************************************************
Completed: create pluggable database pdbbook using '/tmp/pdbbook.xml' nocopy
alter pluggable database pdbbook open
Sun Jan 10 12:17:47 2016
Pluggable database PDBBOOK dictionary check beginning
Pluggable Database PDBBOOK Dictionary check complete
Database Characterset for PDBBOOK is AL32UTF8
Sun Jan 10 12:18:05 2016
Opening pdb PDBBOOK (3) with no Resource Manager plan active
Pluggable database PDBBOOK opened read write
Completed: alter pluggable database pdbbook open
```

The pluggable database PDBBOOK is now open in the destination root container. We have to configure the Web listener for that new PDB.

Source PDB Doesn't Have APEX

- Destination has APEX in CDB

We want to move/copy a PDB, that doesn't have APEX either locally in the PDB or in the CDB. The destination has APEX installed in the root container. Figure 7-8 shows that situation.

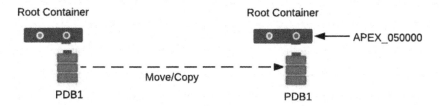

Figure 7-8. *Move/copy PDB between CDBs*

As we have seen earlier, when we have a common installation of APEX in the root container and we are creating a new PDB, the creation takes a copy of the PDB$SEED, which already contains the METADATA LINK pointing to the APEX objects in the CDB$ROOT. Here we want to transfer a PDB that doesn't have APEX locally installed or METADATA LINK that points to a common APEX. We need to previously install APEX locally in the PDB before performing the transfer. Once APEX will be installed, we can refer to the previous example for the transfer of a PDB with APEX locally install to a destination root container with APEX installed in the CDB.

Verify the status of the APEX installation in the source root container.

```
SQL> select r.COMP_NAME, r.VERSION, c.NAME from CDB_REGISTRY r, V$CONTAINERS c where r.CON_
ID=c.CON_ID and r.COMP_ID='APEX' order by c.CON_ID;

no rows selected
```

Verify the status of the APEX installation in the destination root container.

```
SQL> select r.COMP_NAME, r.VERSION, c.NAME from CDB_REGISTRY r, V$CONTAINERS c where r.CON_
ID=c.CON_ID and r.COMP_ID='APEX' order by c.CON_ID;


COMP_NAME                  VERSION       NAME
-----------                ----------    ----------------
Oracle Application Express 5.0.1.00.06   CDB$ROOT
```

First, we have to install APEX locally in the PDB. Follow Chapter 8 for the installation of APEX in the PDB. When the installation is completed, follow the previous example for the transfer between CDBs.

Move or Copy a PDB with Incompatible Versions of APEX

We will have to deal with this situation only if we are working with APEX installed in the CDB. We have to understand that if APEX is locally installed in the PDB, we will never have an issue on the version because APEX is standalone in the PDB. As we will see in Chapter 9, we have minor and major upgrades. Upgrades affect the first two numbers of the version, as an example of going from APEX 4.2 to APEX 5.0 and then, going from APEX 4.2.5 to APEX 4.2.6 will be done by applying a patch.

- Destination has a higher version of APEX

We have APEX version 4.2 installed in the source CDB. We have to move or copy a PDB to the destination CDB which we have installed the version 5.0 of APEX. Figure 7-9 shows that situation.

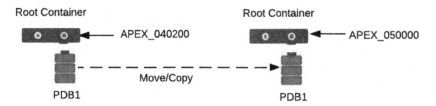

Figure 7-9. *Move/copy PDB between CDBs*

To successfully complete this operation, we have to perform an upgrade of the version of APEX. We will first transfer the PDB to the destination CDB, even though the versions of APEX are not compatible. The next step is to upgrade the version of APEX by running the script "catcon.pl" while you are connected to the new PDB. In that case, we are talking about an upgrade because we are changing the first two numbers of the version, from 4.2 to 5.0.

Before starting this operation, the patch 20618595 needs to be applied. Otherwise the upgrade of APEX 4.2 to APEX 5.0 in the container database will fail.

First, we need to validate the installation of APEX in the source CDB.

```
SQL> select r.COMP_NAME, r.VERSION, c.NAME from CDB_REGISTRY r, V$CONTAINERS c where r.CON_
ID=c.CON_ID and r.COMP_ID='APEX' order by c.CON_ID;


COMP_NAME              VERSION       NAME
-----------           ----------    ----------------
Oracle Application Express    4.2.5.00.08    CDB$ROOT
Oracle Application Express    4.2.5.00.08    PDBBOOK
```

Now verification the installation of APEX in the destination root container:

```
SQL> select r.COMP_NAME, r.VERSION, c.NAME from CDB_REGISTRY r, V$CONTAINERS c where r.CON_
ID=c.CON_ID and r.COMP_ID='APEX' order by c.CON_ID;


COMP_NAME              VERSION       NAME
-----------           ----------    ----------------
Oracle Application Express    5.0.1.00.06    CDB$ROOT
```

Then, use any PDB unplug and plug procedure to transfer the PDB from the source to the destination root container. From the source root container, do the following:

```
SQL> alter pluggable database pdbbook close immediate;
SQL> alter pluggable database pdbbook unplug into '/tmp/pdbbook.xml';
SQL> drop pluggable database pdbbook keep datafiles;
```

Now we are going to the destination root container. First we will validate if the PDB can be plugged into the root container. If everything is ok, we will plug it.

```
set serveroutput on
DECLARE
   compatible BOOLEAN := FALSE;
```

```
BEGIN
   compatible := DBMS_PDB.CHECK_PLUG_COMPATIBILITY(
       pdb_descr_file => '/tmp/pdbbook.xml');
   if compatible then
     DBMS_OUTPUT.PUT_LINE('Is pluggable PDBBOOK compatible? YES');
   else DBMS_OUTPUT.PUT_LINE('Is pluggable PDBBOOK compatible? NO');
   end if;
END;
/
Is pluggable PDBBOOK compatible? NO

PL/SQL procedure successfully completed.

SQL> select message,action from pdb_plug_in_violations;

MESSAGE
--------------------------------------------------------------------------------
ACTION
--------------------------------------------------------------------------------
APEX mismatch: PDB has installed common APEX. CDB has not installed APEX.
Please contact Oracle Support.

APEX mismatch: PDB installed version NULL CDB installed version 5.0.1.00.06
Install or upgrade APEX in the PDB or the CDB

APEX mismatch: PDB installed version 4.2.5.00.08 CDB installed version 5.0.1.00. 06
Install or upgrade APEX in the PDB or the CDB
```

■ **Note** The message "Install or upgrade APEX in the PDB or the CDB" confirmed that we need to upgrade APEX once plugged into the destination CDB.

We need to plug the PDB into the CDB and upgrade the version of APEX.

```
SQL> create pluggable database pdbbook using '/tmp/pdbbook.xml' nocopy;

Pluggable database created.

SQL> alter pluggable database pdbbook open;

Warning: PDB altered with errors.
```

Now let's upgrade the version of APEX. As we were saying, we need to upgrade the version from 4.2 to 5.0. We will then use the script apexins_nocdb.sql. If we would have to change from 4.2.5 to 4.2.6 for example, we would need to apply a patch (instead of an upgrade) and we would use the script "apxpatch.sql".

■ **Note** For more detail on the upgrade or patching process, please refer to Chapter 9.

Make sure APEX 5 is installed under the ORACLE_HOME/apex folder. Remember by default we have APEX 4.2 under ORACLE_HOME/apex.

Make sure you are located into ORACLE_HOME/apex folder.

```
$ cd $ORACLE_HOME/apex
$ $ORACLE_HOME/perl/bin/perl $ORACLE_HOME/rdbms/admin/catcon.pl -d $ORACLE_HOME/apex -b
$ORACLE_HOME/apex/upgrade_plug_pdb -c 'PDBBOOK' apexins_nocdb.sql '--psysaux' '--psysaux'
'--ptemp' '--p/i/'

catcon: ALL catcon-related output will be written to /u01/app/oracle/product/12.1.0.2.0/
dbhome_1/apex/upgrade_plug_pdb_catcon_11098.lst
catcon: See /u01/app/oracle/product/12.1.0.2.0/dbhome_1/apex/upgrade_plug_pdb*.log files for
output generated by scripts
catcon: See /u01/app/oracle/product/12.1.0.2.0/dbhome_1/apex/upgrade_plug_pdb_*.lst files
for spool files, if any
catcon.pl: completed successfully
```

■ **Note**   Make sure to use "perl" from the $ORACLE_HOME/perl/bin folder.

If the patch 20618595 is not applied, this step will fail will this error:

ERROR at line 1:

ORA-00001: unique constraint (APEX_050000.WWV_FLOW_BANNER_U_IDX) violated

Now we can close the PDB and opening it without having the warning. You can also validate in the alert.log file.

```
SQL> alter pluggable database pdbbook close;

Pluggable database altered.

SQL> alter pluggable database pdbbook open;

Pluggable database altered.
```

- Destination has a lower version of APEX

We have the version 5.0 installed in the source root container. We have to move or copy a PDB to another CDB that has APEX version 4.2 installed. Figure 7-10 shows that situation.

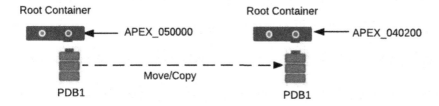

Figure 7-10. *Move/copy PDB between CDBs*

First, we need to validate the installation of APEX in the source CDB.

```
SQL> select r.COMP_NAME, r.VERSION, c.NAME from CDB_REGISTRY r, V$CONTAINERS c where r.CON_
ID=c.CON_ID and r.COMP_ID='APEX' order by c.CON_ID;

COMP_NAME                    VERSION        NAME
-----------                  ----------     ----------------
Oracle Application Express   5.0.1.00.06    CDB$ROOT
Oracle Application Express   5.0.1.00.06    PDBBOOK
```

Now verification the installation of APEX in the destination root container:

```
SQL> select r.COMP_NAME, r.VERSION, c.NAME from CDB_REGISTRY r, V$CONTAINERS c where r.CON_
ID=c.CON_ID and r.COMP_ID='APEX' order by c.CON_ID;

COMP_NAME                    VERSION        NAME
-----------                  ----------     ----------------
Oracle Application Express   4.2.5.00.08    CDB$ROOT
```

Then, use any PDB unplug and plug procedure to transfer the PDB from the source to the destination root container. From the source root container, do the following:

```
SQL> alter pluggable database pdbbook close immediate;
SQL> alter pluggable database pdbbook unplug into '/tmp/pdbbook.xml';
SQL> drop pluggable database pdbbook keep datafiles;
```

Now we are going to the destination root container. First we will validate if the PDB can be plugged into the root container. If everything is ok, we will plug it.

```
set serveroutput on
DECLARE
    compatible BOOLEAN := FALSE;
BEGIN
    compatible := DBMS_PDB.CHECK_PLUG_COMPATIBILITY(
        pdb_descr_file => '/tmp/pdbbook.xml');
    if compatible then
      DBMS_OUTPUT.PUT_LINE('Is pluggable PDBBOOK compatible? YES');
    else DBMS_OUTPUT.PUT_LINE('Is pluggable PDBBOOK compatible? NO');
    end if;
END;
/
Is pluggable PDBBOOK compatible? NO

PL/SQL procedure successfully completed.

SQL> select message,action from pdb_plug_in_violations;

MESSAGE
--------------------------------
```

```
APEX mismatch: PDB installed version 5.0.1.00.06 CDB installed version 4.2.5.00.08
Install or upgrade APEX in the PDB or the CDB
```

Before proceeding with the plug operation of the PDB into the destination root container, we need to upgrade APEX in the destination CDB.

Make sure APEX 5 is installed under the ORACLE_HOME/apex folder. Remember by default we have APEX 4.2 under ORACLE_HOME/apex.

Make sure you are located into ORACLE_HOME/apex folder.

```
SQL> @apexins.sql sysaux sysaux temp /i/
```

■ **Note**   This is an example of the upgrade to APEX 5.0. Please refer to Chapters 8 and 9 for more detail.

Now you can validate again if the plugging process of the PDB will be successful. If everything is ok, we will plug it.

```
set serveroutput on
DECLARE
   compatible BOOLEAN := FALSE;
BEGIN
   compatible := DBMS_PDB.CHECK_PLUG_COMPATIBILITY(
        pdb_descr_file => '/tmp/pdbbook.xml');
   if compatible then
     DBMS_OUTPUT.PUT_LINE('Is pluggable PDBBOOK compatible? YES');
   else DBMS_OUTPUT.PUT_LINE('Is pluggable PDBBOOK compatible? NO');
   end if;
END;
/
Is pluggable PDBBOOK compatible? YES

PL/SQL procedure successfully completed.
```

We are now ready to plug the PDB into the destination root container.

```
SQL> create pluggable database pdbbook using '/tmp/pdbbook.xml' nocopy;

Pluggable database created.

SQL> alter pluggable database pdbbook open;

Pluggable database altered.
```

Here is an excerpt of the alert log showing the plugging in and opening of the new PDB into the destination CDB.

```
Successfully created internal service pdbbook at open
ALTER SYSTEM: Flushing buffer cache inst=0 container=3 local
*************************************************************
Post plug operations are now complete.
```

```
Pluggable database PDBBOOK with pdb id - 3 is now marked as NEW.
******************************************************************
Completed: create pluggable database pdbbook using '/tmp/pdbbook.xml' nocopy
alter pluggable database pdbbook open
Sun Jul 17 14:23:01 2016
Pluggable database PDBBOOK dictionary check beginning
Pluggable Database PDBBOOK Dictionary check complete
Database Characterset for PDBBOOK is AL32UTF8
Sun Jul 17 14:23:16 2016
Opening pdb PDBBOOK (3) with no Resource Manager plan active
Pluggable database PDBBOOK opened read write
Completed: alter pluggable database pdbbook open
```

Summary

We have seen in the chapter the default installation of APEX in a multitenant architecture when you are creating an Oracle database version 12.1. APEX release 4.2 is installed directly in the CDB and it's available for every PDB that has been created in the CDB. Starting with Oracle database version 12.2, APEX is no longer installed by default. We have also presented multiple scenarios, like upgrading the default installation of APEX, deinstallation and installation of APEX in the root container.

The last section was talking about the multiple operation of moving the PDB between root containers. What to do when APEX is locally installed in the PDB? What to do when there is no APEX installed in the target root container? What if the versions of APEX in the root containers are not the same? All the scenarios could happen to you one day.

PART III

Configuration

CHAPTER 8

Installing

This chapter explains the different steps required to install Oracle Application Express. Note that this chapter is not a detailed installation guide. The goal is to explain the different components that need to be installed and also the different steps required for APEX to be functional.

If you already have APEX applications in place and would like to upgrade to another version of APEX, see Chapter 9.

This chapter explains how to install APEX in a standard non-multitenant database or in a PDB 12C instance. For detailed information on multitenant 12c and installing APEX in the Container CDB, or for removing the installation from the CDB before installing APEX in a PDB, please see Chapter 7.

There are two major steps when you install Oracle Application Express:

1. Install APEX in the database

2. Install and configure Oracle Rest Data Services (ORDS)

■ **Note**   Always read and understand the installation guide from Oracle before installing APEX. There may be additional steps required or OS specifics.

Preinstallation Steps

APEX requirements:

- XMLDB has to be installed in your database.

- The system global area (SGA) and program global area (PGA) have at least 300 MB allocated. See the Oracle APEX Installation guide for more details on this.

Before installing APEX, verify if there is already a version of APEX installed in the database. To find the installed version, you can run the following query :

```
SELECT VERSION FROM DBA_REGISTRY WHERE COMP_NAME = 'Oracle Application Express';
```

Also list and note the APEX schemas using the following query:

```
SELECT USERNAME FROM DBA_USERS WHERE USERNAME LIKE 'APEX%';
```

© Francis Mignault and Luc Demanche 2016

F. Mignault and L. Demanche, *Oracle Application Express Administration*, DOI 10.1007/978-1-4842-1958-4_8

Downloads

Oracle Application Express and ORDS are available as free downloads from the OTN website. You can also install the APEX release that comes with the Oracle database software. If this is the case, you can skip the next few sections and read the "**Installing with DBCA**" section. Note that the bundled APEX version with the database will not be the latest since the release cycles of APEX are more frequent than the database one. Because of this, starting with Oracle Database 12C Release 2, APEX will not be included with the database release anymore.

After the download, Always keep the APEX and ORDS zip files on your server in the APEX_HOME and ORDS_HOME directories. Each zip file downloaded from OTN not only contains installation scripts but also contains scripts that will help in managing your APEX installation. Those scripts are release specific so it's important to keep them.

■ **Note**　We will use the term APEX_HOME as a reference to the directory where we keep the downloaded APEX zip files required for the installation. We will also use the term ORDS_HOME as a reference to the directory where we keep the downloaded ORDS zip files required for the installation.

Download APEX

To latest release of APEX is available on the Oracle Technology Network OTN APEX download page: www.oracle.com/technetwork/developer-tools/apex/downloads/. At the moment of writing these lines, the latest available release is 5.0.3 as shown in Figure 8-1.

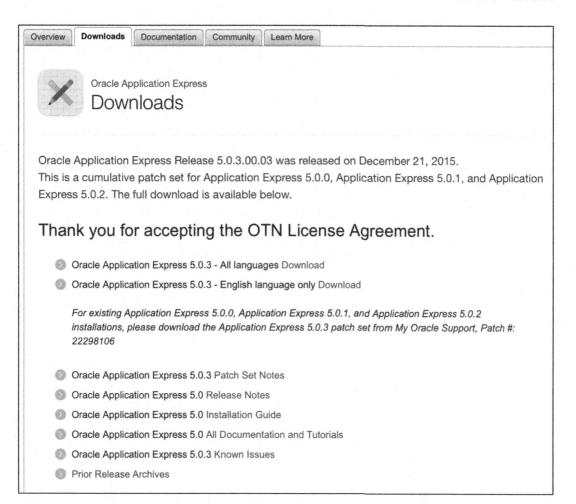

Figure 8-1. *OTN APEX download page*

■ **Note** You will find the downloads for Oracle Application Express, documentation, and a lot of APEX-related information on the OTN web site at `http://OTN.Oracle.com/APEX`. This site is maintained by Oracle.

There are two downloads available, All languages and English only. If you plan on building multilingual applications or would like to use the builder in another language than English, you will have to choose the All languages download. Both downloads contains the English APEX builder and utility scripts.

As you can also see in Figure 8-1, Prior releases of APEX are also available to download.

This is also where you will find the installation documentation like the installation guide, the release notes, and so on.

Accept the License Agreement and click the Download link. This will download a file called apex_5.0.1.zip (5.0.1 being the version of APEX).

Save the apex.zip file in the APEX_HOME directory on the Database Server. APEX_HOME is a term that we will use in this book to reference where the apex.zip and other APEX-related scripts are stored. It could be in /u01/oracle/apex for example.

Create a directory call apex_050000. 050000 is corresponding to the APEX version. As mentioned in Chapter 2, installing APEX 5.0 will create a schema called APEX_050000 and we are keeping that naming convention to differentiate the different downloads of APEX.

Unzip the apex.zip file in the newly created directory apex_050000. This will create an apex directory with all the necessary utilities and scripts to install APEX.

Download ORDS

In this chapter, we will cover the installation of APEX in conjunction with ORDS exclusively. This is the recommended web listener. Using ORDS will allow you to use the latest features of APEX 5 and also allow you to create RESTFull webservices. See Chapter 3 for more information on the different web listeners available for APEX.

If you want to use another web listener like EPG or OHS, please refer to the Oracle APEX installation guide.

The latest release of ORDS is available on the Oracle Technology Network OTN ORDS download: http://www.oracle.com/technetwork/developer-tools/rest-data-services/downloads. At the moment of writing these lines, the latest version of ORDS was 3.0.1 as shown in Figure 8-2.

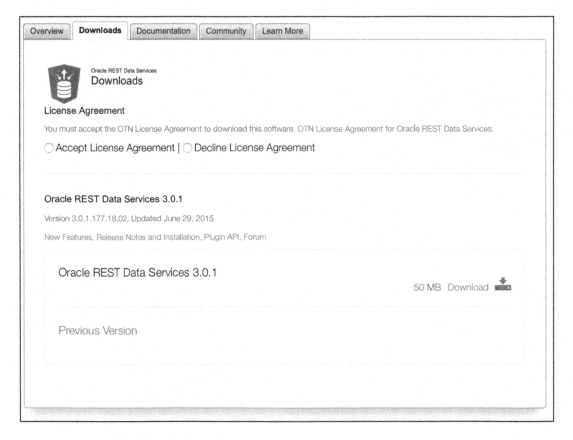

Figure 8-2. OTN ORDS Download page

■ **Note**   You will find the downloads for Oracle REST Data Services (ORDS), documentation, and a lot of ORDS-related information on the OTN web site at www.oracle.com/technetwork/developer-tools/rest-data-services/. This site is maintained by Oracle.

As you can see in Figure 8-2, prior releases of ORDS are also available to download.

This is also where you will find the installation documentation like the installation guide, the release notes, and so on.

Accept the License Agreement and click the Download link. This will download a file called ords.3.0.1.177.18.02 (3.0.1.177.18.02 being the version of ORDS).

Save the ords.zip file in the ORDS_HOME directory on the application server. ORDS_HOME is a term that we will use in this book to reference where the ords.zip and other ORDS-related scripts and configuration are stored. It could be in /Downloads/ords for example.

Create a directory called ords_301. 301 corresponds to the ORDS version.

Unzip the ords.zip file in the newly created directory. This will create directories with all the necessary scripts to install ORDS.

Installing APEX in the Database

Now that you have all the necessary files in place, you can proceed with the installation of the APEX engine in the database. Please refer to Chapter 2 to learn more about the APEX architecture and the different components.

Tablespaces for APEX

In order to ease the maintenance of APEX, it is preferable to install it in its own tablespace. You will see that in the Oracle documentation it uses the SYSAUX tablespace. Database creation assistant (DBCA) also uses SYSAUX as the default option. We strongly recommend not using the SYSAUX tablespace since it is internally used by the database for other purposes. Using a specific tablespace will make installs, upgrades, and maintenance easier since it will contain only APEX-related database objects.

APEX can use three tablespaces:

1. A tablespace for the APEX schema ex: APEX_050000

2. A tablespace for the APEX files schema ex: WWV_FLOW_FILES

3. A temporary tablespace

You can use the same APEX tablespace for the APEX schema and the APEX files schema without any problems. Just make sure that you have enough space allocated. For APEX 5.0.1, you will need at least 220MB for the APEX tablespace plus 60MB per additional installed language. Also, you should keep some more space for future upgrades and for APEX sessions. We usually size this tablespace to 300MB with autoextend to 1GB.

Also note that the installation will use about 100M in the SYSTEM tablespace.

Here is an example of a create tablespace for APEX:

```
Create tablespace apex
datafile '.../apex_01.dbf'
size 300M
autoextend on
next 10m maxsize 1024m;
```

Installing with DBCA

You can install the APEX version that comes with the database. This means that you do not have to download the APEX software; it is bundled with the database software download and available in the *$ORACLE_HOME/apex directory*.

Note that starting with Oracle Database 12C Release 2, APEX will not be included with the database release anymore.

Oracle 12.1.0.2 comes with APEX 4.2.6.00.03. Oracle 11G database downloads also includes a release of APEX. To install APEX using DBCA, simply follow the instructions in the assistant.

When you use DBCA to install APEX while creating a database, there are some things to be aware of:

1. It is not the latest release of APEX available. The release cycle of APEX is much faster than the release cycle of the Oracle Database software.

2. If you create a custom database, and it is not creating a CDB in a 12C multitenant configuration, you will be able to decide not to install Oracle Application Express.

3. The APEX software will be installed in the SYSAUX tablespace by default.

4. It installs the software in the database but does not "Activate" your APEX installation. You will have to do the "**Postinstall" section**.

5. It does not install the web server and web listener to run APEX. See the "**Installing ORDS"** section for that.

If you install a 12C release 1 database using the multitenant architecture, that is, install a CDB and PDBs, APEX will be automatically installed in the CDB and be available in all the PDBs.

■ **Note**   For more information on the 12C multitenant architecture and Oracle Application Express and learn about the different possible scenarios, see Chapter 7.

In most cases, you will want to install the latest version available to have the latest features and latest patch set. If this is the case, you will need to dowload the latest version as mentioned in the Downloads section just before and proceed with the installation as explained in the "**Installing APEX Using the Downloaded Scripts"** section.

Installing APEX Using the Downloaded Scripts

In the APEX_HOME/apex_050000/apex directory, you will find all the necessary scripts for the installation. They are all standard SQL scripts and have to be executed using sqlplus or sqlcl with the Oracle user sys as sysdba.

There are different scripts that can be used to install APEX. In this chapter, we will use the standard installation. The standard installation installs the APEX engine and the APEX builder in the database.

Here is a list of all the available install scripts:

- apexins - Standard Installation including the APEX builder.

- apxrtins - Runtime Install without the APEX builder.

For more information on the runtime install, please see C**hapter 11**.

As mentioned earlier, you can specify a tablespace for the APEX schema and for the APEX files schema FLOWS_FILES. We will use the same tablespace created earlier for both schemas.

You can also use a specific Temp tablespace. Most of the time, the standard database Temp tablespace will do.

The Web directory for the images, CSS, and Javascript used by APEX will be configured when ORDS is installed and configured. The standard is /i/. This can also be changed after the installation using the `APEX_HOME/apex_05000/apex/utilities/reset_image_prefix.sql` script as follows.

1. Change directory to the APEX_HOME/apex_05000/apex directory.

2. Log in the database using `sqlplus / as sysdba`

3. If the Oracle 12C multitenant option is used, make sure that you are connected to the right PDB or to the CDB : `alter session set container = <PDB Name or CDB$ROOT>;`

   APEX can be installed in the CDB or in the PDB. For Oracle 12C Release 1, it may be required to remove APEX default installation from the CDB first in order to be able to install it in the PDBs. For more information about this and the different possible scenarios, please refer to Chapter 7.

4. Run the APEX installation script as follows:

   `@apexins.sql <apex_schema_tbs> <apex_files_tbs> <temp_tbs> <Web directory for apex images>`

Example : `@apexins.sql apex apex temp /i/`
To install APEX without the builder and in runtime only use the `apxrtins.sql` script instead of `apexins.sql`. If APEX 4.2 is installed in the Container Database CDB, run `apexins_con.sql` instead of `apexins.sql`.
A log file called `install2015-01-01-22_13-18-04.log` will be created for the installation where *2015-01-01* is the date when the install was run and *22_13-18-04* is the time.
You should see the following message at the end of the installation to indicate that everything has been installed successfully:

```
Performing Application Express component validation - please wait...

Completing registration process. 17:32:07
Validating installation.  17:32:07
...Starting validation 17:32:07
...Database user "SYS", database schema "APEX_050000", user# "97" 17:32:07
...273 packages
...266 package bodies
...465 tables
...8 functions
...16 procedures
...4 sequences
...498 triggers
...1581 indexes
...254 views
...0 libraries
...14 types
...5 type bodies
...0 operators
...0 index types
...Begin key object existence check 17:32:13
...Completed key object existence check 17:32:13
...Setting DBMS Registry 17:32:13
...Setting DBMS Registry Complete 17:32:13
...Exiting validate 17:32:13
```

PL/SQL procedure successfully completed.

timing for: Validate Installation
Elapsed: 00:00:05.98

Session altered.

timing for: Complete Installation
Elapsed: 00:08:24.69

PL/SQL procedure successfully completed.

Thank you for installing Oracle Application Express 5.0.0.00.31

Oracle Application Express is installed in the APEX_050000 schema.

The structure of the link to the Application Express administration services is as follows:
http://host:port/pls/apex/apex_admin (Oracle HTTP Server with mod_plsql)
http://host:port/apex/apex_admin   (Oracle XML DB HTTP listener with the embedded PL/SQL
                                       gateway)
http://host:port/apex/apex_admin   (Oracle REST Data Services)

The structure of the link to the Application Express development interface is as follows:
http://host:port/pls/apex (Oracle HTTP Server with mod_plsql)
http://host:port/apex   (Oracle XML DB HTTP listener with the embedded PL/SQL gateway)
http://host:port/apex   (Oracle REST Data Services)

PL/SQL procedure successfully completed.

To validate the APEX install, the following query on DBA_REGISTRY can also be run:

select version, status from DBA_REGISTRY where comp_id = 'APEX';

```
VERSION                 STATUS
----------------------- ----------
5.0.3.00.03             VALID
```

APEX is now installed in the database and all the required schemas have been created.

Postinstall

After running the installation script, there are many postinstallation tasks to be done. Removing or adding the builder is optional, as is installing other languages. The other tasks should always be performed for APEX to be able to work properly.

Removing / Adding the Builder

Once APEX is installed, you can decide to remove the APEX builder, to change your installation to runtime only. On the contrary, if you installed APEX in runtime only, you can add the APEX builder back to the installation. Simply run the appropriate script using sqlplus / as sysdba.

- apxdvins - Add the APEX builder to the installation.

- apxdevrm - Remove only the APEX builder.

APEX_PUBLIC_USER

Follow these steps to unlock and change password:

1. Unlock the ***APEX_PUBLIC_USER*** user. This user will be used for connecting to the database : `ALTER USER APEX_PUBLIC_USER account unlock;`

2. Change the APEX_PUBLIC_USER password and note it. You will need that password when configuring ORDS : `ALTER USER APEX_PUBLIC_USER identified by <new password>;`

Make sure that the password will not expire. Since this user is used for the APEX database connections, if it expires APEX will not be available. Check the password policy associated with this user so that it never expires.

Make sure that you never grant any other database privileges to this user as this may cause security vulnerabilities.

APEX Administrator User Password

Reset the APEX administrator password. In order to configure APEX, you will have to connect to the APEX administration console using the workspace Internal and the user ADMIN. For more information on configuring APEX see Chapter 10.

The following script will let you set the ADMIN user password for the Internal workspace:

```
SQLPLUS / as sysdba
@apxchpwd.sql
```

Drop Old APEX Schemas

If you are installing APEX into a database for the first time, you should not need to drop old APEX schemas. But it is possible that an old APEX schema was created with the creation of the database for releases prior to Oracle 12C Release2.

For details on which APEX schemas can be dropped and how to clean up after an install, see the **"Post-Upgrade" section in** Chapter 9.

Installing Other Languages

If you downloaded the all-languages APEX release, you can install the builder in other languages than English. The APEX builder is available in nine different languages in addition to English (default): German, Spanish, French, Italian, Japanese, Korean, Brazilian Portuguese, Simplified Chinese, and Traditional Chinese.

The scripts to install those languages are in the APEX_HOME/apex_050000/apex/builder directory. There is a subdirectory for each language. For example, if you want to install the French version of APEX, all the scripts will be in the fr subdirectory.

1. Change directory to the language subdirectory that you want to install, for example to install the French version : `cd APEX_HOME/apex_050000/apex/builder/fr`

2. Set the NLS_LANG variable so that it is in AL32UTF8 :

```
set NLS_LANG=AMERICAN_AMERICA.AL32UTF8
```

3. Run the load_lang.sql script. For example to load the French language run :

```
SQLPLUS / as sysdba
ALTER SESSION SET CURRENT_SCHEMA = APEX_050000;
@load_fr.sql
```

Enabling Network Services: ACL Security

Network services are disabled by default in Oracle 11 and 12. In order to be able to use APEX to send outbound emails, use Web services or use the PDF report printing option, you must grant connect privileges to any host to the APEX schema APEX_050000.

If you have installed APEX in Oracle 11, see the Oracle APEX install documentation to enable network services.

In 12C you have to run the following script to grant access to any host:

```
BEGIN
    DBMS_NETWORK_ACL_ADMIN.APPEND_HOST_ACE(
        host => '*',
        ace => xs$ace_type(privilege_list => xs$name_list('connect'),
                            principal_name => 'apex_050000',
                            principal_type => xs_acl.ptype_db));
END;
```

■ **Note**   If you installed APEX in an ORACLE 11 database or if you get errors running the preceding ACL script, see the Oracle APEX install documentation for more detail.

Configuring RESTful Services

If you want to create webservices using ORDS, you have to configure it in the database first.

To do so, run the following script from the APEX_HOME/apex_050000/apex directory:

```
SQLPLUS / as sydba
@apex_rest_config.sql
```

This will create two Oracle users: APEX_LISTENER and APEX_REST_PUBLIC_USER.

Take note of the passwords that you assign to those users, it will be required during the configuration of ORDS.

Installing ORDS

Oracle REST Data Services (ORDS) is the recommended web listener for APEX. As mentioned in Chapter 3, it should be installed on its own server. ORDS will allow the use of new and future APEX functionalities and also allow the creation of Web services.

ORDS is essentially a Java class that needs to be deployed on a web container. It is supported on Oracle WebLogic, GlassFish, and Tomcat. See Figure 8-3.

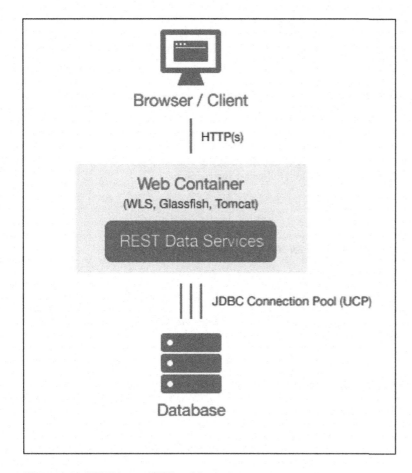

Figure 8-3. *ORDS in an APEX architecture*

1. Installing ORDS is a two-step process.

2. Configure ORDS.

3. Deploy ORDS in the web container.

As explained earlier, the web listener should be configure on its own server for better security, performance, and scalability (see Chapter 3).

Configure ORDS

The first step for installing ORDS is to create and configure the appropriate war files that will then be deployed on the application server.

Java Version

Verify that you have the correct Java version using the following: java -version.

ORDS 3 requires Java 7 or higher.

To download the latest release of Java, go to http://www.oracle.com/technetwork/java/javase/downloads/index.html and select the appropriate JDK release that relates to the right operating system.

Create the Configuration War File

Configuring ORDS means that a war file needs to be updated with the proper parameters. Note that once you have configured the ords.war file, you will have to use the setup parameter instead of install to change the configuration.

Change directory to the ORDS_HOME/ords_301 where the ords.war is located.

To configure ords run the following command and follow the instructions:

```
Java -jar ords.war install
```

Database connection configuration:
The following questions will configure ORDS for the database connection.

```
Enter the location to store configuration data :
Enter the name of the database server [localhost] :
Enter the database listen port [1521] :
Enter 1 to specify the database service name, or 2 to specify the database SID [1] :
Enter the database service name :
```

ORDS users :
The following questions will configure ORDS and create the Oracle database users required.

```
Enter the database password for ORDS_PUBLIC_USER :
Confirm password :

Please login with SYSDBA privileges to verify Oracle REST Data Services schema. Installation
may be required

Enter the username with SYSDBA privileges to verify the installation [SYS] :
Enter the database password for SYS :
Confirm password :

INFO : Oracle REST Data Services Schema does not exist and will be created
```

APEX parameters :
The following questions will configure ORDS for APEX. It is important to use the same passwords used in the postintall of APEX.

```
Enter 1 if you want to use PL/SQL Gateway or 2 to skip this step [1] : 1
Enter the database password for APEX_PUBLIC_USER :
Confirm password :

Enter 1 to specify passwords for Application Express RESTful Services database users (APEX_
LISTENER, APEX_REST_PUBLIC_USER) or 2 to skip this step [1] : 1
Enter the database password for APEX_LISTENER :
Confirm password :

Enter the database password for APEX_REST_PUBLIC_USER:
Confirm password :
```

End of the ORDS configuration:

```
INFO: Updated configurations: defaults, apex, apex_pu, apex_al, apex_rt
Oct 03, 2015 8:21:53 PM oracle.dbtools.installer.Installer installORDS
INFO:
Installing Oracle REST Data Services version 3.0.1.177.18.02
...Log file written to /home/oracle/Downloads/ords_301/logs/
ordsinstall_2015-10-03_202153_00173.log
...Verified database prerequisites
...Created Oracle REST Data Services schema
...Created Oracle REST Data Services proxy user
...Granted privileges to Oracle REST Data Services
...Created Oracle REST Data Services database objects
Oct 03, 2015 8:22:04 PM oracle.dbtools.installer.Installer installORDS
INFO: Completed installation for Oracle REST Data Services version 3.0.1.177.18.02. Elapsed
time: 00:00:11.214

Enter 1 if you wish to start in standalone mode or 2 to exit [1]: 2
```

The ords.war file is now configured.
If you want to change the configuration of the ords.war file, run the following command :

```
Java -jar ords.war setup
```

For more options for the ORDS configuration, run:

```
Java -jar ords.war help
```

■ **Note** By default, "ords" is used in the URL to execute APEX. Ex: `http://<hostname>:<port>/ords`. If you want to use another alias, before configuring the ords.war file, rename it to the alias you would like to use. Ex: apex.war : `http://<hostname>:<port>/apex`.

APEX Images

In the apex.zip file previously downloaded on the database server during the installation of APEX, in the `APEX_HOME/apex_0500/apex` directory, there is an `images` directory. It contains all the images, Javascript, and CSS for the APEX engine. This directory has to be copied on the web server in the appropriate location and will be used by ORDS. As a standard, we copy it in the `ORDS_HOME/ords_301` directory.

For deployment on WebLogic or GlassFish, an image `i.war` file has to be created.

To create the `i.war` file with the path to the APEX images, run the following:

`Java -jar ords.war static <APEX images Path>` where `<APEX images Path>` is equal to the path where the images directory is. In our example it would be `ORDS_HOME/ords_301/images/`

For a Tomcat deployment, simply copy the images directory from `APEX_HOME/apex_0500/apex` into `<Tomcat directory>/webapps/i/`.

Deploying the War Files

For detailed information on how to deploy ORDS on each application servers, see the Oracle Data RESTful Services installation document.

On WebLogic and GlassFish, you will have to deploy the ords.war and the i.war file created in the previous section.

Note that if you are using WebLogic, you also have to disable the HTTP Basic Authentication credentials by changing the config.xml file as follows:

```
...<enforce-valid-basic-auth-credentials>false</enforce-valid-basic-auth-credentials>
</security-configuration> ...
```

See the Oracle Data RESTful Services installation document and the WebLogic documentation for more details on this.

If you are using Tomcat, simply copy the ords.war file from the `ORDS_HOME/ords_301` directory into the Tomcat *webapps* directory.

Once ORDS is deployed on WebLogic, GlassFish, or Tomcat, make sure that the application server is running and that it is listening on the configured network port. For example, if Tomcat is installed and is listening on port 8080, there should be a Tomcat page displayed by simply accessing the URL `<Hostname>:8080`.

The installation is now complete.

To access the APEX builder, open a web browser and go to the following URL: `http://<hostname>:<port>/ords`. You should see the APEX login page, as shown in Figure 8-4.

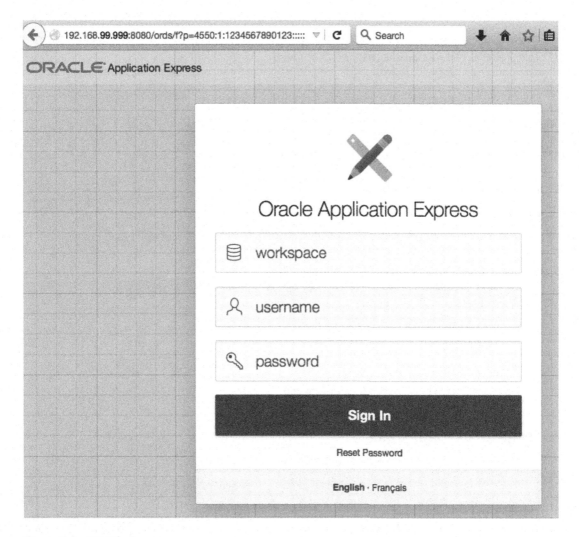

Figure 8-4. *APEX login page*

You are now ready to configure your APEX instance. See Chapter 10 for more information about configuring APEX.

Uninstall

In order to completely remove APEX from the database, there are different steps that need to be performed on the database server and on the application server.

Removing APEX

In the APEX_HOME directory, there is a script called apxremov.sql that removes the latest APEX installation. For example, if the current release installed is APEX 5.0, it will remove the APEX_050000 schema. Be aware that this will also remove all your APEX applications and your APEX configuration.

■ **Caution** Running `apxremov.sql` will drop the current APEX metadata. This means that it will also drop your APEX configuration and your applications.

To uninstall the last installed release of APEX in the database, run the apexremov script.

```
SQLPLUS / as sysdba
@apexremov.sql
```

To completely remove APEX, you also have to do the following steps:

1. Drop All APEX-Related Schemas

As mentioned in Chapter 2, APEX uses multiple Oracle users. To completely remove APEX from the database, those Oracle users have to be dropped.

Here is a list of the Oracle users related to APEX that you should drop:

- APEX_**000000**, where **000000** is the APEX release number. Ex: APEX_040200 is for APEX 4.2.

- APEX_PUBLIC_USER

- FLOWS_FILE

- APEX_LISTENER

- APEX_REST_PUBLIC_USER

2. Drop APEX Tablespaces

After removing all the APEX Oracle users, simply drop the APEX tablespaces.

3. Undeploy ORDS

To uninstall ORDS, drop the ORDS_HOME directory and undeploy ORDS from the java application server used. It could be either Tomcat, GlassFish, or WebLogic. If it is in Tomcat, the images folder will need to be deleted to uninstall it as well.

Summary

Installing APEX is somewhat simple. First run the installation sql script in the database. Then do the postinstallation tasks like unlocking APEX_PUBLIC_USER, change the ADMIN password, and grant network ACL security. And finally deploy ORDS and the APEX images on the application server. Of course, depending on the requirements, there might be some other tasks required but in summary it is that simple.

Once APEX is installed and running, there are some configurations that need to be done and workspaces have to be created in order for the developers to start creating applications. Chapter 10 explains the different configuration options to do so.

CHAPTER 9

Upgrading and Patching

This chapter explains the different steps required to upgrade or patch Oracle Application Express. Note that this chapter is not a detailed upgrade guide but is more about the general process of upgrading and patching. You should always read the Oracle APEX installation guide before performing an upgrade or applying a patch.

If you already have APEX applications in place and would like to upgrade Oracle Application Express to another version, this is the chapter to read.

For detailed information on multitenant 12c, please see Chapter 7.

Note Always read and understand the installation guide from Oracle before upgrading or patching APEX. There may be different steps required or OS specifics.

When Oracle releases a patch, it is usually to fix some issues in a major or a minor release. The first two positions of the version of APEX are the major release and the minor release. For example, `5.1.2.03.04` means it is major release 5 and minor release 1. The final two numbers, 03 and 04, refer to fixes and patches, respectively.

When Oracle releases a major or minor release, it usually includes a full install of APEX. We will call this an upgrade. If Oracle releases changes to fix smaller issues, they usually release it as a patch. Refer to the proper section depending on whether you are planning on upgrading APEX or on patching APEX.

Upgrading APEX

In this section, we will cover how to plan and how to upgrade Oracle Application Express. Upgrading means that you are already using APEX and that you have an existing APEX installation in place containing applications, workspaces, users, and so on.

First, you will need to plan the upgrade in order to make sure that there will be a minimum impact on your existing production.

Once your plan is in place, than you will have to proceed with the upgrade and with testing applications in all of your APEX environments.

After that, there are postupgrade tasks that need to be done to finish the upgrade process.

Upgrading APEX is about the same as installing APEX. There are some installation steps that do not need to be executed. When appropriate, there will be some references to Chapter 8 to avoid having to duplicate the information.

© Francis Mignault and Luc Demanche 2016
F. Mignault and L. Demanche, *Oracle Application Express Administration*, DOI 10.1007/978-1-4842-1958-4_9

Planning an Upgrade

In order to successfully upgrade APEX, good planning is required and important. Upgrading the APEX software is somewhat fairly simple. The most complex part of an upgrade is surely coordinating all the tests and synchronizing the different environments, all while making sure that the development process of applications is impacted as little as possible.

Only one version of APEX can be active in an Oracle database at a time. All applications in a database or in a PDB have to run in the same APEX release. This means that after an upgrade, all the applications of all the workspaces will be running under the new release. In other words, everything is upgraded at once.

The upgrade will copy all the existing applications in the new release metadata. But applications will not be modified or changed. They will stay the same and will run using the upgraded release of APEX. The developers can upgrade applications individually afterward to make use of new features. For example, if you upgrade a 4.2 APEX instance to APEX 5.0, applications will be copied to APEX 5.0 but will have to be individually modified to use the new Universal Theme template feature.

For our examples and for the rest of the explanations in this chapter, we will take into account that there are three APEX environments:

- DEV for development,

- TEST for integrated testing and user acceptance testing, and

- PROD for production.

It is a good practice to upgrade an environment where developers can look and try the new release and the new functionalities before upgrading. This can first be done in a sandbox, training, or another environment that does not impact the development cycle. This allows developers to get acquainted with the new release of APEX, the upgrade process, and major issues, if any.

Once the developers and the testers are comfortable and it is decided to upgrade all the environments, follow these steps:

1. Upgrade the TEST environment

    By upgrading the TEST environment first it will validate the upgrade so that it will not break or change anything major. Also, this will allow the continuity of the current application development in parallel with the upgrade. Since APEX is backward compatible it is possible to develop in DEV, which is an earlier release, move to TEST which is in the upgraded release. When testing is done and accepted, it is possible to finally move to PROD, using DEV as the source, since they are both in the same APEX release. Remember that, in that scenario, you cannot export the application from TEST and import it into PROD. They are not the same release and TEST is using a higher version than PROD.

    Make sure that applications are thoroughly tested. If possible, some of the problems should be fixed in DEV, before the final upgrade. If the issues are related exclusively to the newer release, they will have to be fixed after the upgrade.

2. Upgrade the DEV and PROD environment

    Once the TEST environment has been upgraded and you are ready to upgrade the production environment, DEV and production can be upgraded.

Oracle makes a lot of effort to test and ease the upgrades of APEX. Even then, some issues might arise. They usually are minor problems or are most often caused by old code or nonstandard APEX development like using external libraries. Also be sure that plug-ins are well tested since they are external to APEX and may not have been modified to work with the latest release of APEX you are upgrading to.

Preupgrade Tasks

Before running the upgrade scripts, it is important to make some verification and preparation.

Current Version

Before proceeding with the upgrade, check the current release number of APEX installed in the database.
There are different ways to do so:

```
select * from apex_release

VERSION_NO          API_COMPATIBILITY    PATCH_APPLIED
------------------- -------------------- --------------------
5.0.2.00.07         2013.01.01
```

or

```
select version from sys.dba_registry where comp_id = 'APEX';

VERSION
------------------------------
5.0.2.00.07
```

You can also find the version of APEX in the builder, once you are logged in, at the bottom right corner of the screen.

Download APEX

The latest release of APEX, including the latest patch set, is available on OTN.Oracle.com/APEX.
Please refer to the section **"Download APEX" in** Chapter 8 for the instructions on how to download APEX.

Tablespaces for APEX

As mentioned in Chapter 8, it is preferable to install APEX in its own tablespace instead of using the SYSAUX tablespace.
APEX can use three tablespaces:

1. A tablespace for the APEX schema ex: APEX_050000

2. A tablespace for the APEX files schema ex: WWV_FLOW_FILES

3. A temporary tablespace

In this chapter, we will use the same APEX tablespace for the entire APEX install. For APEX 5.0.1 you will need at least 220MB available plus 60MB per additional installed language. This information is available in the Oracle APEX installation guide document.
Setting your tablespace in autoextend mode is a good practice to allow future growth.

If you do not have an APEX tablespace already in place, you can create one using the following example:

```
Create tablespace apex
datafile '.../apex_01.dbf'
size 300M
autoextend on
next 10m maxsize 1024m;
```

Upgrading APEX

As mentioned in the download section, the apex.zip file and its content should now be in the APEX_HOME/ apex_050000/apex directory. This directory contains all the necessary scripts for the upgrade. They are all standard SQL scripts and have to be executed using sqlplus or sqlcl with the Oracle user sys as sysdba.

There are different scripts that can be used to install APEX. In this chapter, we will use the standard installation. The standard installation installs the APEX engine and the APEX builder in the database.

As mentioned earlier, you can specify a tablespace for the APEX schema and for the APEX files schema FLOWS_FILES. We will use the same tablespace created earlier for both schemas.

You can also use a specific TEMP tablespace. Most of the time the standard database TEMP tablespace will do.

The Web directory for the images, CSS, and Javascript used by APEX is configured in ORDS. We will use /i/ as the alias for the image directory.

1. Change directory to the APEX_HOME/apex_05000/apex directory.

2. Log in the database using sqlplus / as sysdba.

3. If the Oracle 12C multitenant option is used, make sure that you are connected to the right PDB or to the CDB : alter session set container = <PDB Name or CDB$ROOT>;

   APEX can be installed in the CDB or in the PDB. For Oracle 12C Release 1, it may be required to remove APEX default installation from the CDB first in order to be able to install it in the PDBs. For more information about this and the different possible scenarios, please refer to Chapter 7.

4. Run the APEX installation script as follows:

   ```
   @apexins.sql <apex_schema_tbs> <apex_files_tbs> <temp_tbs> <Web directory for
   apex images>
   ```

Example: @apexins.sql apex apex temp /i/

To install APEX without the builder and in runtime only use the apxrtins.sql script instead of apexins.sql.

If APEX 4.2 is installed in the Container Database CDB, run apexins_con.sql instead of apexins.sql.

A log file called install **2015-01-01-22_13-18-04**.log will be created for the installation where **"2015-01-01-22_13-18-04"** is the date and time of when the install was run.

In the log file, you will see that APEX copies all your existing applications metadata in a new APEX schema. This allows the possibility of a rollback to the older version in case of problems.

```
-- Now beginning upgrade. This will take several minutes.-------
-- Ensuring template names are unique -------
-- Migrating metadata to new schema -------
-- Switching Builder to new schema -------
```

```
-- Migrating SQL Workshop metadata -------
-- Upgrading new schema. -------
-- Copying preferences to new schema. -------
-- Upgrading Websheet objects. -------
.
.
.
```

Upgrade completed successfully no errors encountered.
```
-- Upgrade is complete ----------------------------------------
timing for: Upgrade
Elapsed: 00:02:54.57
```

You should also see the following messages indicating that the upgrade completed successfully:

```
Performing Application Express component validation - please wait...

Completing registration process. 09:34:10
Validating installation.  09:34:10
...Starting validation 09:34:10
...Database user "SYS", database schema "APEX_050000", user# "106" 09:34:10
...272 packages
...265 package bodies
...465 tables
...8 functions
...16 procedures
...4 sequences
...497 triggers
...1582 indexes
...254 views
...0 libraries
...14 types
...5 type bodies
...0 operators
...0 index types
...Begin key object existence check 09:34:15
...Completed key object existence check 09:34:15
...Setting DBMS Registry 09:34:15
...Setting DBMS Registry Complete 09:34:15
...Exiting validate 09:34:15

PL/SQL procedure successfully completed.
.
.
.
```

Thank you for installing Oracle Application Express 5.0.2.00.07

Oracle Application Express is installed in the APEX_050000 schema.

APEX is now upgraded in the database and all the required schemas have been created.

Postupgrade

Once APEX has been upgraded, different taks may be executed in order to finalize the upgrade process.

Verify the Validity of the Upgrade

You can verify the validity of the APEX upgrade by running the following query:

```
SELECT STATUS, VERSION FROM DBA_REGISTRY WHERE COMP_ID = 'APEX';
```

If the result is VALID, you can assume the installation was successful.

APEX Metadata Schemas

When you upgrade or install APEX, it creates a new schema and copies all the metadata, which includes all current applications and workspaces, into this new schema. So there is nothing to worry about when upgrading APEX, you can always revert back to the original release.

Find all the APEX master schemas by running the following query:

```
select username from dba_users where regexp_like(username,'(FLOWS|APEX)_\d{6}') ;
```

In our example, we have APEX 5.0 installed and an old copy of APEX 4.2:

```
USERNAME
---------------------------
APEX_050000
APEX_040200
```

In essence, after an APEX upgrade, there are public synonyms that are now referencing the new release of APEX. Downgrading APEX is essentially getting those public synonyms to point back to the previous release.

If you encounter any major problems during, or right after, the upgrade, it is possible to revert back to the older version.

If the problem is due to errors with the database or with a tablespace, it is possible to rerun the install by simply dropping the APEX schema first and rerunning the install script.

See the section **"Reverting to a Previous Release After a Failed Upgrade Installation"** in the Oracle APEX Installation Guide to downgrade to a previous release and for more detailed instructions.

APEX_PUBLIC_USER

After an upgrade, you should not need to unlock APEX_PUBLIC_USER. But you should make sure that the APEX_PUBLIC_USER password will not expire. If it expires, APEX will not be available. Check the password policy associated with this user profile. By default, the profile associated to APEX_PUBLIC_USER is DEFAULT and it has a PASSWORD_LIFE_TIME set to 180 days.

To check the policy of APEX_PUBLIC_USER, run the following query:

```
select profile from dba_users where username = 'APEX_PUBLIC_USER';
```

To find the number of days PASSWORD_LIFE_TIME is set to in the DEFAULT profile, run the following query:

```
select * from dba_profiles where RESOURCE_NAME LIKE 'PASSWORD_LIFE_TIME';
```

You can create a specific profile with a PASSWORD_LIFE_TIME unlimited and associate this new profile to APEX_PUBLIC_USER in order to make sure that the password never expires.

Here is an example on how to do so:

```
SQL> create profile apex_public_user limit password_life_time unlimited;

Profile created.

SQL> alter user APEX_PUBLIC_USER profile apex_public_user;

User altered.

SQL> alter user APEX_PUBLIC_USER identified by <Password>;

User altered.

SQL> select profile from dba_users where username = 'APEX_PUBLIC_USER';

PROFILE
----------------
APEX_PUBLIC_USER
```

If the password of APEX_PUBLIC_USER is changed, the configuration of the web listener has to be changed also. This will allow the web listener to connect to the database and run APEX. If you are using EPG or OHS, please refer to the Oracle Application Express installation document. If you are using ORDS follow these steps:

1. Find the ords.war file (or apex.war file) that is used by the web server.

2. Reconfigure the PLSQL Gateway to set the correct password for APEX_PUBLIC_USER using : $ java -jar ords.war setup

```
Enter the name of the database server [localhost]:
Enter the database listen port [1521]:
Enter 1 to specify the database service name, or 2 to specify the database SID [1]:
Enter the database service name: <Enter the Database Service Name>
Enter 1 if you want to verify/install Oracle REST Data Services schema or 2 to skip this
step [1]:2
Enter 1 if you want to use PL/SQL Gateway or 2 to skip this step [1]:
Enter the PL/SQL Gateway database user name [APEX_PUBLIC_USER]:
Enter the database password for APEX_PUBLIC_USER: <Enter new password>
Confirm password: <Enter new password>
Enter 1 to specify passwords for Application Express RESTful Services database users (APEX_
LISTENER, APEX_REST_PUBLIC_USER) or 2 to skip this step [1]:2
Dec 09, 2015 2:52:06 PM oracle.dbtools.common.config.file.ConfigurationFilesBase update
INFO: Updated configurations: apex
```

3. Redeploy the ords.war file on the web server.

APEX Administrator User Password

After an upgrade, when you will log in the « Internal » workspace, APEX will ask you to reset the existing password. If you do not remember the original password, you can reset it using the following script:

```
SQLPLUS / as sysdba
@apxchpwd.sql
```

Installing Other Languages

Every time APEX is installed or upgraded, the other languages have to be reinstalled.

Simply follow the instructions from the **"Installing Other Languages"** section in Chapter 8 to do so.

Enabling Network Services: ACL Security

Every time APEX is installed or upgraded, the network services ACL security has to be re-enabled because of the new APEX schema created.

Simply follow the instructions from the **"Enabling Network Services: ACL Security"** section in Chapter 8 to do so.

APEX Images

After the upgrade of the APEX metadata, the images for the new APEX release have to be copied on the web server.

If the new images directory is not copied on the web server and APEX is accessed, the error message shown in Figure 9-1 will be displayed:

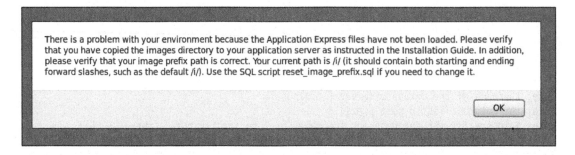

Figure 9-1. Error message when images have not been installed

If you are using EPG or OHS as the web listener, please refer to the Oracle Application Express installation document to find out how to deploy the images directory.

If you are using ORDS, all that is required to do is replace the current images directory with the one provided in the apex.zip file downloaded from OTN and used for the upgrade.

To find were the images are currently stored, you can look in the file called weblogic.xml deployed using the i.war file if GlassFish or WebLogic is used. If Tomcat is used, the images are stored in the webapps directory under the i directory if /i/ is the image alias used.

For example:

```
$ cd /u01/Glassfish/glassfish4/glassfish/domains/domain1/applications/i/WEB-INF

$ ls
sun-web.xml   weblogic.xml   web.xml

$ more weblogic.xml

<weblogic-web-app xmlns="http://www.bea.com/ns/weblogic/weblogic-web-app">
 <!-- This element specifies the context path the static resources are served from -->
 <context-root>/i</context-root>
 <virtual-directory-mapping>
  <!-- This element specifies the location on disk where the static resources are located
-->
  <local-path>/u01/apex_images/images/</local-path>
  <url-pattern>/*</url-pattern>
 </virtual-directory-mapping>
</weblogic-web-app>
```

Keep a copy of the current images in case a rollback to the previous release is required.

Copy the images directory from the apex.zip file downloaded in the same location as the current images directory.

Example (*where APEX_HOME is the directory where* apex.zip *was unzipped and* /u01/apex_images *is the current image directory specified in the preceding weblogic.xml file*):

```
$ cd /u01/apex_images
$ mv images images_50
$ mkdir images
$ cp -pr APEX_HOME/apex_050000/apex/images/* /u01/apex_images/images/
```

Drop Old APEX Schemas

There are APEX users that can be dropped after an upgrade or an install and others than must never be dropped.

NEVER drop the following Oracle users:

- APEX_PUBLIC_USER

- APEX_REST_PUBLIC_USER

- FLOWS_FILES

- APEX_LISTENER

- ORDS_METADATA

- ORDS_PUBLIC_USER

There is one schema used to store the APEX metadata. This schema has the following nomenclature: *APEX_123456*, where 123456 is the release number. For example, the APEX 5.0 metadata schema is APEX_050000.

After making sure that you will not need to revert back to the previous release of APEX, you can drop the Old unused APEX metadata schemas. To list those schemas, you can run the following query:

```
select username from dba_users
where regexp_like(username,'(FLOWS|APEX)_\d{6}')
and username <> (select table_owner from all_synonyms
                 where synonym_name = 'WWV_FLOW'
                 and owner = 'PUBLIC');

USERNAME
------------
APEX_040200
```

In that example, the APEX_040200 Oracle user can be dropped.

Patching

Oracle releases patches periodically. It is important to verify regularly if there are any available patches. Patches fix small bugs and issues and can be applied at any time.

Planning a Patch

APEX patches are delivered the same way as Oracle database patches. It's always good practice to apply patches in TEST and DEV before applying them to production.

Note that APEX applications can be exported and imported between patch releases, higher or lower. This means that for example an application in APEX 5.0.2.00.07 can be exported and imported into an earlier patch set, like for example 5.0.1.00.09.

Because of this, there are no impacts in the development cycle.

Downloading an APEX Patch

Patches are available the same way as database patches (see Figure 9-2).
Follow these steps:

1. Log in to support.oracle.com.

2. In the Patches & Updates tab, select Product or Family (Advanced).

3. In the product drop-down list, select Oracle Application Express (formerly HTMLDB).

4. In the release drop-down list, select the release of Oracle Application Express.

5. Click Search and download the patch on your system.

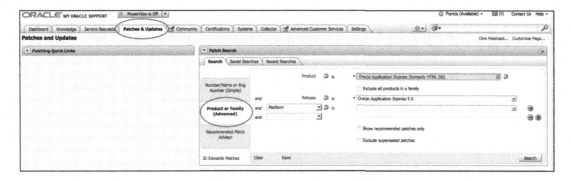

Figure 9-2. *Oracle Support download patch*

Unzip the downloaded patch

```
$ mkdir p21805060_502_Generic
$ mv p21805060_502_Generic.zip p21805060_502_Generic
$ cd p21805060_502_Generic/
$ unzip p21805060_502_Generic.zip
```

Installing an APEX Patch

In the directory where the patch has been unzipped, you will find a readme.html file with instructions on how to apply the patch.

Usually, in the patch directory, there is an apxpatch.sql script that needs to be run with the user sys as sysdba and there is an images directory that needs to be redeployed on the web server. See the subsection "APEX Images" in the section "Postupgrade" for more information on how to deploy images.

If you are using the multitenant option of Oracle 12c and you would like to patch APEX in a specific PDB, the PDB has to be set using the following command before running the script:

```
Alter session set container = <PDB name> ;
```

To apply the patch in the CBD if APEX is installed there, **apxpatch_con.sql** needs to be run instead of apxpatch.sql.

Summary

Upgrading APEX is the same as installing APEX except that for an upgrade, there are existing applications and APEX is already being used. The main thing to remember is to make sure that all the required precautions have been taken before proceeding with an upgrade. That means planning and testing before upgrading production.

Patching APEX on the other hand is usually less intrusive. It does not mean that precautions should not be taken but it is simpler than a major upgrade. Also, remember that patches are only available from the Oracle support portal.

Once APEX is upgraded or patched, some changes to the configuration and to the existing workspaces may need to be done. See Chapter 10 for more information about configuring APEX.

CHAPTER 10

■ ■■ ■

Configuring

In this chapter, we will explain how to configure APEX. There is one central workspace that is associated with the administration of the APEX instance. This administration workspace is called Internal.

Using the Internal Workspace, it is possible to configure the security, the instance settings, the self-service workspace provisioning, workspaces, and much more.

The two major sections of the administration services are Managing the Instance and Managing Workspaces. Managing the Instance is where you will configure the instance after the installation of APEX. Managing Workspaces is where you will edit, create, and manage the schemas and developer accounts associated to workspaces.

It is not intended to mention all the configuration options available in the APEX administration services. Some of the options are not listed in this chapter on purpose for different reasons, maybe because they are self-explanatory, because the online help is detailed enough, or because they are not commonly used. Again, the goal is not to replace the Oracle documentation but more to explain the main configuration options.

It is good to note that the configuration of an instance has to be done per database instance. Only one version of APEX can run at a time in one Oracle database instance or in one PDB.

The sections of this chapter regarding the configuration of APEX are as follows:

- Manage Instance

- Manage Workspaces

- Monitor Activity

For detailed information about the self-provisioning option, **see** Chapter 13. If APEX is installed as Runtime Only, see Chapter 11.

To access the APEX administration services you can either go to http:=//<server name : port number >/ords/**apex_login** and connect with the Internal Workspace, or go to http:=//<server name : port number >/ords/**apex_admin**. The password of the Admin user for the Internal Workspace is configured during the installation using the script APXCHPWD.sql. See Chapter 8 for more detail.

■ **Note**   If APEX is installed in an Oracle 12C Container Database (CDB), the configuration in the APEX administration services (Internal Workspace) has to be done in each Pluggable Database (PDB). Workspaces cannot be created or configured directly in a CDB. See Chapter 7 for more information.

Manage Instance

In the *Manage Instance* page of the administration services, it is possible to configure different settings for the whole APEX instance.

We will cover the most important or relevant configuration options for the following:

- Instance Settings
- Manage Metadata
- Manage Log and Files
- Manage Shared Components
- Messages

Instance Settings

Instance Settings is where you can turn on or off features in the builder for developers. This is where one can configure SQL Workshop for example. It is also where one can set different security features, set instance settings for storage and e-mails, and define the automated workspace purge settings.

Feature Configuration

In the Feature Configuration, you can turn on and off different features for the builder. Here is a description of some of those features that we think are the ones most often used or good to know about.

Create Demonstration Objects in New Workspaces

When this option is set to Yes, it will automatically install the demonstration application "Sample Database Application" and its corresponding database objects when a new workspace is created.

The Sample Database Application can be manually installed from the packaged applications.

Here is the list of all the tables used by the Sample Database Application:

```
TABLE_NAME
--------------------
DEMO_CONSTRAINT_LOOKUP
DEMO_CUSTOMERS
DEMO_ORDERS
DEMO_ORDER_ITEMS
DEMO_PRODUCT_INFO
DEMO_STATES
DEMO_TAGS
DEMO_TAGS_SUM
DEMO_TAGS_TYPE_SUM
```

In an enterprise installation, usually demonstration objects are not required when new workspaces are created, so it is a good practice to set this to No.

Create Websheet Objects in New Workspaces

When set to No, it will not create websheet tables at the workspace creation. Those can be installed manually when creating websheets.

If you do not plan to use websheets, then this option should be set to No.

Here is a list of the tables created for the websheets when this option is set to Yes:

```
TABLE_NAME
----------------------------
APEX$_WS_WEBPG_SECTIONS
APEX$_WS_ROWS
APEX$_WS_HISTORY
APEX$_WS_NOTES
APEX$_WS_LINKS
APEX$_WS_TAGS
APEX$_WS_SEQ
APEX$_WS_FILES
APEX$_WS_WEBPG_SECTION_HISTORY
APEX$_ACL
```

Packaged Application Install Options

As mentioned before, APEX comes with a set of packaged applications that can be used for learning or for real-life usage.

The options in this section are for defining which authentication schemes will be available for packaged applications. When set to Yes, the corresponding authentication will be available as an option during the installation process of the packaged applications. See Figure 10-1. The authentication "Application Express Accounts" is always available.

Figure 10-1. *Packaged application install options*

You can allow the use of the following authentications for packaged applications:

- Allow HTTP Header Variable authentication

- Allow LDAP Directory authentication

- Allow Oracle Application Server Single Sign-On authentication

Enable Transactional SQL Commands

In the **SQL Workshop** section of the **Feature Configuration** page, it is possible to configure different limitations for SQL Workshop like the maximum inactivity, maximum output size, and so on.

The **Enable Transactional SQL Commands** feature is for managing the autocommit in SQL Workshop. When set to No, the autocommit checkbox option from the SQL Commands in SQL Workshop is removed and autocommit is always active as shown in Figure 10-2.

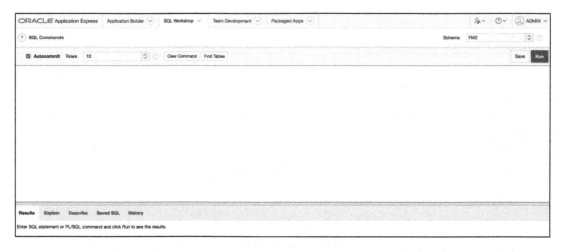

Figure 10-2. *Autocommit checkbox in SQL Workshop when Enable Transactional SQL Commands is set to Yes*

Enable RESTful Services

In SQL Workshop, there is a menu option for configuring and managing RESTful Services. If you do not want developers to see that option in the builder, set the **Enable RESTful Services** to No. By default this option is set to Yes.

Enable Database Monitoring

As shown in Figure 10-3, the workspace administrator can monitor database sessions via a web interface available in the **SQL Workshop utilities**. Of course, credentials of a valid Oracle database user with DBA privileges are required. See **Chapter 14** for more detail on this feature.

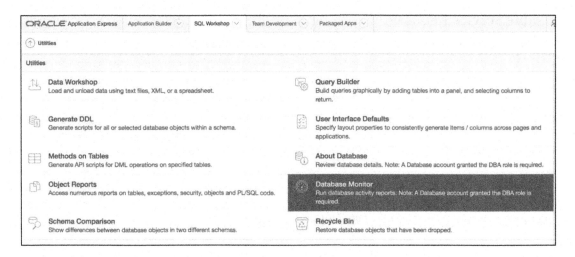

Figure 10-3. *Database Monitor feature in SQL Workshop utilities*

It is possible to enable or disable that feature by setting the ***Enable Database Monitoring*** accordingly.

Using the Database Monitor option, the workspace administrator can manage database sessions, see System Statistic, and see the Top SQL and Long Operations for the whole database instance.

Application Activity Logging

When developers create applications, default activity logging can be configured using this option.

The different possible values are as follows:

- **Use Application Settings**: This will use the activity logging setting at the application level.

- **Never**: This will disable the activity logging for every application in the instance.

- **Always**: This will enable the activity logging for every application in the instance.

- **Initially Disabled for New Applications and Packaged Applications**: This will set the activity logging to No when a new application or a packaged application is created

This option can be useful if, for example, there is a need to stop logging all activities of all applications. You can then set this option to Never temporarily.

Also see **Chapters 14 and 15** for more detail on application activity logging.

Enable Application Tracing

When set to No, developers cannot generate database trace files when running applications. For production environments and security issues it should be set to No. See the chapters 14 and 15 on monitoring and performance tuning for more detail on tracing applications.

Enable Service Requests

This option enables the ability to make Service Requests from the workspace administration menu. See Figure 10-4.

Figure 10-4. *Service Request menu options for workspace administrators*

Service requests can be for requesting a new schema, storage, or termination of the workspace. When this option is disabled, the Make a Service Request menu is not available.

Team Development File Upload Settings

APEX comes with a Team Development feature where end users can provide feedback in applications for developers. For more information on this, see **Chapter 1**.

Enable Team Development's File Repository

This option enables the possibility of file upload in the Team Development feature. When set to Yes a table called **APEX$TEAM_DEV_FILES** is created in the workspace schema when the workspace is created to manage uploaded files. When set to no, file uploads are not permitted in Team Development. This option does not affect existing workspaces.

This option can also be set at the workspace level. When the option Enable File Repository is set to Yes at the workspace administration level, the table is created for the existing workspace.

Security

In the ***Manage Instance / Instance Settings*** section there is a link for configuring ***security*** options. Clicking this link will get you to a page with all of those options grouped under tabs at the top of the page: **Authorized URLs** and **Security Settings** (see Figure 10-5).

Figure 10-5. *Security Settings and Authorized URLs tabs in Manage Instance / Security*

First let's talk about the ***Authorized URLs*** *tab*:

Authorized URLs Tab

Some of the APEX API procedures have an URL parameter, like APEX_UTIL.REDIRECT_URL and APEX_UTIL.COUNT_CLICK. Using authorized URLs, you can list the URLs that can be passed to and used by those procedures. It is a security measure.

When calling those APEX APIs, the URL is compared with this list. If there is an exact match, up to and including the entire length of the Authorized URL value, then the URL parameter is permitted.

And now let's talk about the *Security Settings*:

Security Settings Tab

The Security Settings tab is the default tab for the *Manage Instance / Security* page. Here it is possible to configure different security options. They are all very important and it is good to at least be aware about them. Here is a list of all the options available:

Set Workspace Cookie

This enables the creation of a browser cookie containing the Workspace Name and Username. Set the value to No so that the cookie will not be created. The cookie is called ORACLE_PLATFORM_REMEMBER_UN and has a lifetime of six months. It is used to remember the Workspace Name and User Name in the APEX builder login page.

Disable Administrator Login

This option disables the access to the Internal Workspace.

To re-enable access to the Internal Workspace, use the following API with a privileged account in the database:

```
BEGIN
    APEX_INSTANCE_ADMIN.SET_PARAMETER('DISABLE_ADMIN_LOGIN', 'N');
    commit;
END;
/
```

Disable Workspace Login

When set to Yes, this option disables the access to the application builder and workspaces.

To re-enable access to workspaces, use the following API with a privileged account in the database:

```
BEGIN
    APEX_INSTANCE_ADMIN.SET_PARAMETER('DISABLE_WORKSPACE_LOGIN', 'N');
    commit;
END;
/
```

Allow Public File Upload

Set this option to Yes if applications require file uploads on public pages. By default it is set to No. This option is valid for all the applications in the instance.

Restrict Access by IP Address

This parameter is used to restrict the access to APEX by IP Address. Simply input the IP adresses that are allowed. IP adresses can be specified using a comma-delimited list. Asterisks (*) can be used as a wildcard; for example, 192.168.* would allow all the IP addresses beginning with 192.168. This can essentially be used like a firewall to access APEX.

Be careful not to block the access to the Internal Workspace when changing this parameter.

Instance Proxy

If the network is configured to pass through a proxy server, this is where the proxy information should be entered.

Checksum Hash Function

This is already set to use the most secure hashing algorithms accessible in the database and as such should be left that way as reducing it to a lower function can be a security vulnerability.

It defines how checksums are calculated when using session state protection or other security functions. SHA-2 can only be used with the Oracle database 12c and up. MD5 is not recommended and has been deprecated.

Rejoin Sessions

By default, it is enabled for public sessions. This will automatically use the session in the browser cookie if no session ID is specified in the URL for public sessions only.

When set to Disabled, a new session is created if no session ID is specified in the URL.

When set to Enabled for All Sessions, APEX will reuse the session ID from the cookie when no session ID is specified in URL for all sessions. Using this setting will reduce the security of your application since the session ID validation will be only against the cookie in the browser. Use this option with care. This can be useful when a user would be already logged in an application and would use a link received by e-mail to an authenticated page without having to login again. See the Oracle APEX Documentation for more detail.

Unhandled Errors

This parameter should be set to HTTP 400 for a production server to avoid giving any end user too much information. Otherwise in dev and test the default should be left as the error message can help developers fix issues and bugs.

HTTPS Settings

The HTTPS Settings are for forcing APEX to be accessed via HTTPS and to return all responses via HTTPS. Typically HTTPS will be handled by a reverse proxy and so these options may not be required. However, if HTTPS between the reverse proxy and the application server (GlassFish, Tomcat, or WebLogic) is required, then these options must be set accordingly.

BE VERY CAREFUL! Changing the settings to require HTTPS without having HTTPS up and running in the environment will render APEX inaccessible.

The APEX API APEX_INSTANCE_ADMIN would need to be used to set the values back. Use the following command to reset the Require HTTPS to Application Specific:

```
BEGIN
    APEX_INSTANCE_ADMIN.SET_PARAMETER('REQUIRE_HTTPS', 'N');
    commit;
END;
/
```

RESTful Access

Oracle Application Express reports can be exposed as RESTful Webservices. If this parameter is set to No, then this option is not available to the developers.

See an example of this report attribute setting in Figure 10-6. This option appears for developers in the APEX builder for classic and interactive reports only when this *RESTful Access* option is set to Yes.

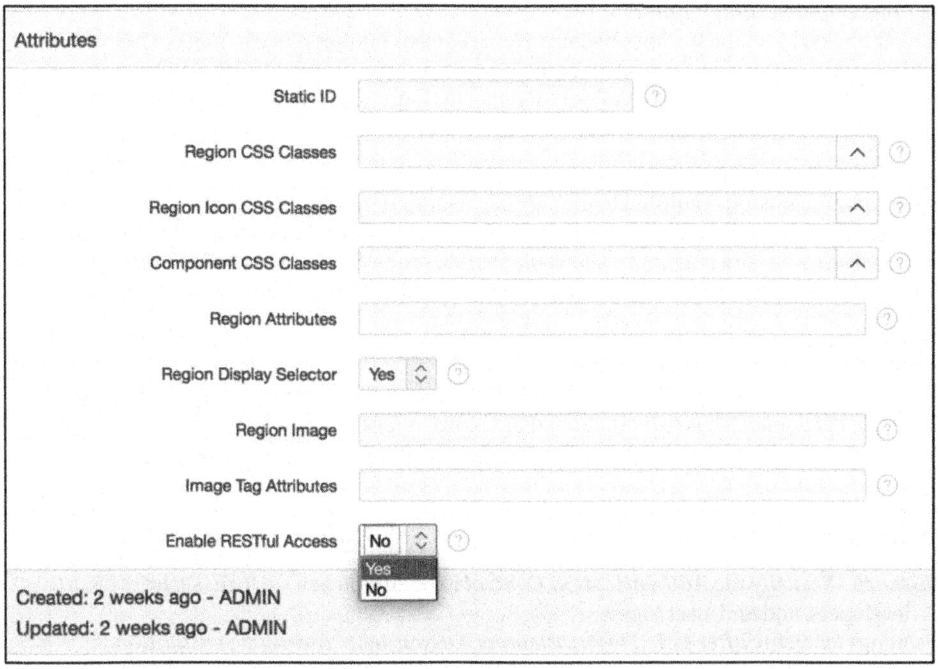

Attributes	
Static ID	
Region CSS Classes	⌄
Region Icon CSS Classes	⌄
Component CSS Classes	⌄
Region Attributes	
Region Display Selector	Yes ⌄
Region Image	
Image Tag Attributes	
Enable RESTful Access	No ⌄
	Yes
	No

Created: 2 weeks ago - ADMIN
Updated: 2 weeks ago - ADMIN

Figure 10-6. *Enable RESTful Access option for an application report, available in the APEX builder*

Session Timeout

Other security options available in Manage Instance / Security are available for managing the timeouts of APEX application sessions. It is possible to set the default ***Maximum Session Length in Seconds*** and the ***Maximum Session Idle Time in Seconds*** globally for all applications.

Workspace Isolation

The ***Workspace Isolation*** settings are for the whole instance and can be overridden at the workspace level. See the ***Manage Workspace*** section for more detail.

Allow Hostnames
With this option we can force the use of certain domains to access APEX. For example, if the DNS has two domains defined for the APEX server such as mywebsite.ca and mywebsite.com. We can input here mywebsite.com and that way only via the .com address can people access APEX. The .ca will not work.

Resource Consumer Group
With this parameter, it is possible to specify the Resource Manage consumer group for the instance. It is possible to override it at the workspace level. The APEX applications as well as the builder will use this setting. See C**hapter 16** for more detail.

Maximum Concurrent Workspace requests
This parameter is used to set the maximum amount of concurrent database transactions for all applications allowed via APEX. If the maximum is reached and a user tries to do something they will get an error message. It uses the CLIENT_INFO information from the database sessions to determine the amount of requests. If this information is changed using DBMS_APPLICATION_INFO.SET_CLIENT_INFO then this feature will not work.

Maximum Concurrent Session requests

This parameter is used to set the number of concurrent requests one session can make. They will also receive an error message if they try doing more than the limit. It uses the CLIENT_IDENTIFIER information from the database sessions to determine the amount of requests. If this information is changed using DBMS_ APPLICATION_INFO.SET_IDENTIFIER then this feature will not work.

Concurrent Session Requests Kill Timeout

Indicate the number of seconds required before APEX can automatically kill a database session tied to an APEX session trying to exceed the limit of Maximum Concurrent Session Requests specified previously. In other words, if a user exceeds the maximum allowable session requests, APEX will kill the oldest active database sessions associated to this same session. If it is left empty, no database sessions will be killed. It is empty by default.

Region and Web Service Excluded Domains

Enter a list of domains, such as mywebsite.com, which will not be allowed to access regions of type URL or Web services. The list of domains has to be separated by colons. A reverse proxy in production would normally manage this functionality. See **Chapter 4** for more information on using a reverse proxy with APEX.

Authentication Control

The **Manage Instance / Security** the **Authentication Control** is where you can set login security for administrators, developers, and end-user logins.

The usual settings for **Delay after failed login attempts**, **Logout URL**, **username validation**, **Maximum Login Failures Allowed**, **Account Password Lifetime**, and so on can be configured in this page.

Here are some of the authentication control settings that could be of interest:

Inbound Proxy Servers

Input here any inbound proxy servers so that APEX can properly determine the source host information or client information. Otherwise the proxy server's information such as IP will be extracted and will not properly reflect the user's origin and information. Use a comma-delimited list.

Require User Account Expiration and Locking

When set to Yes, this feature will force all workspaces to use the expiration and locking features for APEX end-user accounts and workspace administrators will not be able to disable it. When set to No, workspace administrator will be able to enable this feature at the workspace level if they want to.

Development Environment Authentication Schemes

As shown in Figure 10-7, the **Development Environment Authentication Schemes** is where you define which authentication scheme will be used by the APEX builder. The configuration page is available in **Manage Instance / Security / Authentication Control**. This feature definitely facilitates the management of developers' accounts since it now can be linked to an LDAP server. The **Development Environment Authentication Schemes** was introduced with the release of APEX 5.0.

Development Environment Authentication Schemes		
Name	**Description**	**Status**
✐ Application Express Accounts	This is the default authentication scheme. It authenticates users against the workspace user repository.	Current
✐ Database Accounts	This scheme utilizes database credentials. The user name and password of the database account is used to authenticate the user.	Not Current
✐ HTTP Header Variable	This scheme relies on a HTTP header variable to contain the username and on an external login method to log in. Application Express presents the available workspaces for the user.	Not Current
✐ LDAP Directory	This scheme checks credentials against an LDAP repository.	Not Current
✐ Oracle Application Server Single Sign-On	This scheme authenticates developers with Oracle Single Sign-On, using SSO's external login page. After authentication, Application Express presents the available workspaces for the user.	Not Current

Figure 10-7. *Authentication Schemes configuration for the APEX builder*

You have to make sure that the user exists in the authentication scheme you will use. For example, if the **Database Accounts** is selected, there must be an admin user in the database to be able to login to the Internal Workspace with the user admin. It will then use the password of the database user to authenticate the user.

To use another authentication scheme, simply edit it and change the status to current.

You could use your enterprise LDAP server for authenticating developers in the APEX builder and by doing so, simplify the management of the APEX developer accounts.

By default, it is the **Application Express Accounts** that is current and active.

Be careful because changing the authentication scheme can render APEX inaccessible. It is possible to reset the Authentication Schemes configuration to use Application Express accounts using the following API:

```
BEGIN
    APEX_INSTANCE_ADMIN.SET_PARAMETER('APEX_BUILDER_AUTHENTICATION','APEX');
    commit;
END;
/
```

Password Policy

The Password Policy parameters in **Manage Instance / Security** are used for all APEX accounts. It is valid for administrators, developers, and end-user accounts in all workspaces.

We will not list them all here since they are self-explanatory.

To enable the password policy rules defined in this section for the administration services (Internal Workspace), the option *'Use Policy Specified in Workspace Password Policy'*, at the bottom of the page, must be selected. See Figure 10-8.

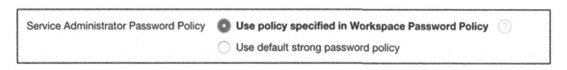

Figure 10-8. *Enabling password policy rules for administration services users*

By default, the password policy settings for the Internal Workspace (Service Administrator) are set to the default strong password policy. It will use the following rules:

- consist of at least six characters

- contain at least one lowercase alphabetic character, one uppercase alphabetic character, one numeric digit, and one punctuation character

- cannot include the username

- cannot include the word Internal

- cannot contain any words shown in the Must Not Contain field specified in Workspace Password Policy

Instance Settings

The Instance Settings are configurable by going to the ***Manage Instance / Instance Settings*** section and using the ***Instance Settings*** link. This will get you to a page where database storage and e-mail settings can be configured.

Require New Schema

This option is used by the self-provisioning option explained in its specific chapter. Essentially, when set to Yes, the end user will be forced to enter the name for a new schema when self-provisioning a new workspace. When set to No, the end user will be able to specify an existing schema.

Auto extend Tablespaces

If Auto Extend Tablespaces is enabled, tablespaces provisioned with Oracle Application Express are created with a data file that is one-tenth the requested size. The data file will automatically extend up to the requested size. For example, if a user requests a 100 MB workspace, the initial size of the datafile will be 10 MB and it will automatically extend up to a maximum size of 100 MB.

Bigfile Tablespaces

When Bigfile Tablespaces is enabled, all the tablespaces created by APEX will be bigfile tablespaces. APEX creates a new tablespace when a new schema is provisioned during the workspace creation.

Encrypted Tablespaces

When Encrypted Tablespaces is enabled, all the tablespaces created by APEX will be encrypted tablespaces. See the Oracle Database documentation about Encrypted Tablespace for the required wallet for this option. APEX creates a new tablespace when a new schema is provisioned during the workspace creation.

Delete Uploaded Files after (days)

This number indicates the number of days when APEX deletes uploaded files. The default value is 14 days. Uploaded files include export and import files, like for example application export. When set to null, no files will be deleted.

E-MAIL

Configuring e-mails in APEX is as simple as setting these SMTP parameters. There is nothing else to configure. APEX will simply relay the e-mails via the database to the specified SMTP server. In the ***Manage Instance / Instance settings / E-mail*** section there are many different configuration options that can be set. Here are some settings that I think are worth mentioning:

SMTP Host Address

For configuring e-mails, this setting is very important. It indicates which SMTP server that APEX will use. By default it is set to localhost, so it will use the SMTP server on the Database Server where the APEX instance is installed.

Use SSL/TLS

No is the default value for this option. It can be set to Yes for using a secure SSL/TLS connection with the SMTP server. It can also be set to "After connection is established"; then APEX will use the STARTTLS command after the connection is opened.

Maximum E-mails per Workspace

This is the maximum number of e-mails that can be sent in a day (24-hour period) by workspace using the APEX_MAIL API.

This is taken into account in all the applications of a workspace. To use the APEX_MAIL API a workspace has to be specified. If an application or a database package is sending a lot of e-mails, it would be worth considering the use of a specific workspace. This would ensure that it does not interfere with the number of e-mails sent by other applications.

Wallet

Here the path and password for an Oracle wallet can be set and saved. The password will never be displayed, which is why the checkbox must be checked to confirm that you wish to change it, if you want to change it. The wallet in the context of APEX would be used to store SSL certificates that need to be authorized to allow an APEX application to access a RESTful service, which is served over HTTPS. It could also be used for regions of type URL.

Report Printing

The **Report Printing** settings in **Manage Instance / Instance settings** are used for PDF printing in applications. This is where the **Print Server** can be configured.

There are three options for the Print Server:

- Oracle Rest Data Service (ORDS)

- External (Apache FOP)

- Oracle BI Publisher

Use the ORDS setting for PDF printing if ORDS is used as the Web Listener. This is the recommended setting and is the easiest one to use.

If the print server is on an external Java J2EE server, use the External (Apache FOP) option.

The Oracle BI Publisher can be used to link to an Oracle BI publisher server. The use of BI Publisher allows advanced printing but requires the proper Oracle licensing.

Depending on the selected print server, different configuration parameters have to be entered.

Application ID Range

Sometimes we may want to restrict the application IDs to be used. This is where you can set a minimum and maximum range for application IDs. As mentioned in C**hapter 2,** application IDs are unique in an APEX instance across all workspaces.

Workspace Purge Settings

Using the self-provisioning option allows end users to provision workspaces themselves. This can lead to having a lot of unused workspaces. The workspace purge process can then be used to purge unused workspaces.

When this feature is enabled, a nightly Oracle job called ORACLE_APEX_DAILY_MAINTENANCE runs and checks for inactive workspaces. If it finds an inactive workspace, it will send an e-mail to the workspace administrator. The workspace administrator can choose to keep or purge the workspace.

This is the content of the e-mail sent when a workspace will be purged:

Dear Oracle Application Express User, Workspace <Workspace Name> on <URL of APEX instance> has not shown any recent activity. Your inactive workspace is currently scheduled to be purged on or after <Date>. To prevent your workspace from being removed, please click the URL below and choose that you do not wish to have your workspace purged. You must do this within the next <Days Until Purge> day(s). If you do not need this workspace any longer, no action is required. Confirmation link: <URL>

A workspace can be specifically marked so that it will not be automatically purged. Go to **Manage Workspaces - Existing Workspaces** and edit the workspace attribute 'Allow workspace to be automatically purged' to No.

This feature is actually the same that is used by APEX.ORACLE.COM to purge inactive workspaces. Here is a description of all the parameters available for the Workspace Purge Settings:

Language

This is the language that will be used in the e-mails generated by APEX for the Workspace Purge. The selection of languages is based on the installed translations for the APEX Builder. See the **List of Installed Translations** in the **Manage Metadata** section later in this chapter.

Purge Administration E-mail address

This e-mail address will be the **"From"** address in e-mails sent by the purge workspace process. It is also the contact e-mail if users have questions or issues.

Send Summary E-mail to

This is a comma-separated list of e-mail addresses that will receive the Workspace Purge report on a daily basis. When there are no workspaces purged, there will not be any e-mails sent.

The Summary e-mail contains the following information:

- Number of workspaces newly added to purge list

- Workspace Remaining

- Workspaces Purged Summary, including number of schemas, tablespaces, and datafiles

- Workspaces Purged Today

- Workspaces to be Purged in 3 Days

- Workspaces Newly Added to Purge List

- Workspaces Added Back to Purge List

- Workspaces Removed from Purge List

Days Until Purge

Indicates the number of days before the Workspace is purged from the time that the workspace administrator receives the e-mail. The default value is 10 days.

Reminder Days in Advance

A reminder can be sent to the workspace administrator when a workspace is marked for deletion. This parameter indicates the number or days, before the workspace will be purged, that a reminder e-mail will be sent. The default value is 3 days.

Days Inactive

A workspace will be marked as inactive when it will not be used for the number of days indicated here. The default value is 45 days.

Grace Period (Days)

If the workspace administrator decides that the workspace should not be purged after receiving the notification e-mail, the number of days of the grace period will be used to determine when to resend a purge notification if the workspace is still not used and stays inactive. The default value is 45 days.

Maximum Execution Time (Hours)

This is the maximum number of hours that the purge process can run per day.

This parameter is for performance issues and is usually set when there are a lot of workspaces defined, especially when the self-service provisioning is used.

Maximum Number of Workspaces

This is the maximum number of workspaces that the purge process can remove each time it runs.

This parameter is for performance issues and is usually set when there are a lot of workspaces defined, especially when the self-service provisioning is used.

Maximum Number of E-mails

This is the number of e-mails that the purge process can send each time it runs.

This parameter is for performance issues and is usually set when there are a lot of workspaces defined, especially when the self-service provisioning is used.

Workspace Purge Dashboard

The Workspace Purge Dashboard gives a global view of the purge process. It displays information about workspaces marked to be purged, inactive, or purged by the nightly job as shown in Figure 10-9.

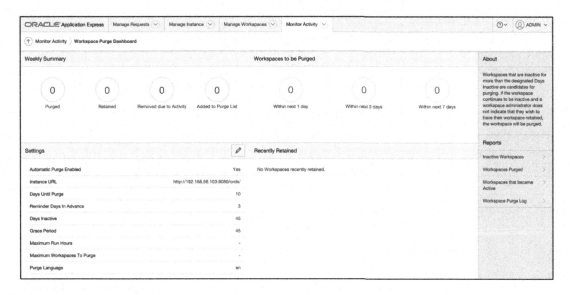

Figure 10-9. *Workspace Purge Dashboard*

Manage Metadata

Manage Instance / Manage Metadata is where you manage session state, manage the mail queue, check installed translations, and manage IR subscriptions.

Manage Session State

In the *Manage Session State* page to see a listing the *Recent Sessions.* There it is possible to see the content of the APEX sessions.

There is also a link to manually *Purge APEX sessions*. When a session is purged, the user is automatically disconnected.

Note that there is an Oracle Scheduled Job that purges sessions older than 12 hours automatically. It is called ORACLE_APEX_PURGE_SESSIONS and runs every hour. If you need to automatically purge sessions more often, you can reschedule this job with different parameters.

Another link called *Session State Statistics* will show the number of sessions, the total session state entries, and the average number of entries per session. It is also possible to purge the sessions from that page.

Manage Mail Queue

There is an APEX API that can be used to send e-mails. This API is called APEX_MAIL. It makes sending mail a lot easier using PL/SQL and provides multiple functionalities like attachments, and so on.

APEX_MAIL uses a mail queue to send mails. A scheduled job called ORACLE_APEX_MAIL_QUEUE regularly reads the queue and sends the e-mails using the SMTP configuration of the APEX instance, see the **"Instance Settings"** section of this chapter. This job runs every 5 minutes by default.

Using the manage mail queue report, it is possible to manually send e-mails that are still in the queue or view any errors that would cause the e-mail not being sent, or remove it from the queue.

When e-mails are not working properly in your APEX instance, this is a good place to go. If there is a problem with the ACL security configuration (see Chapter 10), it will be shown here.

Installed Translations

Installed translations is an interactive report that lists all the languages available for the builder and which ones have been installed for this instance. For more information regarding the installation of other languages for the APEX builder, see Chapters 8 and 9.

Interactive Report Subscriptions

If the option is enabled on the report, end users can subscribe to interactive reports in applications and receive the report via e-mail automatically as shown in Figure 10-10. They simply have to specify their e-mail address and the frequency.

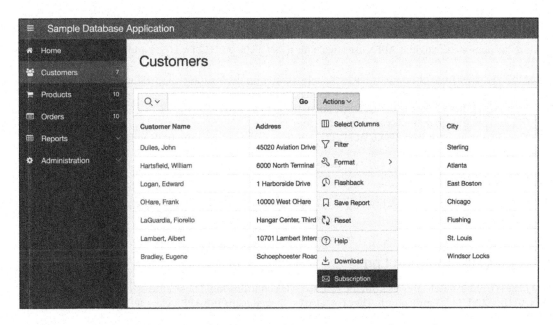

Figure 10-10. *Example of the Subscription feature on an interactive report for an end user*

The ***Interactive Report Subscriptions*** report lists all the user subscriptions. They can be deleted using the checkboxes and the ***Delete Checked*** button. See Figure 10-11.

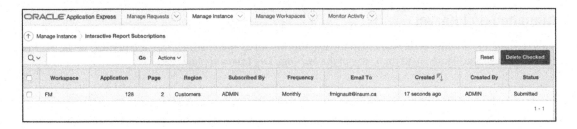

Figure 10-11. *Interactive Report Subscriptions*

Manage Logs and Files

In ***Manage Instance*** there is a section for ***Managing Logs and Files.*** There are multiple links that can be used to manage all the logs available in Oracle Application Express. I listed all those links with a short description and the name of the related underlying APEX table or view.

SQL Workshop Log

Use this option to manually truncate or delete entries from the SQL Workshop Log.
SQL Workshop Log entries are stored in `WWV_FLOW_SW_SQL_CMDS`.

Page View Activity Log

To store the page view activities APEX uses two tables: WWV_FLOW_ACTIVITY_LOG1$ and WWV_FLOW_ACTIVITY_LOG1$.

APEX switches from one activity log to the other based on the log interval specified in Manage Log Interval. When a switch occurs, the log being used is truncated.

This page shows all the details available about the activity logs.

It is also possible to manually truncate each log.

The APEX view APEX_WORKSPACE_ACTIVITY_LOG lists all the entries from both activity tables.

Developer Activity Log

This page is used to delete entries from the developer activity log. Those log entries are stored in WWV_FLOW_BUILDER_AUDIT_TRAIL.

External Click Counting Log

This page is used to delete entries from the external click counting log. Those entries are inserted using the APEX_UTIL.COUNT_CLICK procedure. They can also be viewed using the APEX view APEX_WORKSPACE_CLICKS.

Login Access Log

This page is used to delete entries from the login access log. They can also be viewed using the APEX view APEX_WORKSPACE_ACCESS_LOG.

Manage Log Interval

This is where the number of days to retain the log information is specified. The default number of days is 14 for all the logs. See Figure 10-12 for a view of the *Manage Log Interval* page.

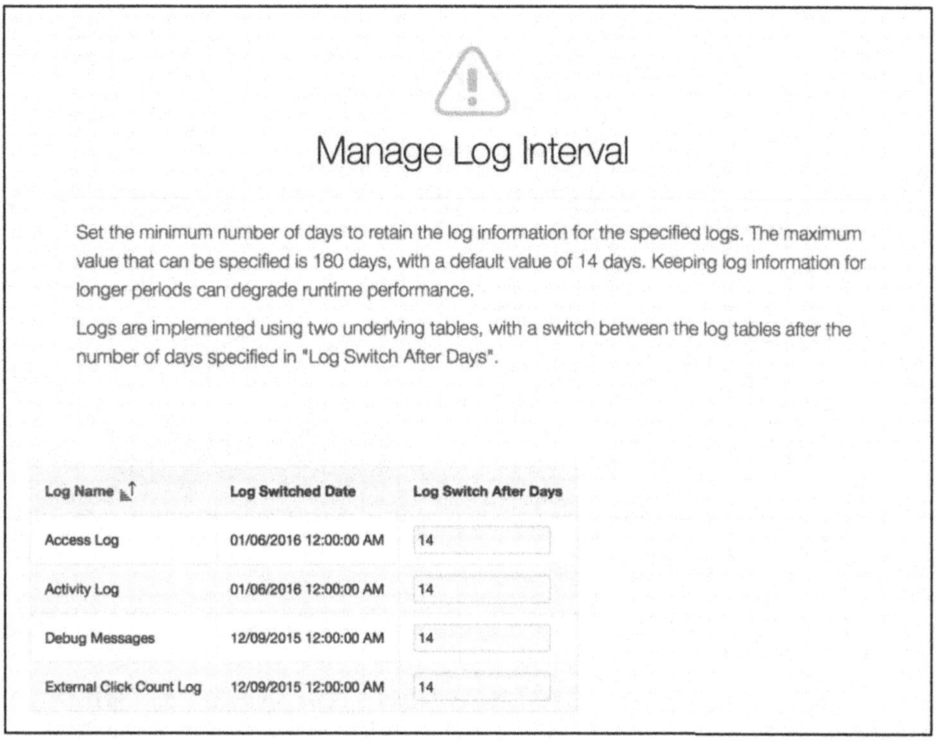

Manage Log Interval

Set the minimum number of days to retain the log information for the specified logs. The maximum value that can be specified is 180 days, with a default value of 14 days. Keeping log information for longer periods can degrade runtime performance.

Logs are implemented using two underlying tables, with a switch between the log tables after the number of days specified in "Log Switch After Days".

Log Name ↑	Log Switched Date	Log Switch After Days
Access Log	01/06/2016 12:00:00 AM	14
Activity Log	01/06/2016 12:00:00 AM	14
Debug Messages	12/09/2015 12:00:00 AM	14
External Click Count Log	12/09/2015 12:00:00 AM	14

Figure 10-12. *Manage Log Interval*

Archive Activity Log

Every night, the APEX_DAILY_MAINTENANCE scheduled job summarizes the APEX_WORKSPACE_ACTIVITY_LOG in a table called WWV_FLOW_LOG_HISTORY. This table is never purged, truncated, or cleaned.

When accessing the Archive Activity Log, it is possible to manually execute this archive process by clicking the Archive Activity Summary button. See Figure 10-13 for an example. The APEX view accessing the history table is APEX_WORKSPACE_LOG_ARCHIVE.

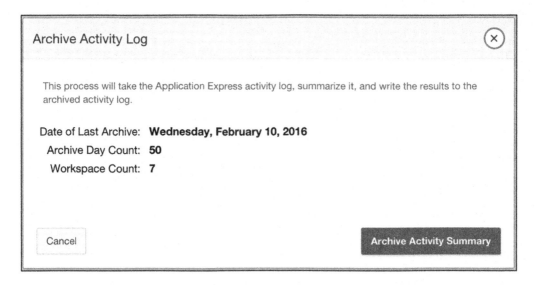

Figure 10-13. *Archive Activity Log example*

Manage Shared Components

In the ***Manage Instance*** page there is also a section for ***Managing Shared Components*** in the top right corner. As explained in the following, with those links it is possible to manage and monitor packaged applications. This is also where you will find the link to manage public themes for applications.

Manage Packaged Applications

This list shows all available packaged applications. It is also possible to add your own custom application in the packaged application catalog. This will make it so that it will be available to all developers in all workspace that have access to packaged applications.

Once created, it is also possible to edit your custom-packaged application attributes like its status and version number. The packaged applications that come built in with APEX cannot be removed or changed.

Monitor Packaged Application Installations

This report gives information on the installation of packaged applications. It is possible to find different statistics about the installation process of packaged applications across the whole instance.

Public Themes

Add your own custom themes that the developer will be able to use in the wizards while creating an application in addition to the built-in themes that comes with APEX.

Messages

In order to communicate to the development team and the administrators in APEX, it is possible to display messages in different places in the builder. Here is a list of available places to use this messaging capability:

Define Login Message

This option is used to enter a custom message that will be displayed on the APEX login page, as shown in the yellow region at the bottom of the page in Figure 10-14.

Figure 10-14. *Login message example*

Define System Message

This option is used to enter a system message for the instance administrators and workspace administrators.

The system message is displayed on the workspace home page of all workspaces, including the instance administration services (Internal Workspace). In the instance administration services, it is also possible to edit it directly where it is displayed by pressing the Edit icon. See an example in Figure 10-15.

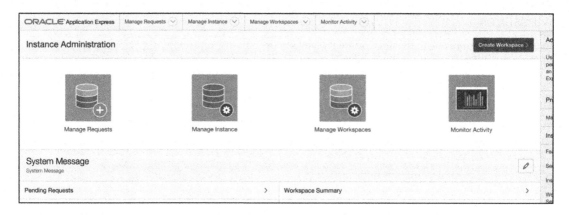

Figure 10-15. *System message in the main page of the instance administration services*

On standard workspaces, it is displayed in the ***News and Messages*** section of the home page, as shown in Figure 10-16.

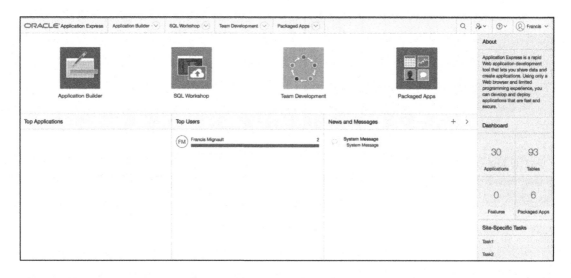

Figure 10-16. *System messages and site-specific tasks on the builder home page*

Manage Site-Specific Tasks

Site-Specific Tasks can be displayed on the ***Workspace Home Page*** on the right side in the ***Site-Specific Tasks*** region, also shown in Figure 10-17. They are not displayed in the APEX administration services (Internal Workspace) home page. It is also possible to set the ***Display Location*** to be on the workspace login page instead.

Manage Workspaces

The *Managing Workspaces* section is probably the most used by the instance administrator. This is where all the maintenance of workspaces is done. This is where it is possible to create, modify, and drop workspaces as well as manage users and assign database schemas to workspaces.

Create a Workspace

The *Create a Workspace* option is, of course, used to create a new workspace.

Make sure that the workspace IDs are the same in all your APEX instances in all your environments for the same workspace. For example, to create an HR workspace in Development, Test, and Production, it would be a good practice to use the same workspace ID everywhere. Create the workspace in Development and APEX will assign a unique ID to it. Then, create the HR Workspace in Test and Production using the Development workspace ID. This will allow the possibility of exporting and importing application pages between those two APEX instances in this workspace. The workspace name can be modified at any time, not the workspace ID.

First, as shown in Figure 10-17, enter a workspace name. This is also where the workspace ID can be specified. Note that there is also a link to create multiple workspaces. This is explained later in this chapter.

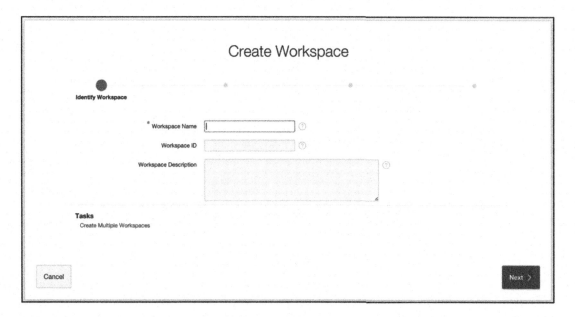

Figure 10-17. *Create Workspace wizard*

On the next page, enter the information for the schema that will be associated with the workspace. See Figure 10-18. Depending on the **Instance Settings**, it can be either a request for a new schema or an existing one.

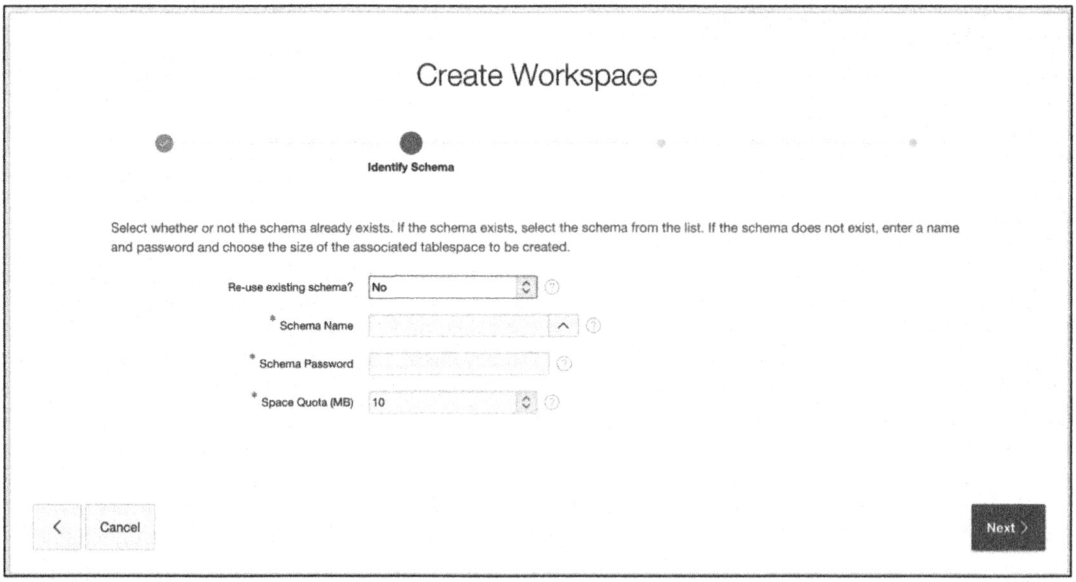

Figure 10-18. *Create Workspace wizard, database schema*

The next step is to enter the workspace administrator information and credentials as shown in Figure 10-19.

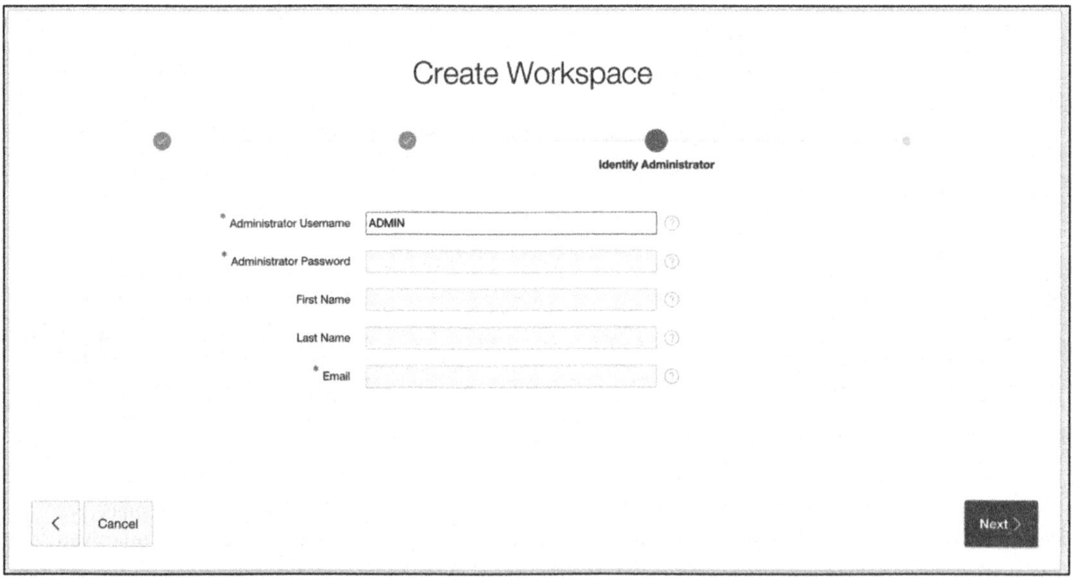

Figure 10-19. *Create Workspace wizard, administrator user information*

CHAPTER 10 ■ CONFIGURING

Click **Next** and a confirmation page will be displayed. Click **Create Workspace** if all the information is correct.

The Workspace is now created with a new Oracle database schema and a new tablespace. The database user account created is locked by default.

You can login to the newly created APEX workspace using the credentials entered. At the first login attempt, APEX will automatically ask for a password change.

Create Multiple Workspaces

It is also possible to create multiple workspaces at the same time. This is particularly useful to create training environments that require multiple workspaces.

Simply specify how the workspace names will be generated, the number of workspaces to create, and other self-explanatory options to create multiple workspaces at once.

There are three different ways that APEX will generate workspace names:

- System Generated

  - APEX will generate Workspace Names.

- Statically Prefixes Workspace Name with Sequential Integer Suffix

  - Specify a Workspace Prefix and APEX will append a sequential number.

- E-mail Domain Name as Workspace Name, with Sequential Integer Suffix for duplicates.

  - APEX will use the domain names from the e-mail list and add a sequential number when there will be duplicate e-mail domain names.

Removing / Locking a Workspace

In the **Manage Workspaces** page, it is possible to remove or lock a workspace.

Remove Workspace

To remove a workspace, go to **Manage Workspaces** and select the **Remove Workspace** option. The same wizard is also available in the **Existing Workspaces** interactive report by clicking the delete link in the Action column.

This will delete the workspace definition, the workspace APEX applications, and the workspace users from the APEX instance.

The remove workspace option does not remove database objects, schemas, and tablespaces. This has to be done manually in the database. The wizard will list the objects related to the workspace being deleted.

Lock Workspace

Locking a workspace essentially is making all the associated user accounts locked, including the administrator of the workspace, and changing the status of all the related applications to unavailable.

To unlock a workspace, follow these steps:

1. Log in the Internal APEX instance administration services (Internal Workspace).

2. Go to Manage Workspaces, Manage Developers and Users, and unlock the workspace user accounts by changing the account availability to Unlock.

3. Login to the workspace as an administrator.

4. Unlock all the applications one by one and change their status to Available in the application properties.

It is also possible to change the status of multiple applications by going to Manage Service and using the Application Build Status link in the "Manage Metadata" section. It is available on the right-hand side of the page as shown in Figure 10-20.

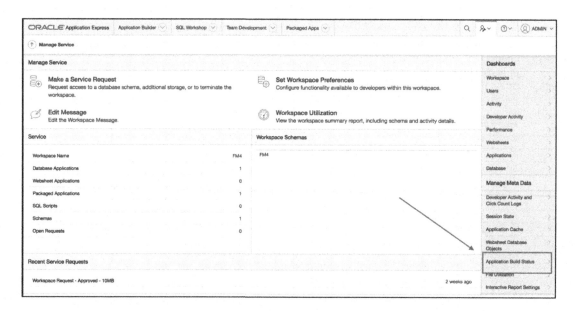

Figure 10-20. *Workspace administration option to bulk edit the application status*

Manage Workspace to Schema Assignments

This is where you manage the assignments of Oracle database schemas to workspaces. The report lists all the schemas used by all workspaces. It is also possible to add existing or new schemas to a workspace here.

As specified in **Chapter 2**, a workspace can have one or many database schemas assigned to it.

Manage Developers and Users

Using this option, you can see and manage all the Application Express users for the instance. The list shows all the users by workspaces. They can be users that only have access to applications and not the builder, developer accounts, workspace administrators, or Instance administrators.

From the report, it is possible to reset user passwords easily and create new users.

Manage Component Availability

For each workspace, components in the Application Builder can be enabled or disabled. For example, if you do not want the developers to use SQL Workshop in a specific workspace, simply set the Enable SQL Workshop to No.

From the *Manage Component Availability* report it is possible to click the workspace name to edit the components availability. See Figure 10-21.

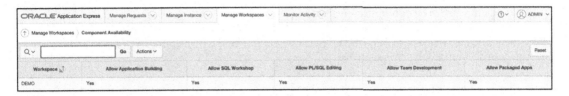

Figure 10-21. *Manage Workspaces, Component Availability report*

Once in the detail page of the component report, the following component can be enabled or disabled:

- Application Builder
- SQL Workshop
- PL/SQL Editing in SQL Workshop
- Team Development
- Packaged Application Installation

Export/Import

The export/import workspace is used to keep a copy of the definition of the workspace. It does not export the applications. This can useful if you want to recreate the same workspace in different environments or keep a backup of the workspace configuration and users. See **Chapter 12** for more detail on how to backup workspaces and applications.

Existing Workspaces

This is probably the option that is used the most in the administration services of APEX and it is available in the *Manage Workspaces* page.

This report will list all the existing workspaces in the APEX instance. It is possible to create or edit a workspace from here. The internal workspace is listed but cannot be modified.

Basically, this is where a workspace can be modified. Simply click the workspace name to get to the edit page for the workspace. The following is a list of some of the options that can be viewed or changed for a workspace.

Workspace Identifier

This is the unique ID number of the workspace. It will be unique across environments. As mentioned before, to be able to copy only one application page from one APEX instance to another, the workspace ID has to be the same in both instances.

Workspace Name

This is the name of the workspace. APEX uses the workspace ID to identify a workspace. The name can be changed at any time without affecting anything.

First Schema Provisioned

Database schema is used to create the workspace. To add more schemas to the workspace, use the Manage Workspace to Schema Assignments option in the Workspace Actions section. Or use the Add Schema link on the right side of the page.

Feedback Synchronization Source Identifier

This is used to link Feedback exports for a workspace. It is possible to export application feedbacks using the APEXExport java class. See **Chapter 12** for more detail on this feature.

Allow workspace to be automatically purged

When the Purge Workspace process is enabled, it will automatically look for inactive workspaces and purge them. See the "Workspace Purge Settings" section of this chapter. The purge process will not take this workspace in account when this is set to No.

Display Name

This is used in some reports. It can be seen as a description of the workspace name. We recommend that you always keep the same value as the workspace name to avoid any confusion.

Login Control

The Login controls here have the same functionalities as the one configured at the instance level but can be changed specifically for a workspace.

Component Availability

As in the Workspace Settings of the manage component settings option, it is possible to enable or disable the application builder, SQL Workshop, PL/SQL Editing in SQL Workshop, Team Development, and Packaged Application Installation.

Session Timeout

It is possible to override the session timeout settings from the global APEX instance setting specifically for a workspace.

Workspace Isolation

The Workspace Isolation settings are the same as the ones at the instance level specified earlier in this chapter. These settings are to override them for the workspace specifically.

Workspace Reports

The Workspace Reports section contains reports that can be very useful. The Existing Workspaces report is where workspaces can be edited and configured. The other reports are mostly used for auditing purposes.

Here is a description of each report:

Workspace Details

This is a report that shows the details of a workspace. First select a workspace and a reporting period and click the Set button. The report can also be sent via e-mail.

Amongst other information, it is possible to see the schemas assigned to the workspace information like tablespaces, database roles, database privileges and database object counts in this report.

Workspace Database Privileges

This report lists the database privileges associated to database schemas assigned to workspaces.

Workspaces with Only Sample Application

This report lists workspaces that have only the Sample Application installed.

Manage File Utilization

This report lists the Total File Size, Count of Files, Newest File, and Oldest File per workspace.

Find an E-mail Workspace Summary

This report allows you to see and search workspaces using the interactive report and get to the workspace summary mentioned before. It lists the Workspace Name, First Schema Provisioned, Last Login, Workspace ID, Number of Applications, Number of Schemas, and an indicator of active sessions.

Manage Applications

In the *Manage Workspaces* page, it is also possible to manage application attributes, application build status, and application parsing schemas. Those links are in the *Manage Applications* section in the bottom right of this page.

Application Attributes

The application attributes report lists all applications in the instance in an APEX interactive report. For example, it is possible to see the build status, workspace name, language, parsing schema, and so on for all applications. This report is very useful to search and see application attributes information in one simple report.

Build Status

The applications build status can be changed here. If an application has been set to run only, this is the only place, other than using an API, that you can reset an application to *run and build* so that developers can have access to it. Simply click the edit button in the report for a specific application to get to the edit build status page shown in Figure 10-22.

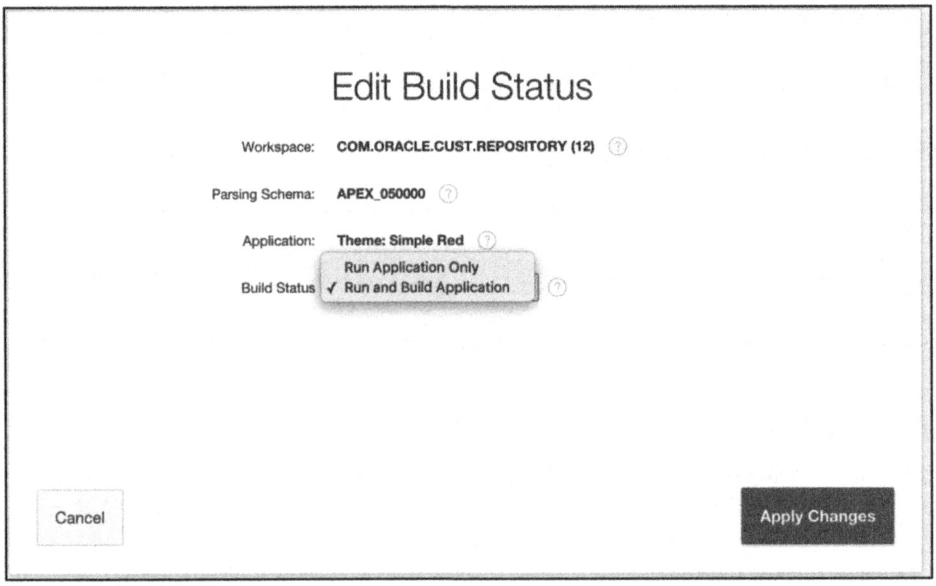

Figure 10-22. *Edit Build Status*

When an application as a ***Run Application Only*** build status, it is not visible in the APEX builder. To make it visible to the developers again, change the build status to ***Run and Build Application***.

Parsing Schemas

This report lists all the parsing schemas associated to workspaces. A workspace can have more than one schema associated to it. To add or remove a parsing schema to a workspace, go to ***Manage Workspaces*** and select ***Manage Workspace to Schema Assignments*** as explained earlier in this chapter.

Monitor Activity

The last main option of the APEX administration services is ***Monitory Activity***. In this page, you will have access to different reports that will help monitoring the instance.

Monitoring Reports

The monitoring reports list different information about the instance. Reports are based on the APEX views available directly in the database.

The ***Page Views*** section contains reports showing the activity on the Instance applications. This includes the builder and end-user applications.

The other sections give access to different reports. For example, the ***Mail Log*** report lists e-mails that have been sent by APEX. This is a good place to look when there are e-mail problems. If the e-mails sent are not listed here it is maybe due to an ACL problem or a bad e-mail configuration. Verify the mail queue report in Manage Instance – Manage Meta Data to see if there are any errors with the mail queue. For more detail on the e-mail configuration see the subsections "E-Mails" under "Instance Settings".

There are also other self-explanatory reports for different things like database jobs, packaged applications, service requests, and developer activity.

Summary

Once APEX is installed and running, the place to go to for configuring it is the APEX administration services. It is accessible by logging into APEX using the Internal Workspace. There it is possible to manage the instance, manage workspaces, and monitor activity. This is also where Self-Provisioning is configured, and that is covered in Chapter 13. The instance administrator, usually the Oracle DBA, will have to login to administration services on a regular basis mainly to create or manage workspaces and manage users, so it is important to understand the different available settings and where they are. Hopefully this chapter will be a good reference.

When APEX is installed as Runtime only the administration services web pages will not be available. It is then required to do all of those configurations via APIs. The next chapter is exactly about managing APEX when it is installed as Runtime only.

CHAPTER 11

Administering APEX in a Runtime-Only Mode

An APEX installation usually consists of the APEX builder applications and the required schema and objects for the APEX instance to work. The APEX applications built by developers also require those APEX database schemas and objects to run. That is why APEX has to be installed in all the environments where the applications have to be executed.

For development and test environments, it is normal to have access to the APEX builder. It facilitates the maintenance and deployment of applications. For production environments it is possible to install APEX without the builder. This way it would be more secure and it would prevent hackers from trying to force the APEX builder login page and consequently access the development tool.

As explained in the first chapters of this book, APEX is essentially a collection of database tables, packages, and schemas. In order to be able to maintain an APEX installation in a runtime environment without the builder or for scripting purposes, APEX provides a lot of different APIs.

This chapter explains how to configure APEX to be in runtime-only mode, how to manage and deploy applications, and how to manage the APEX instance without the web interface.

APEX Runtime-Only Setup

APEX can be installed in runtime only. It is also possible to add and remove the builder on an existing installation without affecting the workspaces, users, and applications in place. APEX has been built using APEX. So the builder is essentially made of APEX applications. Of course, switching to a runtime-only installation not only removes those applications but adds more security and removes any database rights and objects required only by them.

■ **Note**   Make sure that you are using the corresponding scripts related to the installed version of APEX. They are available in the apex.zip file download from OTN. Older versions are also available. A good practice is to keep the apex.zip of the version installed in the database on the database server.

Install APEX in Runtime Only

To install APEX in runtime only, use the `apxrtins.sql` script for the installation.

Follow the installation instructions for everything else including the postinstall scripts. For detailed information on how to install APEX, see Chapter 8.

© Francis Mignault and Luc Demanche 2016
F. Mignault and L. Demanche, *Oracle Application Express Administration*, DOI 10.1007/978-1-4842-1958-4_11

Remove the APEX Builder

If APEX is already installed, it is possible to remove the APEX builder only.

To do so, connect to the database instance using `sqlplus / as sysdba` and run the following script available in the downloaded apex.zip file: `apxdevrm.sql`.

Install APEX Builder

If APEX is installed in runtime mode, it is possible to add the APEX builder back.

To do so, connect to the database instance using `sqlplus / as sysdba` and run the following script available in the downloaded apex.zip file: `apexdvins.sql`.

Managing Applications

Most of the options available in the builder are available using APIs. This section explains how to deploy and maintain applications in a runtime environment. Those APIs are always available, even if the APEX builder is installed. They could be used for automating the deployment process.

Deploying Applications

Again, since APEX is essentially using PL/SQL, it is very simple to deploy application from the command line. An APEX export file is a runnable SQL Script. SQL Developer also has built-in features to deploy APEX applications.

Setting Import Options During the Export

To simplify the import of applications in a runtime environment, it is possible to define some options when the application is exported from the builder. This will avoid making changes during or after the application import since the sql export file will already contain those changes.

Here are the export parameters that can impact the import of the application:

Owner Override

By default, the associated schema of the application is defined in the application attribute owner. Changing the value of the owner at export time will make the import use this new value. At import time, the application will be associated to this Oracle database schema if it is part of the workspace. Otherwise it will be associated to the default workspace schema.

Build Status Override

The build status can also be changed at export time. It should be set to "Run Application Only" for applications that will be deployed in a runtime-only production instance for more security. Setting the build status to "Run Application Only" will disable the possibility to debug and trace the application. (See chapter 14 on monitoring for more detail.)

Debugging

Debugging can be set to No in the export file so that at import time the application will automatically have debugging the option set to that value.

Debugging is a useful feature for applications under development. However, as a best practice, turn off debugging for production applications to prevent users from viewing application logic.

Export Translations

Export Translations indicates whether the translations will be included in the export file. Set this to Yes if you have translations. When deploying the application the translation repository will be populated automatically. The translated applications will still need to be published. See the "Manage Translations" section for more detail on this.

Simple Application Deployment

To deploy an APEX application, an export file is required. The export file is a SQL script using the following naming standard by default: f9999.sql, where 9999 is the application ID.

To deploy the application, connect to the database and run the sql script using SQLcl, SQLDeveloper, or SQLPLUS. Here is an example of how to deploy application 123 using SQLPLUS:

```
SQLPLUS / as sysdba
@f123.sql
```

You have to be connected as an Oracle database user with the DBA or APEX_ADMINISTRATOR_ROLE privilege or with the schema associated to the application being imported, for the import to work.

This will deploy the application using the same application ID and the same workspace ID. If the application ID already exists, the application will be replaced. If the schema user does not have the proper privileges or the workspace does not exist, an error ORA-20001: Package variable g_security_group_id must be set will be displayed. See the following example of this error when trying to import into a schema that does not have the workspace ID (g_security_goup_id) associated with the application being imported:

```
SQL> @f133.sql
--application/set_environment
APPLICATION 133 - demo switch lang
--application/delete_application
begin
*
ERROR at line 1:
ORA-20001: Package variable g_security_group_id must be set.
ORA-06512: at "APEX_050000.WWV_FLOW_API", line 1338
ORA-06512: at "APEX_050000.WWV_FLOW_API", line 1373
ORA-06512: at "APEX_050000.WWV_FLOW_API", line 2094
ORA-06512: at line 2
```

APEX_APPLICATION_INSTALL API

If an application has to be installed into a different configuration, other then what it was exported from, it is possible to change some settings using the APEX_APPLICATION_INSTALL API. As stated before, an error will be raised if the schema does not have access to the workspace ID associated with the application export.

Here is an example that changes the Workspace ID before the import. First we select the workspace ID for the workspace 'FM', we make it the Workspace ID that will be used by the import script and then we generate a unique offset number:

```
declare
    l_workspace_id number;
begin
    select workspace_id into l_workspace_id
      from apex_workspaces
     where workspace = 'FM';
    --
    apex_application_install.set_workspace_id( l_workspace_id );
    apex_application_install.generate_offset;
end;
/
@f999.sql
```

With APEX_APPLICATION_INSTALL the following functions and procedures can be used before the import:

GENERATE_OFFSET and GET_OFFSET

In order to make sure that the primary keys in the APEX metadata are unique, an offset has to be generated. It has to be generated when the workspace ID and/or the application ID is modified.

The GET_OFFSET function will return the offset number used during the import.

SET_WORKSPACE_ID and GET_WORKSPACE_ID

As shown in the previous example, it is possible to set a workspace ID that will replace the one in the import file. Make sure that it is a valid workspace ID. To find a specific workspace ID, use the APEX_WORKSPACES view. To see the workspace ID used by the import script, use the GET_WORKSPACE_ID function.

GENERATE_APPLICATION_ID, SET_APPLICATION_ID, and GET_APPLICATION_ID

The application ID can be changed to a specific ID using the SET_APPLICATION_ID procedure. If the application ID already exists in the workspace, the existing application will be replaced by the import. The application IDs in the reserved range of 3000 to 8999 cannot be used. To automatically set the application ID with the next one available, use the GENERATE_APPLICATION_ID procedure.

Here is an example that generated a new application ID:

```
begin
    apex_application_install.generate_application_id;
    apex_application_install.generate_offset;
end;
/
@f999.sql
```

SET_APPLICATION_ALIAS and GET_APPLICATION_ALIAS

To define and change the application alias, use the SET_APPLICATION_ALIAS procedure. The application alias has to be unique in a workspace. After the import, the GET_APPLICATION_ALIAS function can be used to get the alias applied during the import.

SET APPLICATION NAME and GET APPLICATION NAME

It is possible to set the application name before the import and to get the application name after the import.

SET SCHEMA and GET SCHEMA

Set Schema is used to define the new schema owner of the application. Get Schema will retrieve the schema name used during the import.

SET IMAGE PREFIX and GET IMAGE PREFIX

Set Image Prefix will change the image prefix alias for the import and Get Image Prefix will retrieve the image prefix used during the import.

SET PROXY and GET PROXY

The Set Proxy procedure can be used to change the proxy setting for the application and Get Proxy can be used to see the proxy attribute used during the import.

SET AUTO INSTALL SUP OBJ and GET AUTO INSTALL SUP OBJ

In the application builder, there is a utility called Supporting objects that is related to the APEX applications. Developers can use this feature to associate install scripts, upgrade scripts, and delete scripts. It is a bit like an installer that will run after the application is installed.

Installing an application using the command line and the import scripts does not execute the supporting objects' installation scripts associated to the application unless they are flagged with the automatic install status.

The Set Auto Install Sup Obj can be used to change the status of the supporting object installation script to automatic or not.

As for the other APIs, the get function will return the status of the auto install supporting objects after the import.

CLEAR ALL

The clear all procedure clears all the values configured by the APEX_APPLICATION_INSTALL API.

Deploying Using SQL Developer

In a runtime-only instance, another way of deploying applications is by using SQLDeveloper. There are built-in functionalities in SQLDeveloper for importing applications and for looking at the application definition. There are also some predefined reports available to query the APEX dictionary views.

In the connection tree, there is a node for Application Express. In that node, the connected user will see the available applications. See Figure 11-1.

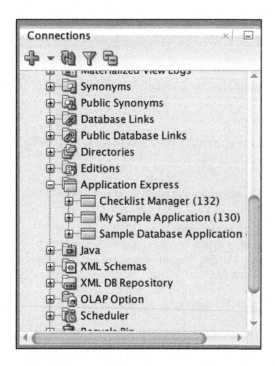

Figure 11-1. *SQLDeveloper Application Express node*

To import an application, open the contextual menu by right-clicking Application Express, selecting the import option, and following the wizard instructions. See Figures 11-2 and 11-3.

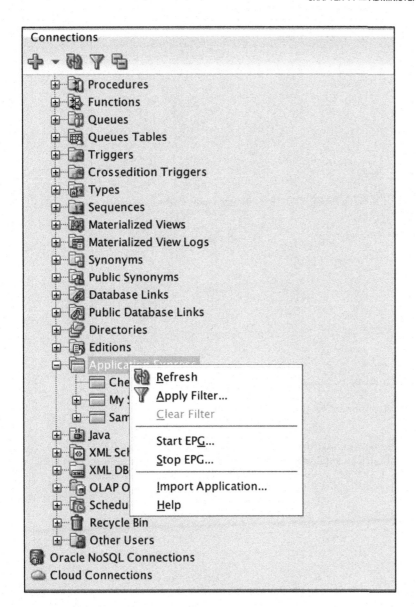

Figure 11-2. *SQLDeveloper importing APEX application*

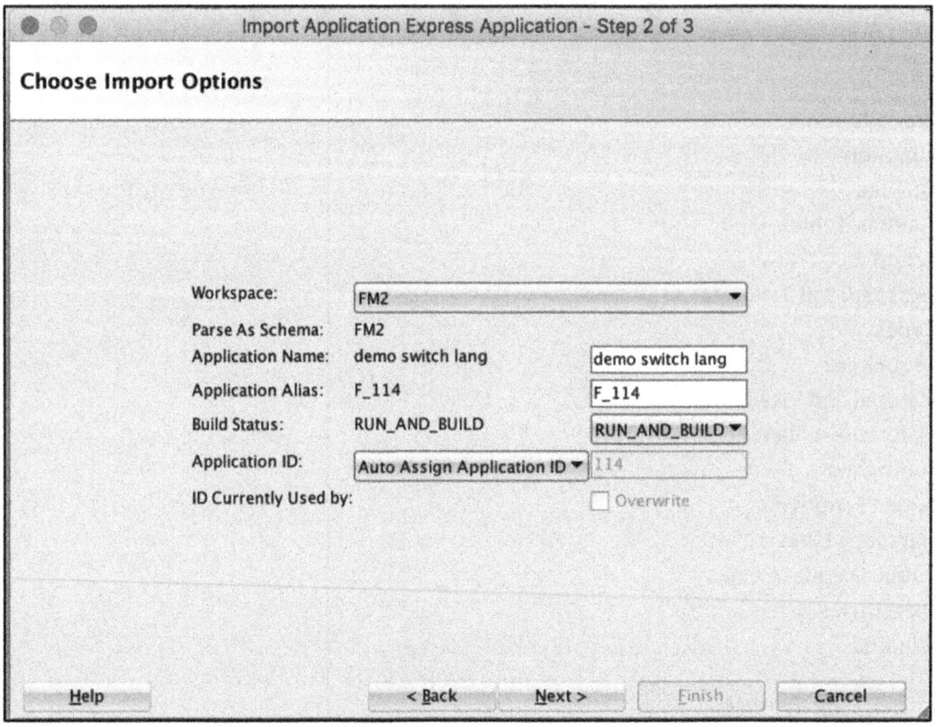

Figure 11-3. *SQLDeveloper wizard for importing APEX application*

It is possible to select the workspace, change the application name, alias, status, and ID.

To export an application, right-click an application to open the contextual menu and select the Quick DDL option as shown in Figure 11-4. This will generate the sql for the import of this application.

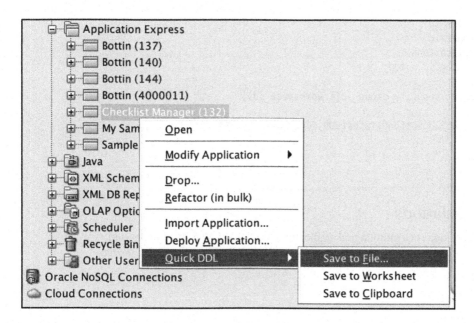

Figure 11-4. *SQLDeveloper exporting an APEX application*

Using the same contextual menu, it is also possible to drop an application or to modify an application. To export a page, open the application node and right-click the page to be exported.

Change Application Build Status

The build status for an application can be changed using the APEX_UTIL API. This API can be called at any time once the application is imported.

To see the build option for an application, the APEX view APEX_APPLICATION_BUILD_OPTIONS used.
For example:

```
select BUILD_OPTION_NAME
     , BUILD_OPTION_STATUS
, BUILD_OPTION_ID
from apex_application_build_options
where application_id = 100;

BUILD_OPTION_NAME    BUILD_OPTION_STATUS    BUILD_OPTION_ID
------------------   --------------------   ------------------
demo_build_option    Include                16840634768094756
```

Here is an example that changes the build option for the application ID 100 to exclude:

```
declare
  l_workspace_id number;

begin
```

```
SELECT workspace_id
INTO l_workspace_id
FROM apex_applications
WHERE application_id = 100;

wwv_flow_api.set_security_group_id(l_workspace_id);

apex_util.set_build_option_status(100,16840634768094756,'EXCLUDE');

end;
/
```

Manage Translations

To manage the translations of a multilingual application, the APEX_LANG API can be used.

In the context of a runtime-only installation, the APEX_LANG API can do the following:

- Seed

- Publish

- Manage Mappings

After importing the application using the export sql script, the translated applications have to be published. To do so, use the apex_lang.publish_application procedure.

For example:

```
begin

  for c1 in (select workspace_id
             from   apex_applications
             where  application_id = 100) loop
      apex_util.set_security_group_id( c1.workspace_id );
      exit;
  end loop;

  -- Now, publish the translated version of the application
  apex_lang.publish_application(
     p_application_id => 100,
     p_language       => 'en-ca' );
end;
/
```

Exporting Applications

It is possible to export application from the command line using the APEXExport.class utility. This program is included in the apex.zip installation files in the utilities directory of that zip file.

■ **Note**   see Chapter 12 for more information on APEX backups and how to export applications on the command line using APEXExport.

SQLDeveloper can also be used to export APEX application with the Quick DDL menu option, as explained earlier in this chapter.

There is now a new sql command-line tool available. It is called SQLcl. To download it go to the following URL: www.oracle.com/technetwork/developer-tools/sql-developer/downloads/index.html

SQLcl comes with different commands to administering APEX on the command line. For example to see all the APEX applications simply use the "apex" command.

```
[oracle@oraclevm Downloads]$ sql

SQLcl: Release 4.1.0 Release Candidate on Sat Mar 19 13:42:07 2016

Copyright (c) 1982, 2016, Oracle.  All rights reserved.

Username? (''?) demo
Password? (*********?) ****
Database? (''?) demo
Connected to:
Oracle Database 12c Enterprise Edition Release 12.1.0.1.0 - 64bit Production
With the Partitioning, OLAP, Advanced Analytics and Real Application Testing options

SQL> apex

WORKSPACE   APPLICATION_ID  APPLICATION_NAME             BUILD_STATUS     LAST_UPDATED_ON
DEMO        111             Sample Charts                Run and Develop  16-01-22
DEMO        100             Sample Database Application  Run and Develop  16-03-11

SQL>
```

And to export, spool the output to a file and use the apex export command. For example, to export the application ID 100:

```
SQL> spool f100.sql
SQL> apex export 100
```

Managing the Instance

Manage the Instance with APEX_INSTANCE_ADMIN

To be able to manage a runtime instance, there is an API called APEX_INSTANCE_ADMIN available. Refer to the Oracle documentation for all the details on all the procedures and functions available in this API.

For example, to add a new schema to a workspace, the ADD_SCHEMA procedure can be used or to add a new workspace the ADD_WORKSPACE procedure can be used.

In order to be able to use the APEX_INSTANCE_ADMIN, the database user has to be *SYS, SYSTEM, APEX_050000* or have the database role APEX_ADMINISTRATOR role granted.

Also see Chapter 10 about the configuration of an APEX instance.

Manage Users and Developers

To manage APEX user accounts in a runtime application, use the `APEX_UTIL` API.

With `APEX_UTIL`, it is possible to create users, delete users, manage user groups, reset the user password, and so on.

For detailed information and to learn more about the available procedures and functions, see the Oracle APEX documentation.

■ **Note** For more information on APEX 5.0 APIs, see `http://apex.oracle.com/doc50` and look for the *Application Express API Reference* document.

APEX Administrator Role

Executing APIs in sqlplus or sqlcl requires special privileges. There is a database role called `APEX_ADMINISTRATOR_ROLE`. A database user with this database role can install applications.

When a database connection is made with a schema that is assigned to a workspace, this user will only see the information related to this workspace. If the same database user has the `APEX_ADMISTRATOR_ROLE` granted, it will then be able to see the information of all workspaces in the instance. This can be useful if you want to run global queries on the APEX views to do some verification or impact analysis.

APEX Dictionary Views

APEX has different views available to see information on the instance objects like workspaces, applications, users, and so on. Those views are especially practical in a runtime-only installation.

See Chapter 2 for more detail on APEX views.

Summary

For a production installation, APEX can be installed without the builder. This secures the installation even more because, in that case, the graphical interface is not accessible. Since everything is stored in the database in a metadata, most if not all of the APEX builder functionalities are available via APIs. And it is possible to add or remove the builder at any time.

Exporting and importing applications can be done using scripts, and the APEX_APPLICATION_INSTALL API can be very useful for application imports, if some IDs need to be changed. Maintenance of a runtime-only install is really knowing how to use the APEX APIs. In the next chapter, we will talk about database backups and application backups.

CHAPTER 12

Database and APEX Backups

One of the main duties and responsibilities of a database administrator (DBA) is to implement, manage, and monitor backup processes. The purpose of a backup is to recover from media failure, data loss, or human error. A DBA's worst nightmare is a call in the middle of the night asking for a full or partial restore of the production database. A DBA should always be ready for such a situation and should have all the possible scenarios documented and tested. But for a database running APEX applications, there may be a few particularities relating to the restore process that a DBA may not be aware of.

In this chapter, we will explain these particularities and we will propose a backup strategy that covers both aspects; backup and recovery for the database itself and backup and recovery for the APEX components. Having backups of the database and APEX components, we are in a position to restore and recover database in any cases.

Note DBAs should be aware that the Oracle database running APEX applications is like any other database and should be backed up using the regular Oracle tools.

Note APEX components should be taken care of separately from the database backup procedure.

Database Backup

Let's start with the Oracle database backups. Database backups are divided in two different kinds:

- Physical backup
- Logical backup

Physical Backup

Physical backups are copies of the physical files that composed the database. By physical files, I mean the control files, datafiles, and the archived log files. The resulting backup files can be stored either on physical disk or directly on tape if we are using Recovery Manager (RMAN) in conjunction with a media management tool

---

Note Any Oracle backup strategy is based on a physical backup. It is the foundation of the strategy.

F. Mignault and L. Demanche, *Oracle Application Express Administration*, DOI 10.1007/978-1-4842-1958-4_12

How to Implement Physical Backup

To implement database physical backup, Oracle provides the following main solutions:

- RMAN
- Oracle Enterprise Manager Cloud Control
- User-managed backup and recovery
- Zero Data Loss Recovery Appliance

These solutions are fully supported by Oracle but the preferred solution for the backup and recovery deployment is RMAN. RMAN provides a unique interface for backup and recovery of a database and also provides techniques not even possible with any of the other solutions like the following:

- Incremental backups
- Block media recovery
- And so on

How to Deploy a Backup/Restore Procedure with RMAN

The following examples show the simplicity of RMAN. We assume that the option "configure controlfile autobackup" is set to "on" and the database is on archivelog mode. The first example is a full backup of the database, and the resulting file would be stored in '/u04/backup/rman' folder.

```
run {

        backup database plus archivelog;
        release channel ch1;
}
```

■ **Note**   We assume that the option "controlfile autobackup" is on and the database is running in archivelog mode.

To configure this option, run the following:

configure controlfile autobackup on;

configure controlfile autobackup format for device type disk to <path>;

The second example shows the simplicity of the full restore.

```
run {
        restore database;
        recover database;
        release channel ch1;
}
```

Logical Database Backups

Logical backups are exports of schema objects into a binary file. These files store the information about objects and store also the data for a specific point in time. DataPump Export is the utility that reads the source database and creates the export files. DataPump Import is the utility that reads the export files and imports the data into the existing database. Whether we use RMAN or user-managed backup procedure to perform the physical backup, we are recommending deploying logical database backups using DataPump as well.

We have to distinguish the Oracle schemas related to APEX, engine, and applications, and the other schemas of the database. As you have seen in Chapter 11 on the installation of APEX, the installation process is creating three Oracle users, APEX_050000, APEX_PUBLIC_USER, and FLOWS_FILES. Since Oracle12c, DataPump Export doesn't export the content of these Oracle schemas. It means that you can't recover the APEX engine using DataPump Import. On the other hand, DataPump is necessary to transfer (Export and Import) the content of the application data.

How to Deploy a Backup Procedure with DataPump

In order to use DataPump, the DBA must create a directory object and grant privileges to the user on that directory. In the following example, a directory called "datapump_dir" is created and mapped to the folder "/u04/backups":

```
create directory datapump_dir as '/u04/backups';
grant read,write on directory datapump_dir to scott;
```

■ **Note**   Privileged users like sys and system already have the grants.

Once the directory is created, we can perform a logical backup using DataPump Export. The first example is a full export of the database and the second example is an export of a specific schema.

```
expdp scott/password directory=datapump_dir dumpfile=expdp_full_database.dmp logfile=expdp_
full_database.log full=y
```

```
expdp scott/password directory=datapump_dir dumpfile=expdp_schema_book.dmp logfile=expdp_
schema_book.log schemas=sch_book
```

■ **Note**   The Oracle schemas that contains the APEX engine (schemas APEX_050000, APEX_PUBLIC_USER, and FLOWS_FILES) are not exported by Data Pump. This is new behavior with an Oracle12c database.

Flashback Technology

Oracle Flashback Technology is a group of database features that allow you to view past states of database objects. Database Flashback features are primarily to recover from data corruption. DBA will mainly use these three types of Flashback features:

- Oracle Flashback Table
- Oracle Flashback Drop
- Oracle Flashback Database

In this section, we will focus on the Oracle Flashback Database. This feature provides a more efficient alternative to point-in-time recovery and does not require a full restore of the database.

Flashback Database is accessible through both RMAN and SQL. We will demonstrate it using SQLPlus.

Configuring Flashback Technology

Two parameters need to be set to enable the Flashback Technology:

- db_recovery_file_dest_size

- db_recovery_file_dest

```
alter system set db_recovery_file_dest_size=10G scope=both;
alter system set db_recovery_file_dest='+FRA' scope=both;
```

■ **Note**　In this example, the Flashback is located in ASM, in the diskgroup +FRA.

When this is done, we can switch the Flashback Technology to on using this SQL statement:

```
alter database flashback on;
```

■ **Note**　The database needs to be in archivelog mode.

Oracle12c Container Database required the database to be down to enable the Flashback option.

APEX Components Backup

Now that we know that the database itself is backed up, we have to deploy the backup procedure for the APEX components. I want to remind you that a full DataPump export of the database doesn't export the APEX engine, workspaces, and applications.

Two components need to be backed up:

- APEX workspace

- APEX application

APEX workspace is like a container for the APEX application. Every application belongs to a workspace and that workspace needs to exist in order to import the application.

We will see in this section how to export the definition of the workspace. We will also see how to export an application and all the components that belong to the application. With these two elements as well as with the DataPump export file of the Oracle schema associated to the workspace, we will be able to import the workspace and application in all other APEX environments.

We will demonstrate how to perform the export of workspace definition and application using different methods.

- Using Application Express Developer website

- Using APEXExport java tool

Using Application Express Developer

When the user is connecting to the Application Express Website, he should mention on which workspace he would like to be connected with: either the "Internal" workspace or the "application specific" workspace. To perform the backups, the administrator has to be connected to the Internal workspace.

■ **Note** Refer to Chapter 2 for the differences between workspaces, roles, and users.

Workspace Backup

The first method we will use to export the workspace definition is by connecting to the INTERNAL workspace.

Figure 12-1 shows the "Application Express" login page.

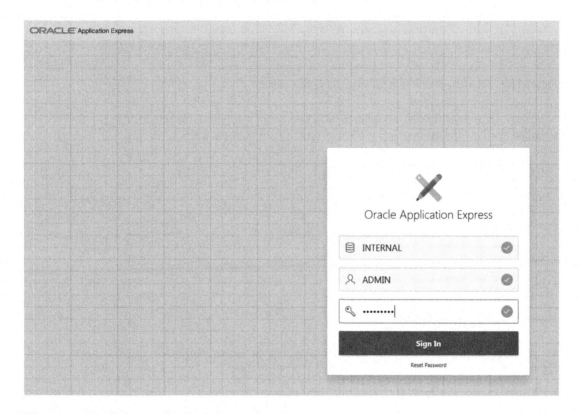

Figure 12-1. *Login into Application Express webpage*

Once connected to Application Express (webpage), Figure 12-2 shows how to select "Manage Workspaces" and "Export."

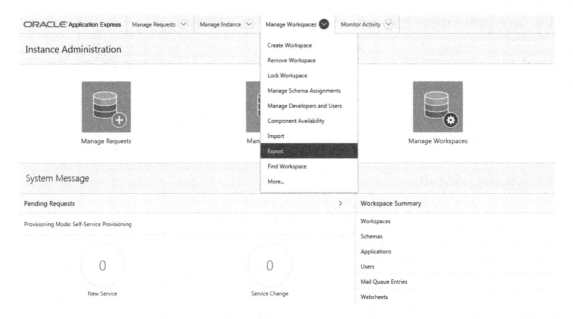

Figure 12-2. *Selection of Export in Manage Workspaces menu*

You will have to select the workspace for which you want to export the definition. In Figure 12-3 you can see where you have to click in order to select the appropriate workspace.

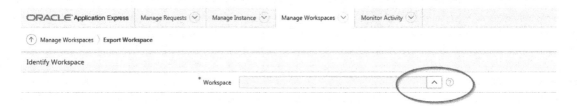

Figure 12-3. *Workspace selection*

When the workspace is selected, you continue by clicking "Export Workspace" as we can see in Figure 12-4.

Figure 12-4. *Workspace selection confirmation*

Figure 12-4 shows the confirmation of the export. You will see three different options, and you can click the question mark to have more details. We recommend keeping the default values. We also recommend taking note of the "File Character Set," as you will need it for the Import process. As we can see in Figure 12-5, click "Save File" and the utility will create the SQL file that contains the definition of the selected workspace.

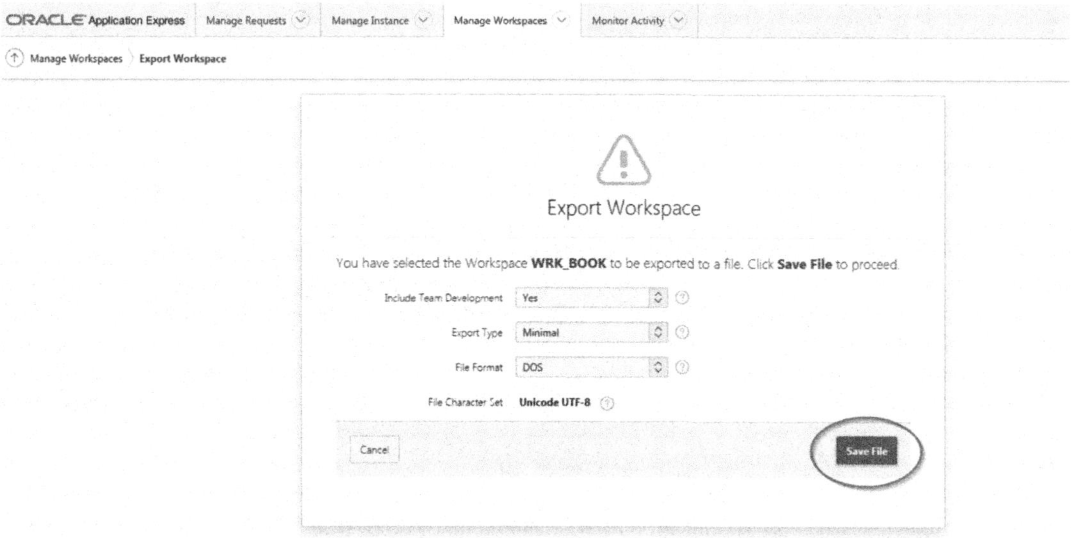

Figure 12-5. *Creation of the SQL file*

You have the script for the creation of the workspace, but don't forget to use Data Pump to export the schema associated to this workspace.

■ **Note**   The Oracle schema associated with this workspace has to be exported with Data Pump.

Application Export

The first method we will use to export the application is by using the Application Express graphical interface and logging into the workspace where the APEX application we would like to export is located. In our case, we will be connecting to the WRK_BOOK workspace.

Figure 12-6 shows the login page of the "Application Express" webpage.

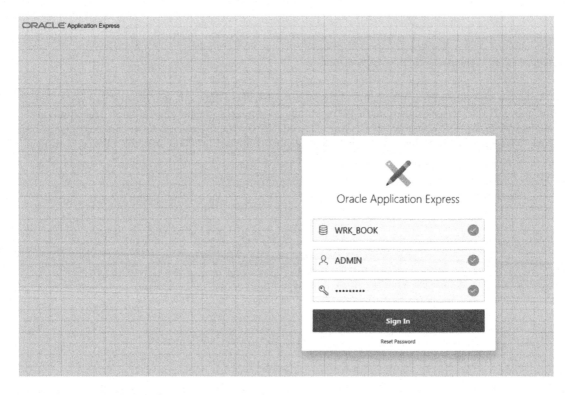

Figure 12-6. *Login into Application Express Developer*

Once connected, select the "Application Builder" menu followed by the "Export" option, as you can see in Figure 12-7.

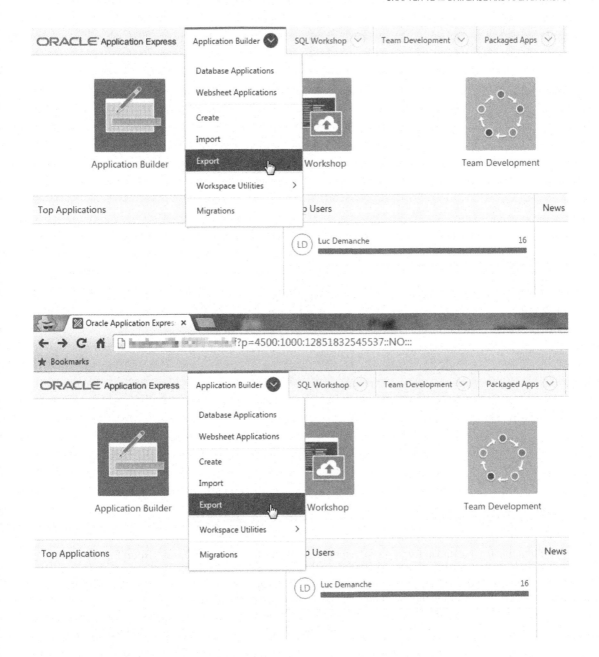

Figure 12-7. *Application Builder export menu*

Once you are in the "Export" main page, click "Application." You will then be able to select using the drop-down list the application you want to export, as we can see in Figure 12-8.

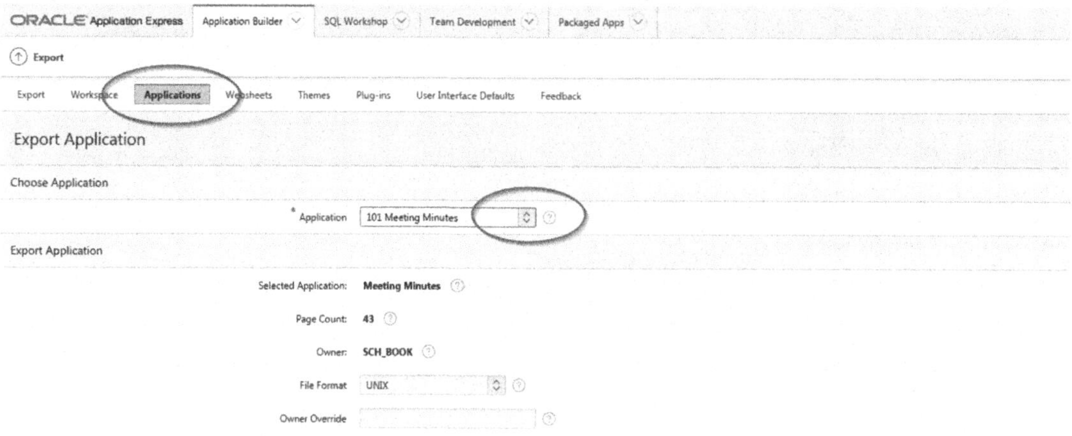

Figure 12-8. *Selection and backup of the application*

In the bottom of the page, you have the Export Preferences section. Figure 12-9 shows the Export Preferences.

Figure 12-9. *Export Preferences*

From that list, I would like to discuss "Export Private Interactive Reports" and "Export Interactive Report Subscriptions." Export Private Interactive to "Yes" will export the private customized settings of all users of the application. If you set "Yes" to Export Interactive Report Subscriptions, the export will include Interactive Report subscriptions for the reports you are exporting in the application export.

When the selection is done, perform the backup of the application by clicking "Export." You now have the script that you can use to import that application in the same or another APEX environment.

Using APEXExport

We can also export APEX components by using the tool APEXExport. This tool, located in $APEX_HOME/utilities/oracle/apex, will generate sql files depending on the parameters we are providing.

Here is the table that contains a list of the main parameters we can use:

Parameter name	Description
-db	Database connect url
-user	Database user
-password	User password
-applicationid	ID of the application to be exported
-workspaceid	Export the workspace definition as well as all the application of this workspace ID
-instance	Export all the application of this instance
-expWorkspace	Export only the workspaces definition
-expTranslation	Export the translation mapping

■ **Note**   Please refer to the Oracle Support document ID 742670.1, which gives the exact list and description of the parameters.

Workspace Export

To perform an APEX workspace export, we will use APEXExport with these parameters:

- workspaceid

- expWorkspace

First of all, we need to know the ID of the workspace we want to export. There are two ways to get that information.

The first way is by using the Application Express Developer using the INTERNAL workspace. In our example, you see in Figure 12-10 the Workspace Identifier 5380439404026964.

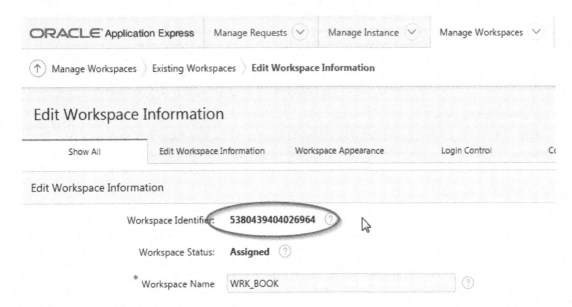

Figure 12-10. *Finding the ID of the workspace*

Another way to find the ID of the workspace is by querying the APEX data dictionary.

```
alter session set current_schema=APEX_050000;
select to_char(workspace_id),substr(workspace_display_name,1,10) from apex_workspaces;
```

We now have the workspace ID, and we can perform the export using APEXExport. Connected to the database server, run these commands:

```
$ export CLASSPATH=.:${ORACLE_HOME}/jdbc/lib/ojdbc7.jar
$ cd $APEX_HOME/utilities
$ java oracle.apex.APEXExport -db hostname:1527/pdb001 -user system -password pass123
-workspaceid 5380439404026964 -expWorkspace

Exporting Workspace 5380439404026964:'WRK_BOOK'
  Completed at Fri Oct 09 14:39:00 EDT 2015
```

■ **Note** This is a connection to a Pluggable Database called pdb001. The URL format for a JDBC format is [HOST]:[PORT]/SERVICE.

This execution is generating a SQL file called w5380439404026964.sql, in $APEX_HOME/utilities. This file contains the necessary information to create the same workspace in another APEX environment.

If we are running the same command without the "expWorkspace" parameter

```
$ java oracle.apex.APEXExport -db 10.1.3.243:1527/pdb001 -user system -password Mdx#3b0Z1#k
-workspaceid 5380439404026964

Exporting Application 100:'Sample Database Application'
  Completed at Fri Oct 09 14:43:41 EDT 2015
Exporting Application 101:'Meeting Minutes'
  Completed at Fri Oct 09 14:43:50 EDT 2015
Exporting Application 102:'Sample Calendar'
  Completed at Fri Oct 09 14:43:52 EDT 2015
```

This execution will generate the SQL file called w5380439404026964.sql, which contains the definition of the workspace and also generate one SQL file per application that resides in this workspace.

■ **Note** The Oracle schema associated with this workspace has to be exported with Data Pump.

Application Export

To perform this APEX application export, we will use APEXExport with this parameter:

- applicationid

First of all we need to know the ID of the application we want to export. There are two ways to get that information.

The first way is by using the Application Express Developer. In our example, you see in Figure 12-11 the application identifiers.

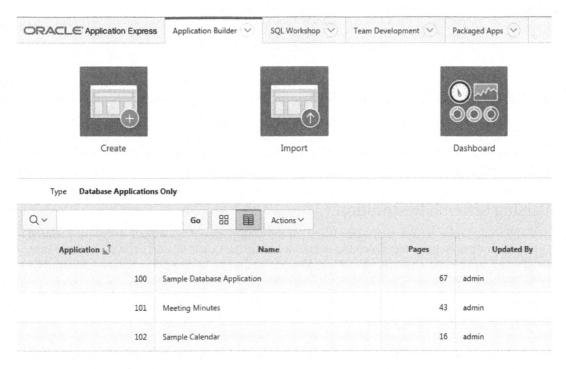

Figure 12-11. *Finding the ID of the application*

Another way to find the ID of the application is by querying the APEX data dictionary.

```
alter session set current_schema=APEX_050000;
select application_id,application_name from apex_applications;
```

When we have the ID, we can perform the export using APEXExport. From the database server, run these commands:

```
$ export CLASSPATH=.:${ORACLE_HOME}/jdbc/lib/ojdbc7.jar
$ cd $APEX_HOME/utilities
$ java oracle.apex.APEXExport -db hostname:1527/pdb001 -user system -password Mdx#3b0Z1#k
-applicationid 102

Exporting application 102
  Completed at Fri Oct 09 15:01:41 EDT 2015
```

■ **Note**   This is a connection to a Pluggable Database called pdb001. The URL format for a JDBC format is the following [HOST]:[PORT]/SERVICE.

This call is generating a SQL file call f102.sql, in $APEX_HOME/utilities. This file contains the necessary information to create the application in another APEX environment.

Another interesting option is to use –instance. This option will generate a sql file for every application and shared component. Oracle Support Doc 1995509.1 explains the exact steps for the export of every workspaces as well as the export of every applications using the option –instance.

APEX Components Restore

We might have to restore the APEX components into another APEX environment. We will see in this section how to, first of all, import the parsing schema related to the workspace and applications. We will demonstrate how to import the definition of the workspace and we will finish by demonstrating how to import the APEX application.

Parsing Schema Restoration

As we have said earlier, even though we are importing the workspace and application, we have to import the Oracle schema that contains the objects like tables, views, etc. The Oracle schema as been backed up using DataPump Export, so we need to use DataPump Import to restore in the destination database where APEX is running. Here is the way to import the Oracle schema associated with our workspace.

```
impdp username/password directory=datapump_dir dumpfile=expdp_schema_book.dmp logfile=impdp_
schema_book.log schemas=sch_book
```

Now that the Oracle schema exists, we can perform the APEX component imports.

■ **Note** You might have to create the necessary tablespaces prior to importing the Oracle schema.

Workspace Import

We have been asked to import the workspace WRK_BOOK into another APEX environment. We know that the Oracle schema SCH_BOOK associated to the workspace is already imported, so we could perform the workspace definition import.

We will use the Application Express webpage to import the workspace. Figure 12-12 shows the login page of the "Application Express" webpage.

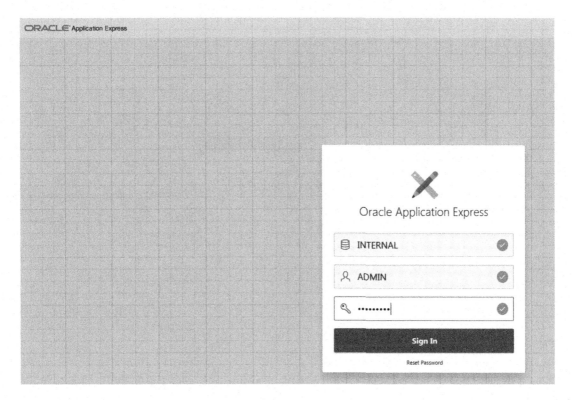

Figure 12-12. *Login into Application Express webpage*

Once connected, we will select "Manage Workspace" and "Import" as we can see in Figure 12-13.

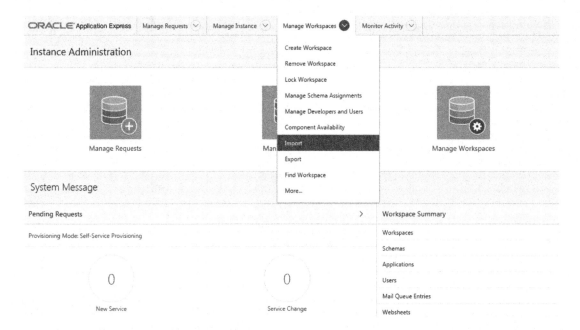

Figure 12-13. *Manage Workspace and Import*

Select the SQL file generated at the export workspace definition step earlier. Figure 12-14 shows that step. When selected, click "Next."

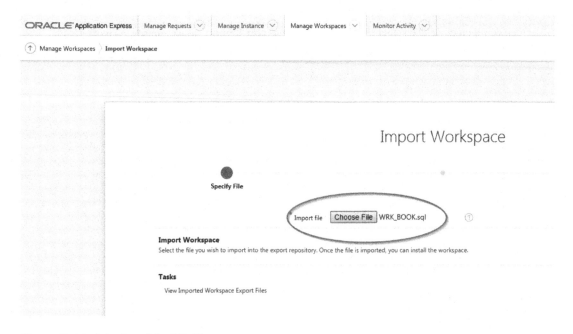

Figure 12-14. *Selection of the SQL file*

Application Express is loading the SQL file and it is asking you to click "Install" as for a confirmation.

The next page is related to the Oracle schema. As we have already transferred the associated schema, we just have to confirm the existence of the schema, then click "Next." Figure 12-15 demonstrates that step.

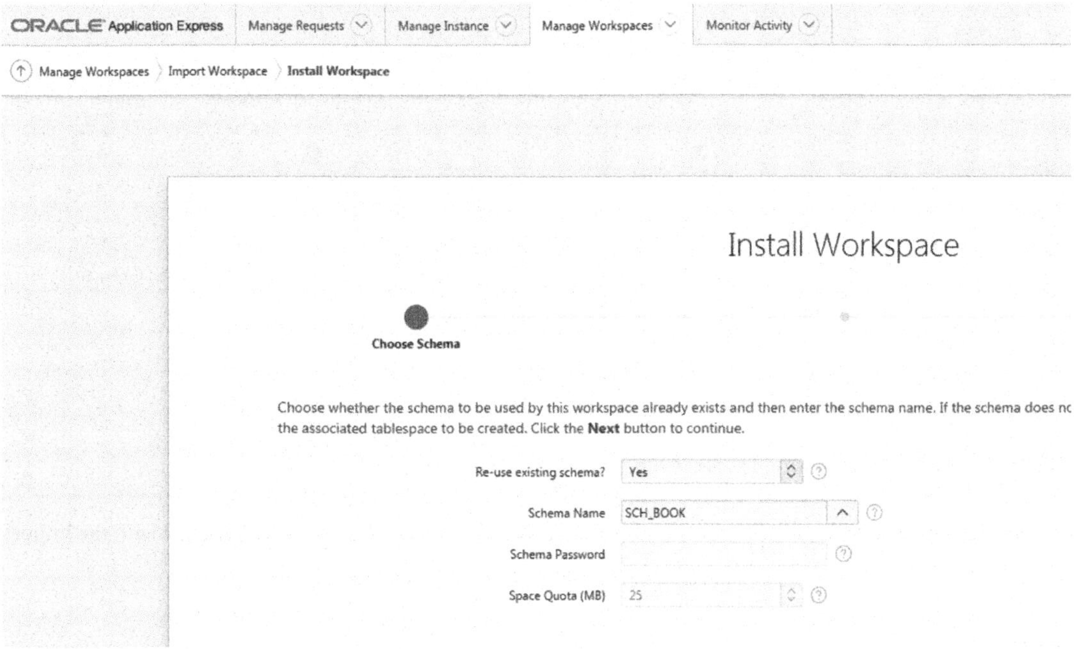

Figure 12-15. *Oracle schema information*

Application Express is again asking us for a confirmation prior to the execution of the import. You should confirm by checking the box. Figure 12-16 shows that step.

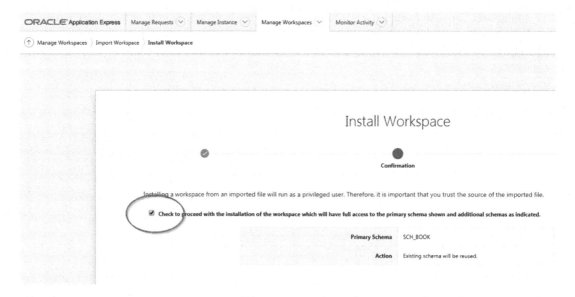

Figure 12-16. *Last confirmation prior to the import*

The workspace WRK_BOOK now exists in the APEX environment. We can now proceed with the import of the application.

Application Import

We want to import the APEX application into the workspace we have restored earlier. We will be using "Application Express Developer" webpage connecting to the application workspace to perform the restore. In our case, we will be connecting to the workspace WRK_BOOK.

Figure 12-17 shows the login page of the "Application Express" webpage.

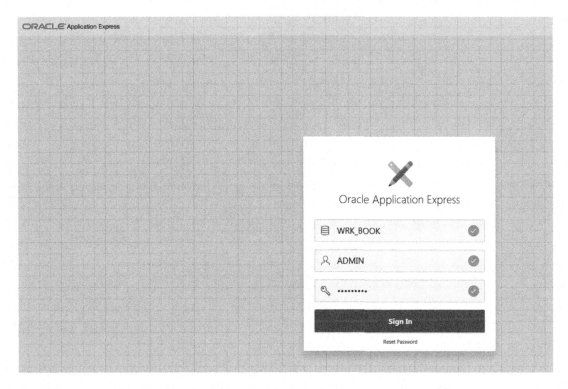

Figure 12-17. *Login into Application Express Developer*

Once you are connected into the application, click the "Application Builder" icon and then on "Import." You will be at the page where you have to choose the SQL file generated from the backup process. As for the file type, make sure the "Database Application, Page or Component Export" is selected. Figure 12-18 shows that page where you are mentioning the SQL file and the file type and where you then click "Next."

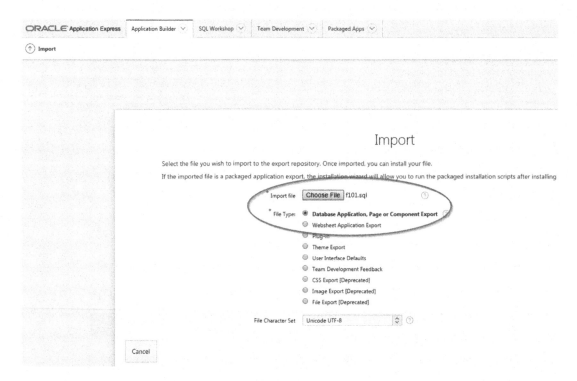

Figure 12-18. *Selection of the SQL file and the file type*

Once the file is selected, APEX loads it. If you are ready to install the application, click "Next." You will see the details of the application, including workspace ID, application ID, and Oracle schema. You will have the possibility to change the application ID but we are recommending not changing the ID. The management of the application is easier, as we are keeping the same ID throughout the development process and/or the lifetime of the application. If you agree on all the details, click "Install Application."

Figure 12-19 shows that page.

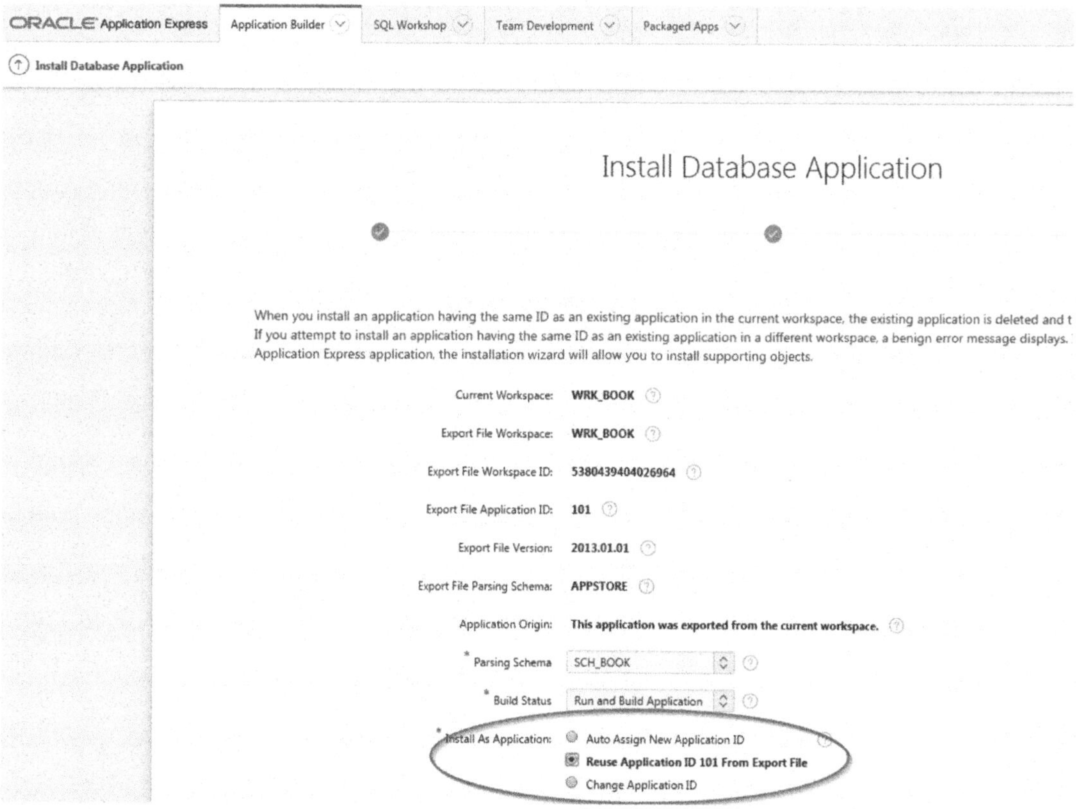

Figure 12-19. Confirmation of the installation of the application

---

■ **Note**   We recommend keeping the same application ID.

If the installation process detects that the application is already installed, it will propose to upgrade the components of the application. If the installation process detects that the ID is already used by another application, you will have to cancel the import process, restart the process, and assign a new ID.

When the verifications are completed by the installation process, you have to click "Next" to launch the process. APEX will also ask you to confirm the installation of the supporting objects. When it's completed, you can run the application by clicking "Run Application."

Summary

In this chapter we have talked about backup and restore procedures. First, we have covered the backup and restore of the database itself by explaining the two different kinds of backup: physical and logical. We have also talked about an option called Flashback Technology that allows rewinding the database in case of human errors or data corruptions.

In the second section, we have talked about the export and import of the APEX components. We explained using different tools, and how to export and import APEX workspaces as well as for APEX applications.

CHAPTER 13

Self-Provisioning Workspaces

This feature is probably one of the less known built-in functionalities available out of the box with APEX. It is a workspace provisioning request workflow.

APEX is the ideal tool for the cloud and always has been because of its multitenant capability and because it is entirely web based. As you probably know, there is a free APEX cloud offering accessible at APEX.ORACLE.COM. When going to that web page, it is possible to request a workspace and test Oracle Application Express for free. The Oracle APEX team included that functionality in APEX itself and so it is possible to have the same feature in an Enterprise private cloud. Simply enable and configure this feature in your APEX instance as explained in this chapter.

There is another associated workflow available for workspace requests. Workspace administrators can create change requests and the instance administrator just has to complete the workflow to accept or decline those change requests. This is also described in this chapter.

To complete the process, there is also an automated workspace purge process. This process automatically identifies inactive workspaces, sends notifications to the workspace administrator, and purges workspaces. For more detail on the workspace purge process see the section "Workspace Purge Settings" in Chapter 10.

Self-Service Provisioning Setup

The first step before utilizing the self-service provisioning workflow, of course, is to configure it. There are many options that affect self-provisioning and they are available in the internal administration services of the instance (Internal workspace).

Enabling Self-Provisioning

Different settings can be configured for self-provisioning and this has to be done using the administration workspace of the APEX instance.

Self Service Instance Settings

To enable the self-service provisioning, first, log into the Internal workspace. Then go to Manage Instance, Instance Settings. Select the Self Service Tab as shown in Figure 13-1.

© Francis Mignault and Luc Demanche 2016
F. Mignault and L. Demanche, *Oracle Application Express Administration*, DOI 10.1007/978-1-4842-1958-4_13

Figure 13-1. *Instance Settings / Self Service tab.*

There are three settings for self-provisioning: Manual, Request, and Request with E-mail Verification:

- ***Manual***

  When the Provisioning status is set to Manual, it basically means that the self-service provisioning is disabled. No link will appear on the login page.

- ***Request***

  When the Provisioning status is set to Request, the self-service provisioning is enabled. A 'Request Workspace' link will appear in the login screen, see Figure 13-2.

  The Workspace will be physically created when the Instance Administrator approves the request. The e-mail sent to the requestor will contain the temporary password to access the newly created workspace.

  See the section "How Self-Provisioning Works" for more detail.

- ***Request with E-mail Verification***

  When the Provisioning status is set to Request with E-mail Verification, the self-service provisioning is enabled. A 'Request Workspace' link will appear in the login screen, see Figure 13-2.

  The Workspace will be physically created when the user requesting the workspace clicks the activation link in the New Workspace Request acceptance e-mail.

  See the section "How Self-Provisioning Works" for more detail.

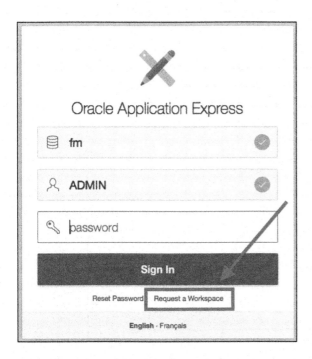

Figure 13-2. *Requesting a Workspace link*

Other options can also be set for self-provisioning in the instance settings:

Require Verification Code

When this option is set to Yes, a verification code will be required by the requestor before completing the request as shown in Figure 13-3. This is also a feature used to avoid having automated robots requesting workspaces.

Figure 13-3. *Requesting a Workspace Verification Code*

Notification E-mail Address

When the self-provisioning is enabled, an e-mail address should be specified here. This is the e-mail of the Instance Administrator in charge of managing the self-provisioning requests. It will send notification e-mails to this address for new or change workspace requests. When it is blank, no e-mails will be sent.

E-mail Provisioning

The e-mail provisioning section is used to notify end users requesting new workspaces that the service is temporarily not available. Simply enter a message and set the e-mail provisioning to Disabled. See Figure 13-4. This is effective only when the self-provisioning is enabled using Request with E-mail Validation. The message will be display when the requestor clicks the activation link in the acceptance e-mail and when the e-mail provisioning is set to Disabled.

Figure 13-4. *Instance Settings / E-mail Provisioning*

Storage Options

In the Manage Instance – Instance Settings – Storage tab, there is the Require New Schema configuration that needs to be configured for self-provisioning.

Of course, the other storage options will be taken in account when create the tablespace for the new requested workspace.

Require New Schema

As mentioned in Chapter 12, when set to Yes, the end user will be forced to enter the name for a new schema. When set to No, the end user will be able to specify an existing schema. See Figures 13-5 and 13-6.

Figure 13-5. *Example of the Workspace Request when Require New Schema is set to Yes*

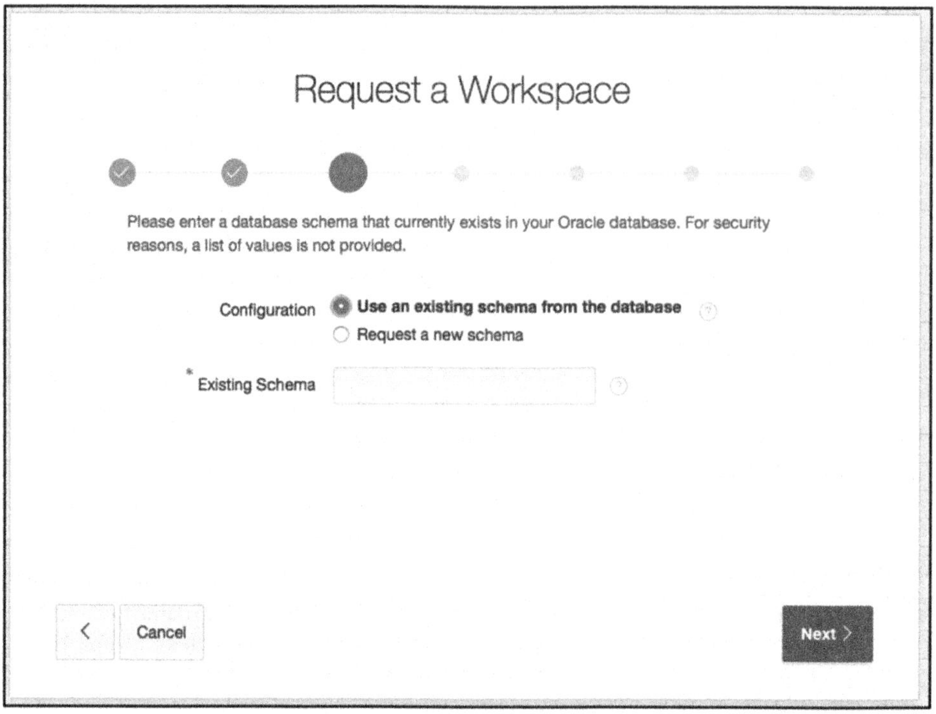

Figure 13-6. Example of the Workspace Request when Require New Schema is set to No

Manage New Service Signup Wizard

In the Manage Instance, self-service signup section there are two options:

- **Manage New Service Signup Wizard**

  Used for creating an agreement text; requires a justification and creates a survey that will be used during the request of a new workspace. More detail on this option follows.

- **Run New Service Signup Wizard**

  Obviously used to run the new service signup wizard and test the survey and agreement text.

Justification and Agreement

It may be required to ask the end user requesting a new workspace a justification for his request.

It is also possible to add terms and agreements and ask the requestor to accept them before continuing with the new workspace request as shown in Figure 13-7.

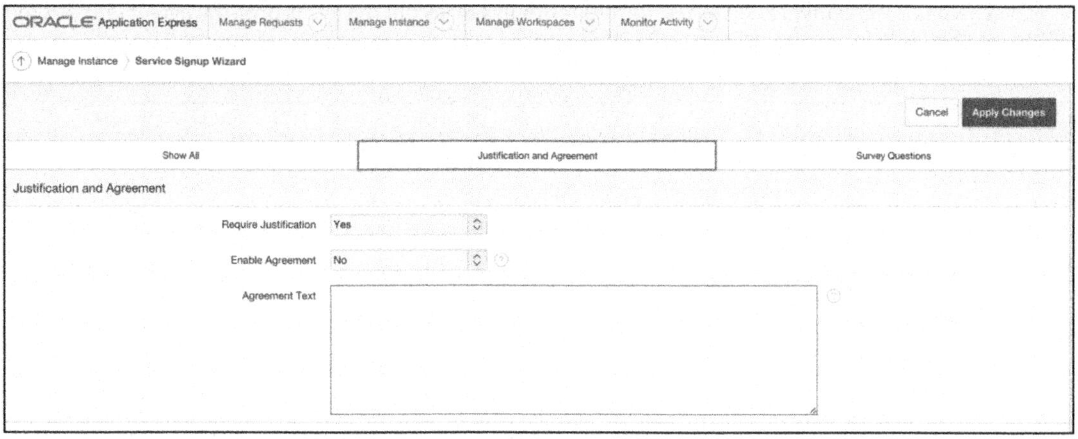

Figure 13-7. Enabling justification and agreement

When Require Justification is set to Yes, the requestor has to enter some justification text before continuing his request. See Figure 13-8.

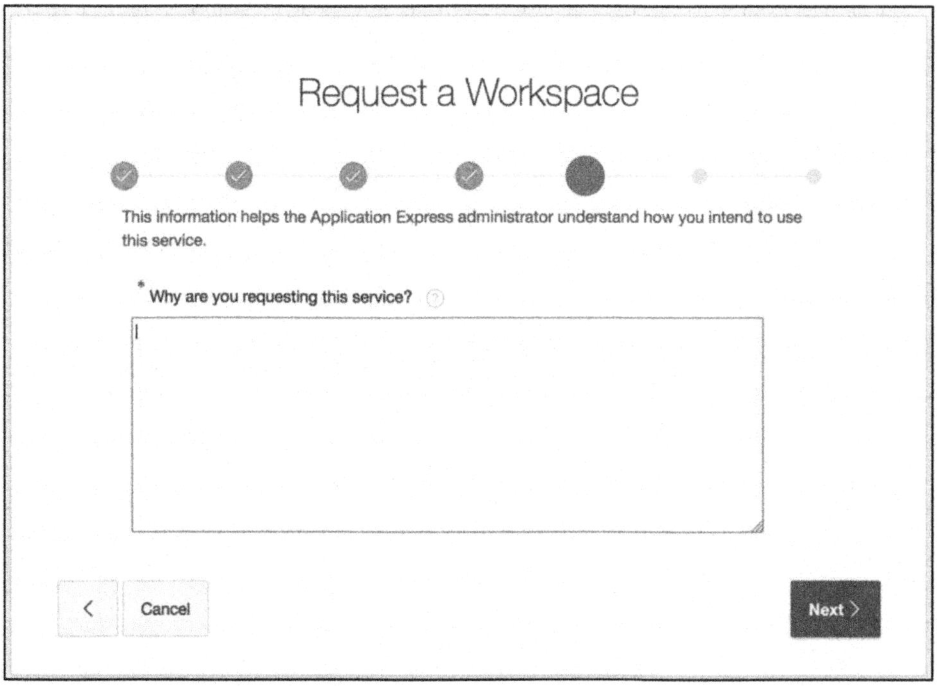

Figure 13-8. Requiring justification

When Enable Agreement is set to Yes, the requestor has to accept the terms from the agreement text to be able to finalize his request by checking the "I accept the terms" checkbox. See Figure 13-9.

Figure 13-9. *Enabling agreement*

Survey Questions

To define a survey that will be used during the new workspace request, first enable the survey and enter questions and answers. For multiple answers, they have to be entered on separate lines. A new line delimits each answer. See Figures 13-10 and 13-11.

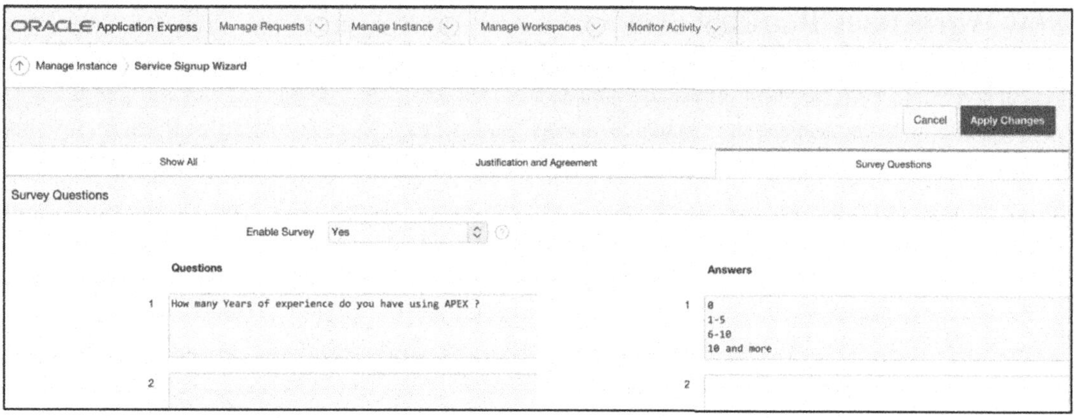

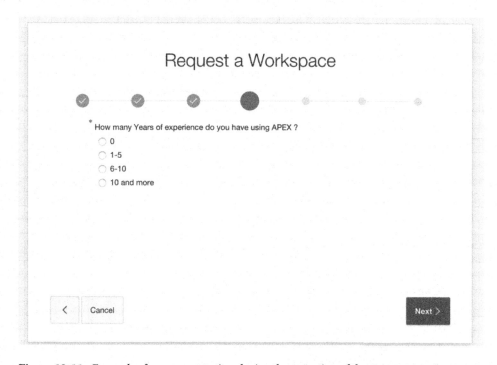

Figure 13-10. *Configuring survey questions with multiple answers*

Figure 13-11. *Example of a survey question during the execution of the signup wizard*

To look at the results of the survey, go to Monitor Activity, Signup Survey. See the "Service Requests Monitoring section" in this chapter.

New Workspace Request Size

Another configuration that can be done is setting the different available tablespace sizes for the schema created that will be associated with the new workspace.

To configure the tablespace sizes available for new workspace requests, go to Manage Instance, Instance Settings and select the New Workspace Request Size tab or scroll to that section as shown in Figure 13-12.

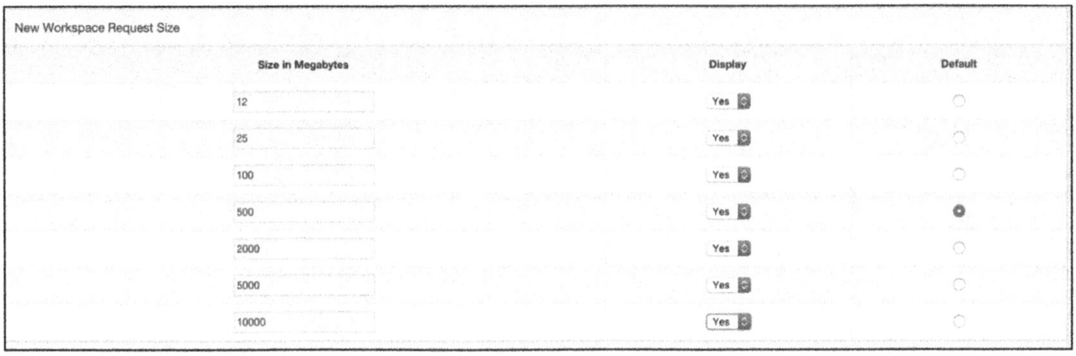

Figure 13-12. *Defining new workspace request sizes*

Here you can define how many sizes you wish to display and which one will be the default.

See the list of values that will be available in the wizard during the provisioning process in Figure 13-13.

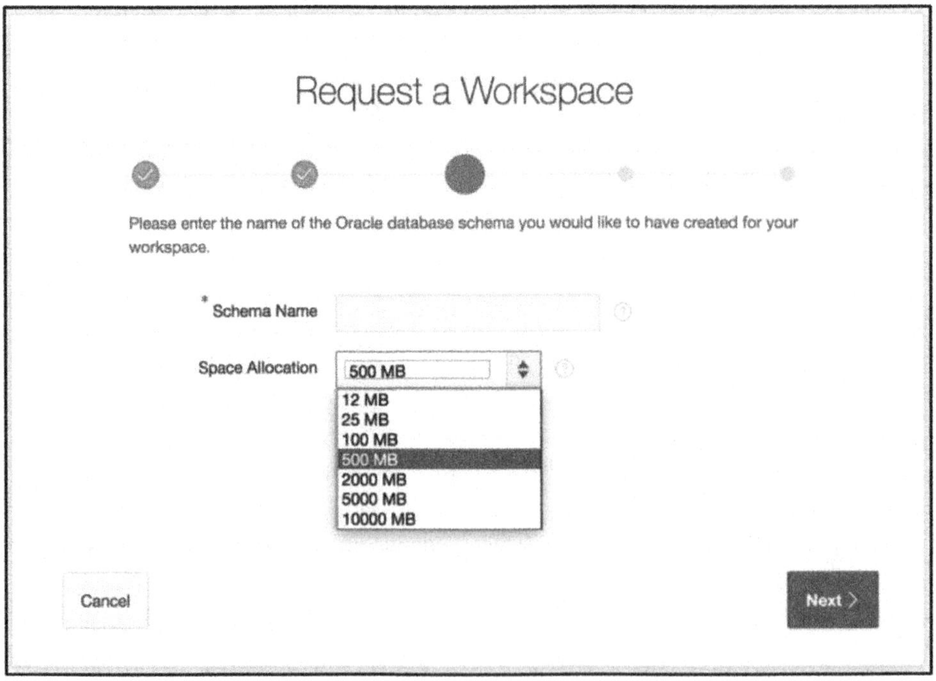

Figure 13-13. *Example of the sizes available at runtime*

Manage Requests

The Manage Requests report lists all the requests. It could be a change workspace request or a new workspace request. This report is available from the main menu of the instance administration when you are logged in the Internal workspace.

To act on a request, click the edit button of the request in the report.

It is possible to see open requests, all workspace request, or all change requests by clicking the appropriate tab.

This is where the instance administrator has to look for any new requests. An e-mail is also sent to the notification e-mail defined in the Manage Instance, Instance Settings, self service section every time a request is made by a user.

How Self-Provisioning Works

Once the self-provisioning is configured and turned on, users will be able to make workspace requests.

Request a New Workspace

The workflow for requesting a new workspace is the following:

The end user requesting a new workspace

   1.   Goes to the APEX login page and clicks the Request a Workspace link (Figure 13-14).

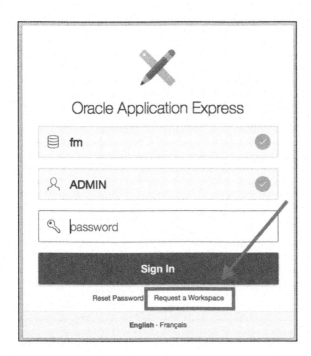

Figure 13-14. Requesting a Workspace link

2. Selects if he wants a workspace for application development or packaged applications only (Figure 13-15).

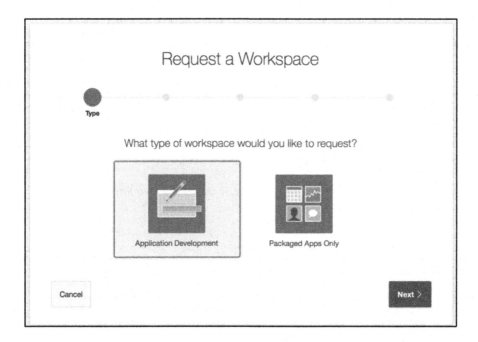

Figure 13-15. *Selecting the type of workspace*

3. Goes through the Request a workspace wizard filling up his information (Figure 13-16). He will then specify the schema that will be associated to the workspace (Figure 13-17). And if required, he will answer the survey, specify the justification, and accept the terms and agreement.

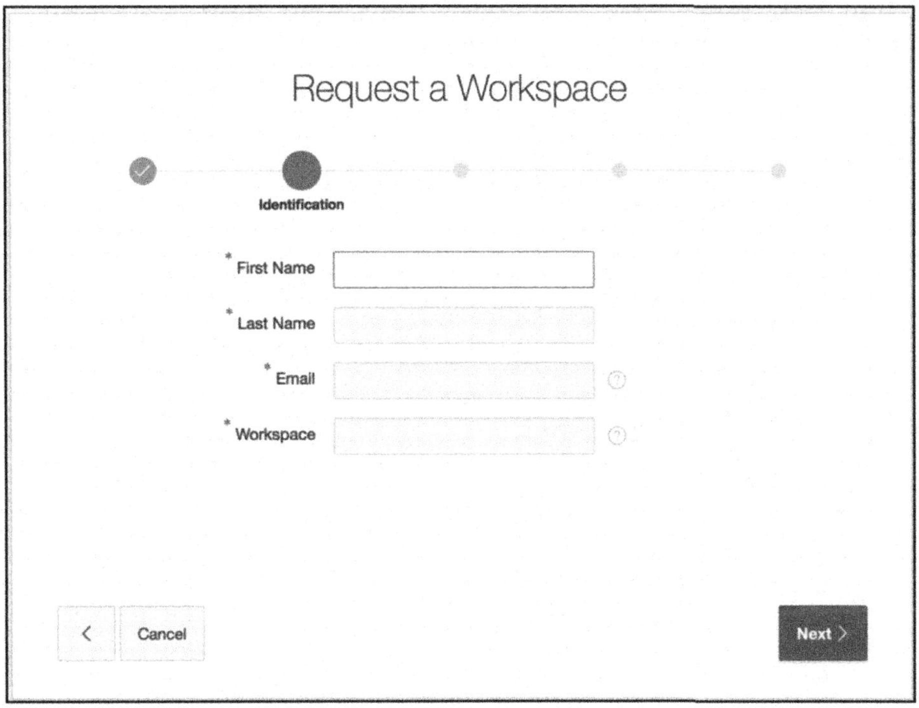

Figure 13-16. *User information and workspace name*

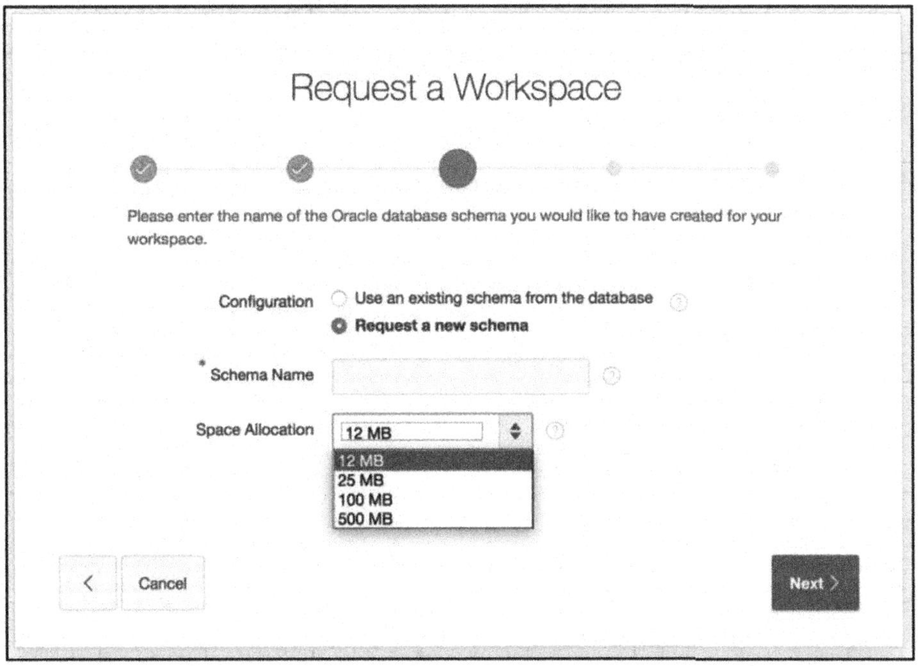

Figure 13-17. *Database schema for the workspace*

4. A summary of the request is shown to the end user and has to be submitted (Figure 13-18).

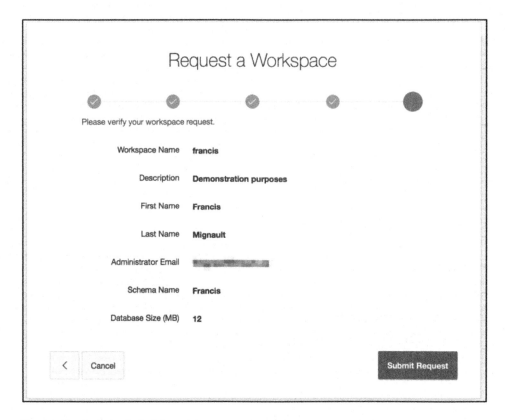

Figure 13-18. *Summary of the request*

5. A new request is created and ready to be approved (Figure 13-19).

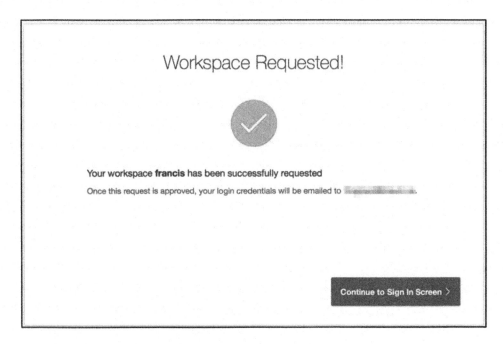

Figure 13-19. *Workspace requested confirmation page*

Now that the request has been submitted, the Instance Administrator has to approve or decline it.

The Instance Administrator:

1. Lists all the open requests in the Manage Requests, Open Requests report. To act on this request, the instance administrator has to click the edit button as shown in Figure 13-20.

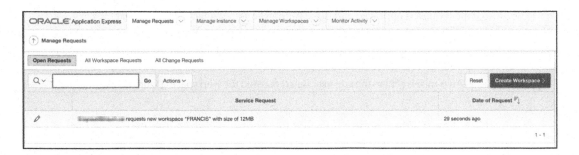

Figure 13-20. *Managing Requests report*

2. Decides if he approves or declines the request (Figure 13-21).

Figure 13-21. *Declining or approving the workspace request*

a. If the request is approved and the self-provision is enabled using 'Request':

i. The Workspace is created and schema is associated.

ii. A password is generated.

iii. An e-mail is sent to the end user that requested the workspace (Figure 13-22).

Figure 13-22. Approval without e-mail verification

   b.   If the request is approved and the self-provision is enabled using 'Request with E-mail Verification':

       i.   A verification e-mail is sent to the end user as shown in Figure 13-23.

      ii.   The end user has to click the acceptation link in the e-mail.

     iii.   The workspace is created and schema is associated.

     iv.   The end user has to enter a new password.

Figure 13-23. Approval with e-mail verification

    c.   If the request is declined:

         i.   The workspace is not created.

       ii.   A decline e-mail is sent to the end user (Figure 13-24).

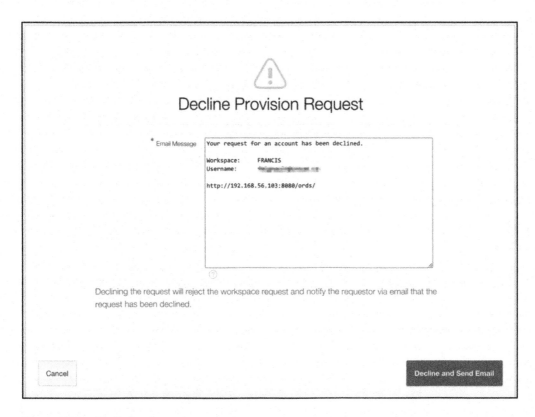

Figure 13-24. *Declining the workspace request*

Workspace Change Requests

Once the workspace is provisioned, the workspace administrator can create change requests for more storage, for a new schema, or for terminating the workspace.

Enable Service Requests

The self-provisioning does not have to be enabled for workspace change requests. To enable workspace change requests, go to Manage Instance, Feature Configuration, and in the workspace administration section, set Enable Service Requests to Yes.

This will activate a Make a Service Request menu option in the workspace administration section in every workspace as shown in Figure 13-25. Of course, this is available for workspace administrators only.

Figure 13-25. *Manage Service Request menu available for the workspace administrator*

Workspace Change Request Size

It is possible to set the different available tablespace sizes for the schema that is associated with the workspace when a change request for storage is made.

To configure the tablespace sizes available for storage change requests, go to Manage Instance, Instance Settings and select the Workspace Change Request Size tab or scroll that to that section.

As Figure 13-26 shows, you can define how many sizes you wish to display and which one will be the default.

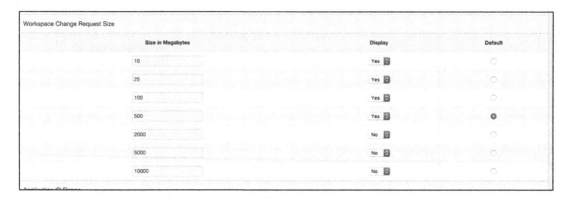

Figure 13-26. *Workspace change request available sizes*

Request Schema

The workspace administrator can make a schema change request from the workspace administration Manage Service menu as shown in Figure 13-27.

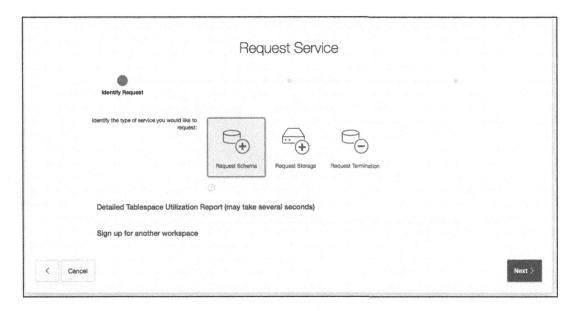

Figure 13-27. *Requesting schema*

At the bottom of the page in this wizard, if self-provisioning is enabled, the workspace administrator can sign up for another workspace. See the "How Self-Provisioning Works" section in this chapter for more detail on how new workspace requests works. The Workspace administrator can also see the detailed tablespace utilization for the database schemas associated with the workspace using the link for this on the same page.

The request schema option can be used to request a new schema or an existing schema. Note that the *Require New Schema* parameter in Manage Instance, Instance Settings, Storage does not apply to workspace change requests.

Once the request is created, the instance administrator can deny the request or create the requested schema in the instance administration services using the manage requests report, as explained previously. There is an e-mail that is sent to the notification e-mail defined in Manage Instance, Instance Settings for all change requests.

An e-mail is also sent to the workspace administrator when the request is denied or approved.

Request Storage

The workspace administrator can make a storage change request from the workspace administration Manage Service menu as shown in Figure 13-28.

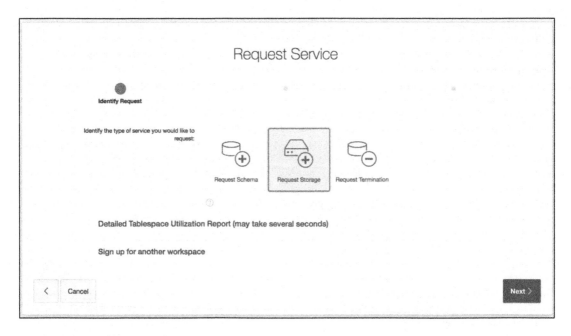

Figure 13-28. *Requesting storage*

The workspace administrator has to select the amount of storage he wishes to add to the tablespace. This will affect only the tablespace associated with the primary (first) schema associated with the workspace.

The Workspace administrator can also see the detailed tablespace utilization for the database schemas associated with the workspace using the link at the bottom of the page.

Once the request is created, the instance administrator can deny or accept the request to add space using the manage requests report by logging in the instance administration services. See Figure 13-29 for an example of the storage change request. An e-mail is sent to the notification e-mail address defined in Manage Instance, Instance Settings for all change requests.

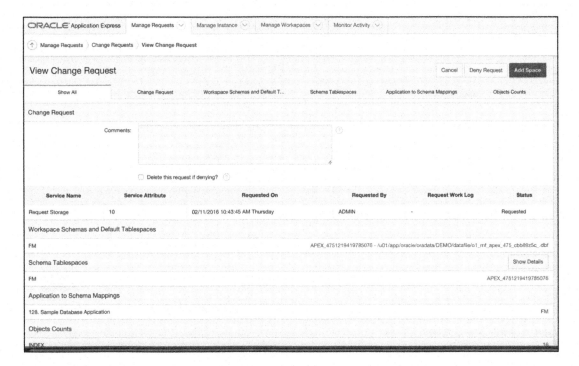

Figure 13-29. *Workspace change request page*

An e-mail is also sent to the workspace administrator when the request is denied or approved.

Request Termination

And finally, the workspace administrator can make a workspace termination request from the workspace administration Manage Service menu as shown in Figure 13-30.

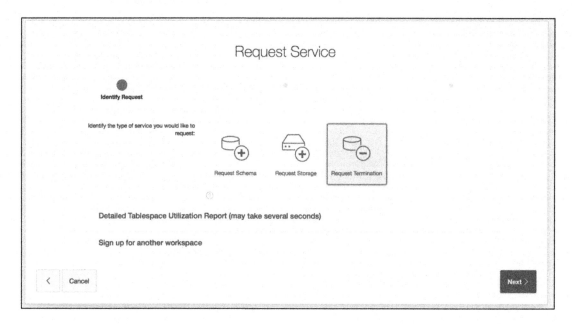

Figure 13-30. Request termination

Before confirming and finalizing the service termination request, the workspace administrator can verify and look at the list of schemas and list of application developers associated with the current workspace. See Figure 13-31 for an example of the list of schemas in the request service termination wizard.

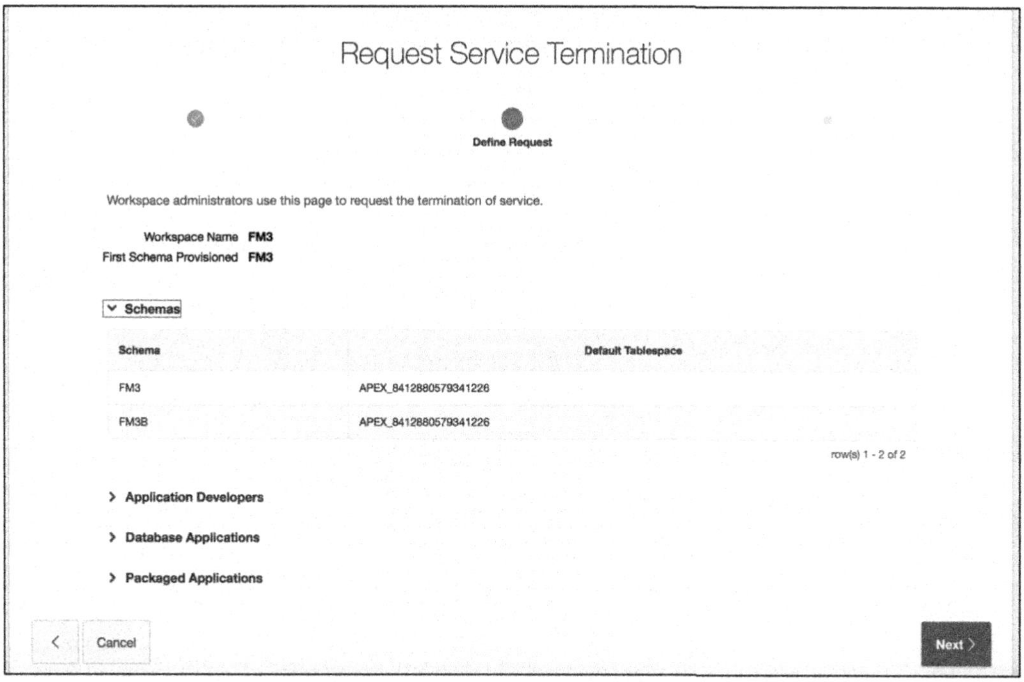

Figure 13-31. *Schemas associated to the workspace that will be dropped*

The schemas, database objects, tablespaces, applications, files, and so forth associated with the workspace will be deleted when the request is accepted. As shown in Figure 13-32, a warning message at this effect is displayed in the confirmation page.

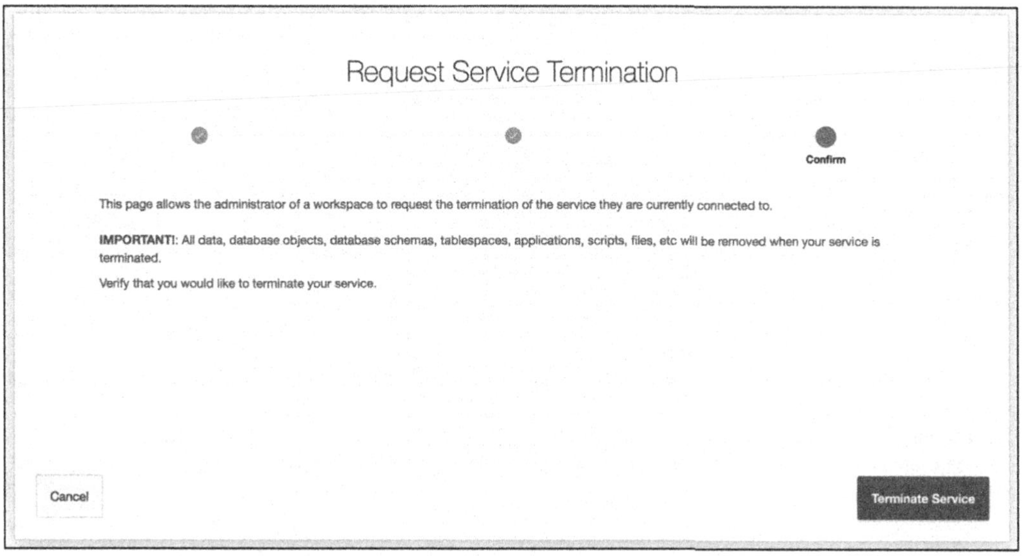

Figure 13-32. *Warning message on Service Termination confirmation page*

Once the request is created, the instance administrator can deny or accept the request to terminate the service in the instance administration services. See Figures 13-33 and 13-34 for an example of the service termination request.

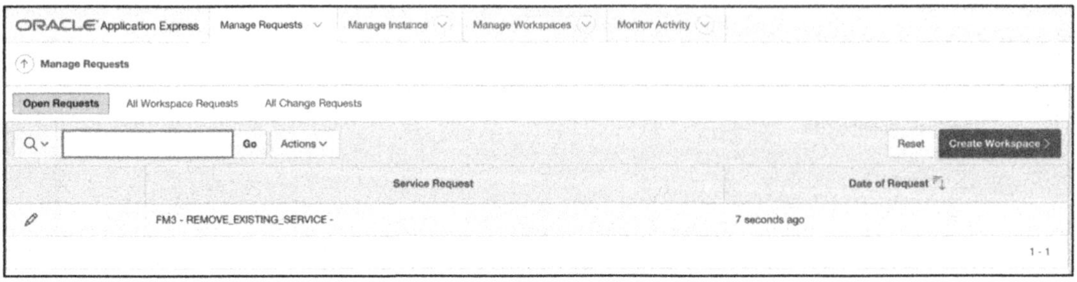

Figure 13-33. Managing Request report with a Service Termination request

Figure 13-34. Example of a termination request

An e-mail is sent to the notification e-mail address defined in Manage Instance, Instance Settings for all change requests.

An e-mail is also sent to the workspace administrator when the request is denied or approved.

In the change request details, the instance administrator can choose to drop the database users and/or the database-associated tablespaces when accepting the terminate service request.

Service Requests Monitoring

In the instance administration services (Internal workspace), there are two reports regarding service requests in the *Monitor activity – Service Requests* section: one for monitoring all the new service requests and another for the surveys as explained in the following.

New Service Requests

The New Service Requests report lists all the service requests in the APEX instance. See Figure 13-35 for an example.

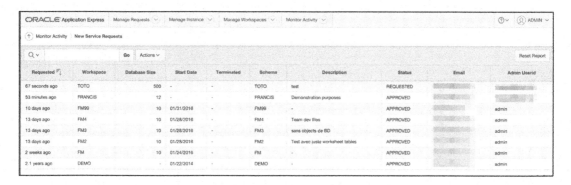

Figure 13-35. *Monitor Activity / New Service Requests report*

Signup Survey

The Signup Survey report will show the results of the surveys that were used in the new workspace requests process. See the section *Manage New Service Signup Wizard – Survey Questions* for more detail on how to configure a survey for new workspace requests.

Summary

Self-provisioning can be a very useful feature to use in a private cloud environment. Users can ask for workspaces and workspace administrator can ask for more storage or new schemas. This self-serve option can ease the management of workspaces by letting users make the requests via the APEX builder interface.

Keep in mind that the self-provisioning option available in APEX is the same thing that Oracle uses for provisioning workspaces on *APEX.ORACLE.COM*.

In the next chapter, we will talk about database monitoring when using APEX applications.

PART IV

Tuning

CHAPTER 14

■ ■ ■

Monitoring

Monitoring the health of the database is an important task for a DBA. Personally I prefer to be proactive by consistently monitoring the database rather than waiting for a call from the end users, usually to tell me that the database is "slow."

In this chapter, we will explain how a DBA can monitor his database that runs APEX applications. We have to keep in mind that monitoring a database that runs APEX is not different than monitoring any other Oracle database. We will use the basic monitoring processes and tools that every DBA knows and we will try to recognize the different components from the different performance reports. As you already know and as covered in previous chapters, APEX architecture is very simple in the sense that everything resides in the database. That is why it is very important for the DBA to distinguish the different components and to identify the process specific to an APEX application that can be brought to the developer for improvement before it can cause a major degradation of performance. The database is the major component here: the objective is to have an optimal database response time.

Another important point is that even though the DBA may not be noticing any performance issue at the database level, the bottleneck can come from other components like APEX Listener, network, and so on.

Database Monitoring

A DBA can use different methods to monitor his Oracle database. Some DBAs prefer to work with their own scripts, accumulated over the years, analyze the outputs, and come up with a conclusion. Some DBAs prefer to work with GUI tools like TOAD, Oracle SQLDeveloper, or Oracle Enterprise Manager that help monitor the database and ease the verification of the general health of the database. Also provided by Oracle, Automatic Workload Repository (AWR) and Active Session History (ASH) give the ability to collect, process, and maintain statistics for problem detection and analysis. Another possibility for monitoring the database is to use a utility called "Database Monitor," which the Oracle APEX team decided to provide from the APEX builder; this utility gives information on sessions, SQL, system statistics, and so on.

We will be focusing on Oracle Enterprise Manager, ASH, AWR, and the tool "Database Monitor" in this chapter.

Oracle Enterprise Manager

We will present how efficiently we can monitor the health of the database using Oracle Enterprise Manager. To evaluate the health of the database, we also have to evaluate how the server is performing. One of the first things I do is to check the overall health of the server by going to its Enterprise Manager home page. Figure 14-1 shows the home page of the server.

© Francis Mignault and Luc Demanche 2016
F. Mignault and L. Demanche, *Oracle Application Express Administration*, DOI 10.1007/978-1-4842-1958-4_14

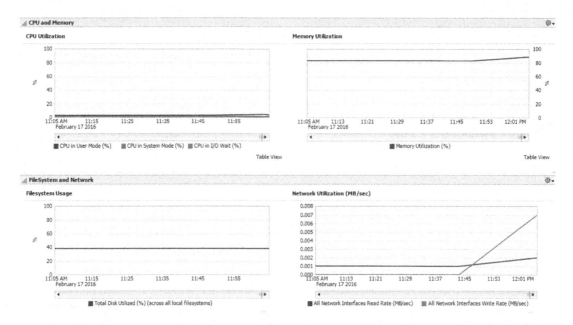

Figure 14-1. *Home page of server running the container database (CDB)*

We can see four main graphs that represent the CPU/Memory/Network Utilization as well as the Filesystem Usage. By looking at these graphs, we can quickly confirm that the system is not heavily used. To go deeper in this analysis, we can also explore a lot of metrics related to the server. Under the "Host" menu, select "Monitoring" and "All metrics"; you will find metrics collected from the server and you can generate reports related on CPU Utilization, Disk Activity, Network Interfaces, and more. This is an excellent source of information to either find any system issues or to validate the health of the system.

Since we have confirmed the low load on the server, let's concentrate on the database health itself. Figure 14-2 shows the pluggable database PDB001 Enterprise Manager home page.

Figure 14-2. *Home page of pluggable database (PDB) running APEX*

I usually have a quick look at the SQL statement in the "SQL Monitor – Last Hour" section for any SQL that seems to go outside of the reasonable boundaries. From there you can already drill down into a specific SQL by clicking its SQL_ID. This view is giving you a quick idea of what is running at that moment on the system. If you want to go deeper in the database performance analysis, we can use ASH to have a more complete view of the overall performance of the PDB. Every second, ASH polls the database to gather statistics on active session and keeps that information into the ASH buffer in the SGA. Once the buffer is filled, the data is written to disk and snapshots are taken every 10 seconds. Then, ASH provides us the ability to see second-by-second snapshots of the activities in the database. From the PDB home page, select "ASH Analytics" under the "Performance" menu. Figure 14-3 shows the main page of ASH Analytics.

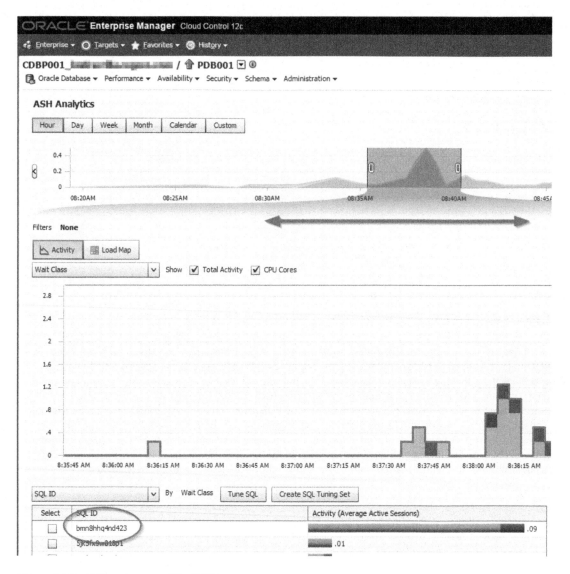

Figure 14-3. *ASH main page of the PDB*

The idea here is to slide the time windows to covert different periods in time. It's an excellent way to see the SQL statements that were running in the busiest period of time. Again, we can decide to drill down into a specific statement by clicking the SQL_ID.

There are multiple ways of having an overview of the health of the system using Oracle Enterprise Manager. We have seen just a couple of examples, but Oracle Enterprise Manager provides a lot of metrics related to different target types like server, CDB, PDB, and so on. We can't cover all of them here, but I would suggest you to go and explore that avenue. To access the monitoring section, select "Monitoring" and "All Metrics" from the target main menu. Figure 14-4 represents an example of "All Metrics" page.

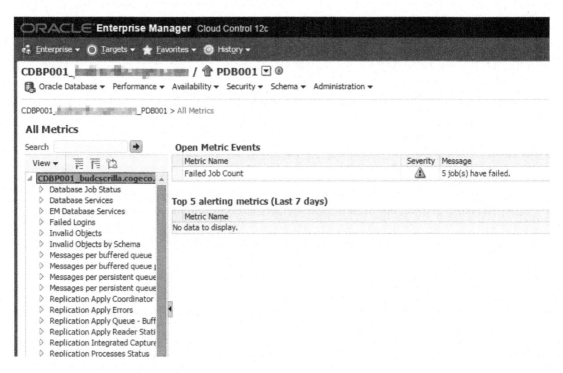

Figure 14-4. *All Metrics page for a pluggable database*

Depending of the target type, you will see the metrics collected by Enterprise Manager and you will be able to generate reports for a specific period of time.

AWR

AWR is a build-on repository in the database that gathers operational statistics. Regularly, by default every hour, AWR gathers, processes, and maintains the necessary information related to the performance of the system and keeps it into the repository. These snapshots are mainly used to identify performance problems over time by comparing two snapshots together. Using Enterprise Manager, you can manage and generate AWR reports, but I will show you how to generate reports using the Oracle-provided script called "$ORACLE_HOME/rdbms/admin/awrrpt.sql".

■ **Note**   As mentioned, the generation of the AWR report could also be done by using Oracle Enterprise Manager. From the database home page, go under Performance menu, and you will find the AWR submenu.

Here is an example of an AWR report. The first interesting table is about the "Instance Efficiency Percentage," which gives ratios of performance. As mentioned in the title of the table, values should be around 100%.

```
Instance Efficiency Percentages (Target 100%)
~~~~~~~~~~~~~~~~~~~~~~~~~~~~~~~~~~~~~~~~~~~~~~~~
           Buffer Nowait %:  100.00      Redo NoWait %:  100.00
           Buffer  Hit  %:    98.17   In-memory Sort %:   99.88
           Library Hit  %:    92.13      Soft Parse %:    89.00
      Execute to Parse %:     54.27      Latch Hit %:     99.37
Parse CPU to Parse Elapsd %:  84.99   % Non-Parse CPU:    87.74
       Flash Cache Hit %:      0.00
```

Anything not close enough to the target of 100% should be investigated by the DBA.

The next table is probably one of the most important sources of information when you are trying to troubleshoot a performance issue, the "Top 10 Foreground Events by Total Wait Time." The table shows the most important event during the selected periods, the number of waits for these events, and the time spent per event. Here is an example.

```
Top 10 Foreground Events by Total Wait Time
~~~~~~~~~~~~~~~~~~~~~~~~~~~~~~~~~~~~~~~~~~~~~
```

Event	Waits	Total Wait Time (sec)	Wait Avg(ms)	% DB time	Wait Class
DB CPU		**111.4**		**87.5**	
db file sequential read	1,177	10	8.47	7.8	User I/O
direct path read	322	4.5	14.11	3.6	User I/O
cursor: pin S wait on X	9	.7	72.94	.5	Concurre
control file sequential read	655	.4	0.59	.3	System I
db file scattered read	21	.3	14.81	.2	User I/O
kksfbc child completion	5	.3	50.07	.2	Other
library cache lock	5	.2	41.41	.2	Concurre
SQL*Net more data to client	258	.2	0.75	.2	Network
direct path write temp	26	.2	7.20	.1	User I/O

The most important event during that period (in bold) is the "DB CPU"; as you can see, it was 87.5% of the time spent for all the events together. Knowing this fact, we will focus our troubleshooting on processes directly related to database process. If the main event would be something related to I/O, we would focus our troubleshooting of SQL, which does a lot of I/O and related tasks.

It is important to note that the AWR report covers the entire CDB. The next section gives the information related to services, so it helps knowing which service in the CDB is the most resource-consuming service. Here is an example that shows that the service "pdb001" is the main service and represents the PDB where the APEX engine and applications are running from.

Service Name	DB Time (s)	DB CPU (s)	Physical Reads (K)	Logical Reads (K)
pdb001	100	89	228	274
SYS$USERS	23	19	0	22
SYS$BACKGROUND	1	1	1	17
CDBP001	0	0	0	0
CDBP001XDB	0	0	0	0

The next section in the AWR report that I would like to focus on is the SQL Statement details. In our example, the main event is "DB CPU," so I will have a deeper look at the section "SQL ordered by CPU Time." Here are the first lines of that section:

```
SQL ordered by CPU Time DB/Inst: CDBP001/CDBP001 Snaps: 6036-6037
-> Resources reported for PL/SQL code includes the resources used by all SQL
   statements called by the code.
-> %Total - CPU Time as a percentage of Total DB CPU
-> %CPU   - CPU Time as a percentage of Elapsed Time
-> %IO    - User I/O Time as a percentage of Elapsed Time
-> Captured SQL account for 63.9% of Total CPU Time (s): 111
-> Captured PL/SQL account for 90.5% of Total CPU Time (s): 111


    CPU                    CPU per        Elapsed
   Time (s) Executions   Exec (s) %Total  Time (s)   %CPU   %IO   SQL Id
---------- ------------ ---------- ------ ---------- ------ ------ -------------
     49.2            6       8.20   44.2       53.9   91.2    8.9 ggd5jwdy4j0b3
  PDB: PDB001
begin wwv_flow.show(p_widget_action=>:1, p_debug=>:2, p_request=>:3, p_widg
et_num_return=>:4, p_arg_values=>:5, p_flow_id=>:6, x01=>:7, x02=>:8, p_flo
w_step_id=>:9, p_widget_name=>:10, p_arg_names=>:11, p_widget_mod=>:12, p_in
stance=>:13 ); commit; end;

     31.0            3      10.32   27.8       34.9   88.9   11.3 65bz6jt25hd9a
Module: SCH_BOOK/APEX:APP 152:1
  PDB: PDB001
select "VENDOR_LAST_NAME", "VENDOR_FIRST_NAME", "VEHICLE", "STATE", "NB_VEHICLE",
"VENDOR_USERNAME", "COMMISSION", count(*) over () as apxws_row_cnt from
( select * from ( select * from ford_sales ) r where ("NB_VEHICLE" > to_number
(:APXWS_EXPR_1)) ) r where

     27.4           13       2.11   24.6       32.5   84.3   15.9 50kx8nhsdqr74
Module: APEX Listener
  PDB: PDB001
begin f(p=>:1 ); commit; end;

     10.9            2       5.45    9.8       11.1   98.6    1.4 4jcw2k3ntyj51
Module: SCH_BOOK/APEX:APP 152:1
  PDB: PDB001
select "VENDOR_LAST_NAME", "VENDOR_FIRST_NAME", "VEHICLE", "STATE", "NB_VEHICLE",
"VENDOR_USERNAME", "COMMISSION", count(*) over () as apxws_row_cnt from
( select * from ( select * from ford_sales ) r where ("VEHICLE" = :APXWS_EXPR_1) )
r where rownum <= to_n

      6.1            1       6.07    5.5        6.7   89.9   10.2 bmn8hhq4nd423
```

The "SQL Ordered by CPU Time" section has a lot of interesting information. You will find the SQL that consumed the most CPU during that period. That is most of the time, where we will focus our troubleshooting task.

At the beginning of this chapter, I was mentioning that is was important to distinguish between the different components of the APEX infrastructure. Let's use the preceding example to show how to distinguish them.

First of all, you can notice the key word "Module." In this example, two different modules are mentioned, "SCH_BOOK/APEX:APP 152:1" and "APEX Listener." Let's take the first module.

```
    CPU                       CPU per           Elapsed
  Time (s)  Executions      Exec (s) %Total    Time (s)    %CPU     %IO    SQL Id
---------- ------------   ---------- ------   ---------- ------  ------  -------------
     31.0             3        10.32   27.8        34.9   88.9    11.3 65bz6jt25hd9a
Module: SCH_BOOK/APEX:APP 152:1
   PDB: PDB001
select "VENDOR_LAST_NAME", "VENDOR_FIRST_NAME", "VEHICLE",
 "STATE", "NB_VEHICLE", "VENDOR_USERNAME", "COMMISSI
ON", count(*) over () as apxws_row_cnt from ( select * from ( select *
 from ford_sales ) r where ("NB_VEHICLE" > to_number(:APXWS_EXPR_1)) ) r where
```

The module information refers to workspace SCH_BOOK, application 152, and page 1. In bold, we can see that this process ran three times and consumed a total of 27.8% of all the CPU used during that period. We already have enough information to go see the developer and ask him to have a look at the SQL statement running in application 152, page 1.

Here is the other module reported in the AWR report.

```
    CPU                       CPU per           Elapsed
  Time (s)  Executions      Exec (s) %Total    Time (s)    %CPU     %IO    SQL Id
---------- ------------   ---------- ------   ---------- ------  ------  -------------
     27.4            13         2.11   24.6        32.5   84.3    15.9 50kx8nhsdqr74
Module: APEX Listener
   PDB: PDB001
begin f(p=>:1 ); commit; end;
```

Unfortunately, this module refers to the APEX Listener and there is nothing we can perform or change at the database level to improve this process.

Let's have a look at another portion of information. This block is not referring to a module. This statement is part of the APEX engine itself, and by looking at the statistics, it's the most CPU-consuming process.

```
    CPU                       CPU per           Elapsed
  Time (s)  Executions      Exec (s) %Total    Time (s)    %CPU     %IO    SQL Id
---------- ------------   ---------- ------   ---------- ------  ------  -------------
     49.2             6         8.20   44.2        53.9   91.2     8.9 ggd5jwdy4j0b3
   PDB: PDB001
begin wwv_flow.show(p_widget_action=>:1 , p_debug=>:2 , p_request=>:3 , p_widg
et_num_return=>:4 , p_arg_values=>:5 , p_flow_id=>:6 , x01=>:7 , x02=>:8 , p_flo
w_step_id=>:9 , p_widget_name=>:10 , p_arg_names=>:11 , p_widget_mod=>:12 , p_instance=>:13
); commit; end;
```

What is the "wwv_flow.show" process? I would like to refer to a document from Oracle Support, "Application Express (APEX) Performance Tuning and Scalability Factor" (Doc ID 1418234.1), which gives an excellent definition of the component "wwv_flow". This component is the main piece in the APEX engine and it's been called by every APEX application. Unfortunately, there is no way we can improve the execution of this component. You might also have, in your AWR report, a statement related to "wwv_flow.accept", but again, this is one of the main components of the APEX engine, the execution of which we cannot improve.

Database Monitor

The Oracle APEX team decided to provide a tool, from the APEX builder, that gives DBA information like we can find with the tools discussed previously in this chapter.

First of all, from the "INTERNAL" workspace we have to permit the usage of that utility. Once connected to the workspace, navigate to "Manage Instance," "Feature Configuration" and scroll down to the "Monitoring" section. As you can see in Figure 14-5, make sure to "Enable Database Monitoring" to "Yes."

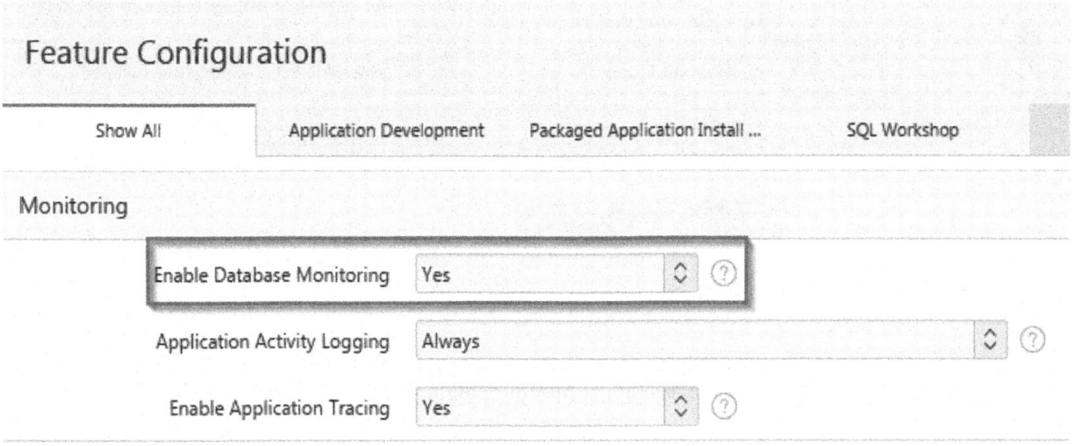

Figure 14-5. *Enabling the Database Monitor utility*

When you are connected to the application workspace, select the "SQLWorkshop" menu, "Utilities" and "Database Monitor" as we can see in Figure 14-6.

Figure 14-6. *Database Monitor utility*

You will be asked to login with a database user that has been granted the DBA role. After the authentication process is completed, you will have the "Database Monitor" main page, as we can see in Figure 14-7.

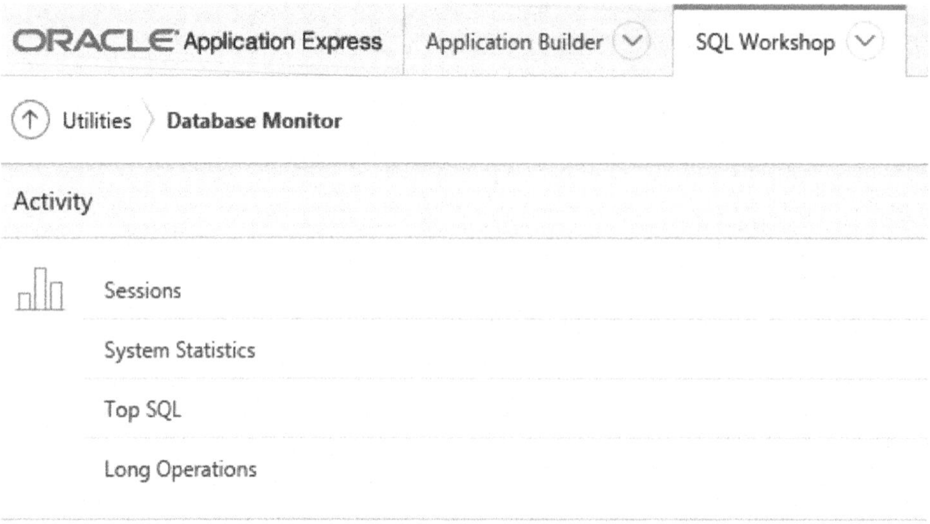

ORACLE' Application Express   Application Builder ⌄   SQL Workshop ⌄

(↑) Utilities 〉 **Database Monitor**

Activity

Sessions

System Statistics

Top SQL

Long Operations

Figure 14-7. *Four areas of monitoring*

We have four areas of database monitoring:

- **Sessions**: we will see information about sessions, locks, waits, I/O, SQL, and open cursors. Figure 14-8 shows an example of session monitoring while application 152 is querying the database.

Figure 14-8. *Example of active session*

We can see SID 171 actually running page 1 of application 152. This session is using the database user "XS$NULL" as it is using Real Application Security (RAS) policies. Notice that I have ordered by the column "Seconds in Database." This way we are seeing the sessions that are consuming the most resources. Please notice the column "Module," which gives all the necessary information to recognize which APEX application is running.

While this session is still active, we can click the "SQL" menu to see the statement that is actually running. Figure 14-9 shows that page.

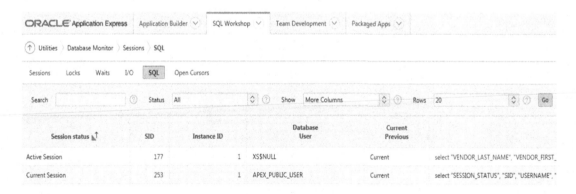

Figure 14-9. *Example of active queries*

The query is running by XS$NULL and by clicking the SQL statement, we will have more detail about this execution as we can see in Figure 14-10.

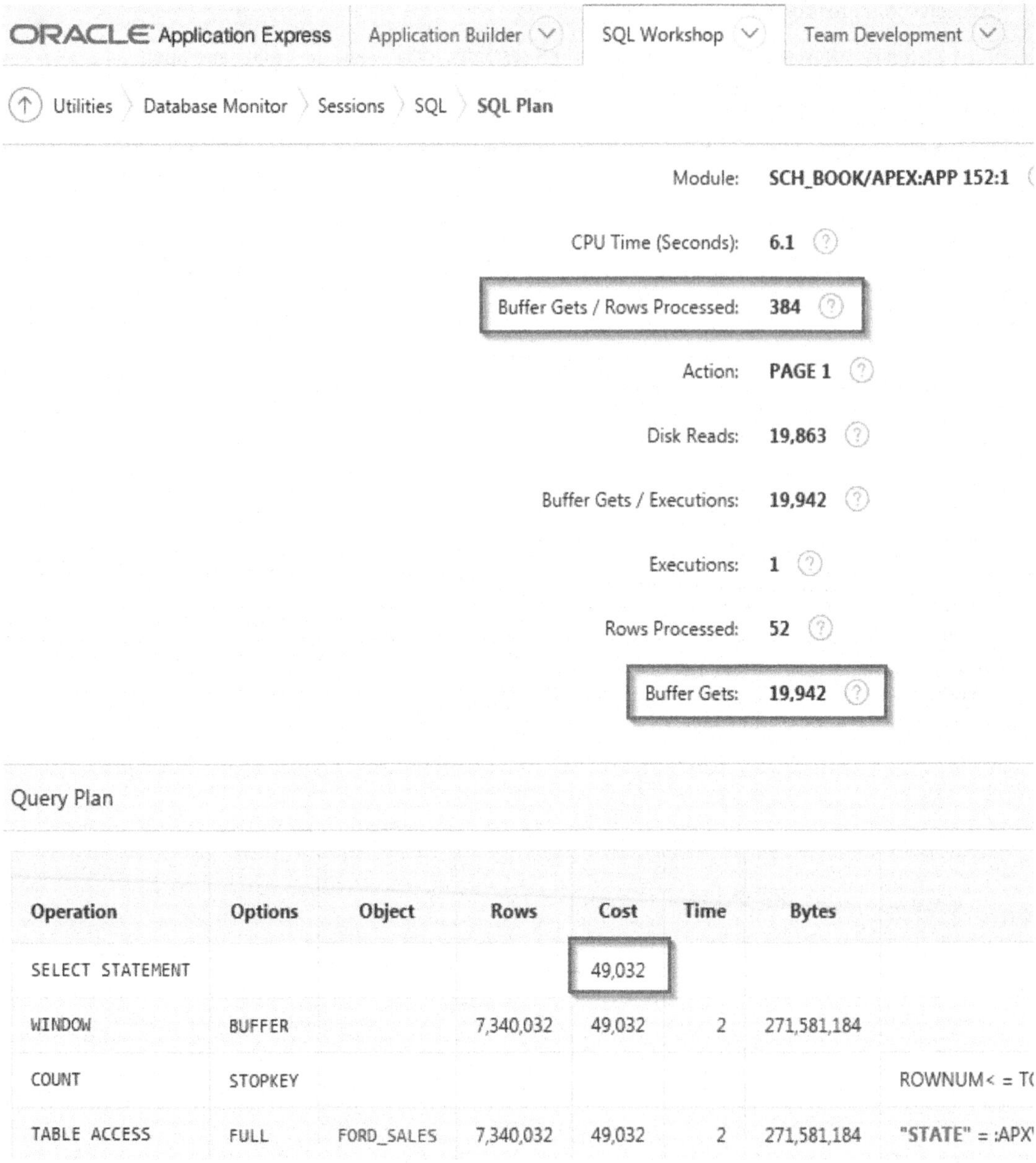

ORACLE' Application Express | Application Builder ⌄ | SQL Workshop ⌄ | Team Development ⌄

(↑) Utilities 〉 Database Monitor 〉 Sessions 〉 SQL 〉 **SQL Plan**

Module:	**SCH_BOOK/APEX:APP 152:1** (
CPU Time (Seconds):	**6.1** ⑦
Buffer Gets / Rows Processed:	**384** ⑦
Action:	**PAGE 1** ⑦
Disk Reads:	**19,863** ⑦
Buffer Gets / Executions:	**19,942** ⑦
Executions:	**1** ⑦
Rows Processed:	**52** ⑦
Buffer Gets:	**19,942** ⑦

Query Plan

Operation	Options	Object	Rows	Cost	Time	Bytes	
SELECT STATEMENT				49,032			
WINDOW	BUFFER		7,340,032	49,032	2	271,581,184	
COUNT	STOPKEY						ROWNUM< = T(
TABLE ACCESS	FULL	FORD_SALES	7,340,032	49,032	2	271,581,184	"STATE" = :APX'

Figure 14-10. *Example of SQL execution*

From this page, we can see the number of Buffer Gets and Rows Processed, as well as the Cost of the SQL statement as well as the Explain Plan. All these information could be helpful to identify a process that can be improved by the developer.

- **System Statistics**: we will see information about system statistics, live statistics, or delta between current and saved statistics. Figure 14-11 is showing the main page, with delta of system statistics in the last 1984 seconds.

Figure 14-11. *Example of system statistics*

This page is giving us the general view of the database activity during that period. We can have the number of physical reads and writes, DB time in seconds, application and user I/O wait time, and so on.

- **Top SQL**: represents the SQL statements that are executed most often, using more system resources and helpful to identify poorly performing SQL as we can see in Figure 14-12.

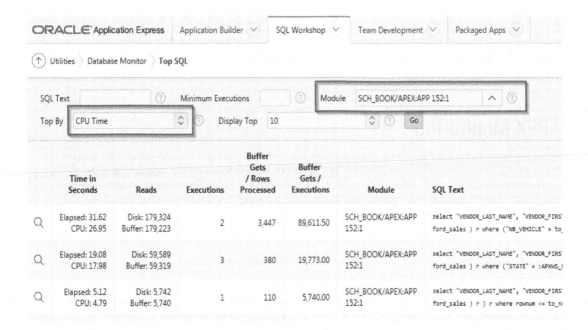

Figure 14-12. *Top SQL*

As we can see, I have selected the module "SCH_BOOK/APEX:APP 152:1" which represents the Ford Sales application. I have also asked to sort by "CPU Time." The first request of the output is showing that the statement ran two times for a total of more than 179,000 buffer gets. This could be a candidate for improvement.

■ **Note** If we remove the filter on "Module," we will get the Top SQL for the entire database as we have in the AWR for example.

- **Long Operations**: this page is showing the operations that run longer than 6 seconds. They are considered as "long operations" by the database.

In this database monitoring section we have seen that the process of monitoring a database that runs APEX engine and application is not different from monitoring any other Oracle database. We have seen how to use Oracle Enterprise Manager, to monitor the database server, and to validate the health of the PDB itself. Of course, Oracle Enterprise Manager collects a lot of information and I invite you to explore the metrics of the different types, such as server, CDB and PDB, and so on. We have also seen two other utilities called ASH and AWR. Both utilities can be used through Enterprise Manager, or if you prefer, you can use command lines to generate the reports as well. I have presented ASH using Enterprise Manager and we have seen how great that tool is to see and analyze, second by second, what is or was happening in the database. I have also presented AWR (in command line) and showed what kind of information it can bring. AWR will help you compare database performance over time. I have concluded this section by presenting the APEX utility "Database Monitor" and shown a few examples of information it could bring.

■ **Note** The usage of AWR and ASH in the section requires the Diagnostic Pack.

APEX Monitoring

In the last section, we have seen how to validate the health of the database by using Oracle Enterprise Manager, ASH, AWR, and Database Monitor. In this section we will focus on the monitoring of the APEX applications themselves. We will see how to view statistics on the applications, pages viewed, which workspace is more actively used, which page has the biggest weight in the workspace, and so on.

We have three ways of monitoring:

1. Monitoring APEX applications from the workspace "INTERNAL"

2. Monitoring APEX applications from the application workspace

3. Monitoring APEX applications using APEX view

Depending of the size of your company or your role, you can monitor the APEX applications either for the entire database in the workspace "INTERNAL" or at the application workspace level. The difference is the workspace that you will be connecting on. We can have the same level of detail from both workspaces; the difference is the visibility of applications. If you want to use SQL statements or scripts, we also have access to a view called "apex_activity_log" that keeps statistics on specified applications. We will show an example of query that could be run against that view to monitor the applications.

Monitoring APEX Applications at the Database Level

While connected on the "INTERNAL" workspace, select the "Monitor Activity" icon as you can see in Figure 14-13.

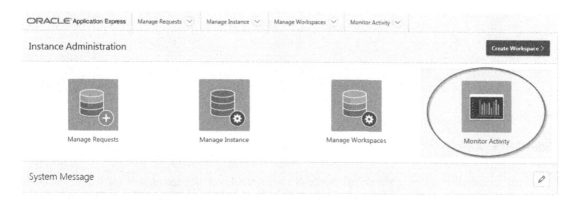

Figure 14-13. *Select "Monitor Activity"*

This page is giving us a lot of possibilities. First of all I would like to have an overview of the activities in the last period, so I select "By Day by Application and User" in the "Calendar Reports" section. Figure 14-14 shows this selection.

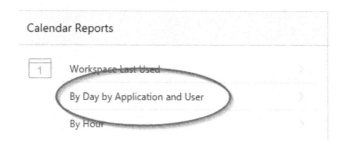

Figure 14-14. *Select "Calendar Reports"*

The idea here is to have a graphical view of the activity throughout the weeks and months. We can easily see which period is the busiest from the application point of view and then relate to the same period on the database point of view. As a DBA, I like to understand and confirm why we had an increase of load on the database performance reports. Figure 14-15 is showing this view.

Figure 14-15. *"Calendar Reports"*

In my AWR reports covering March 3rd to March 4th, I should have noticed an increase of the load and now I can relate this increase on the database side to the increase of activity in the APEX application. From there, I can decide to use ASH to go deeper in that period and extract any processes that might be improved by the developers.

That is an example of how the DBA can monitor his database, as any other Oracle database, and can relate an "abnormal" load on the database with an increase of activity in the application side.

Another interesting section to have statistics on application activities is the "Dashboard." From the main page, select "Dashboard" as we can see in Figure 14-16.

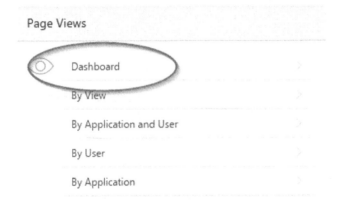

Figure 14-16. *Selecting "Dashboard" from the Monitor Activity page*

The page is quickly showing the "Top Users," "Top Workspaces," and "Top Applications" for a specific period of time. From there you can drill down into the specific application to have more details. For example, we can see that in the last week, the application "Ford Sales" is one of the most used application, so let's have more details by clicking the application's name. Figure 14-17 shows the page with information.

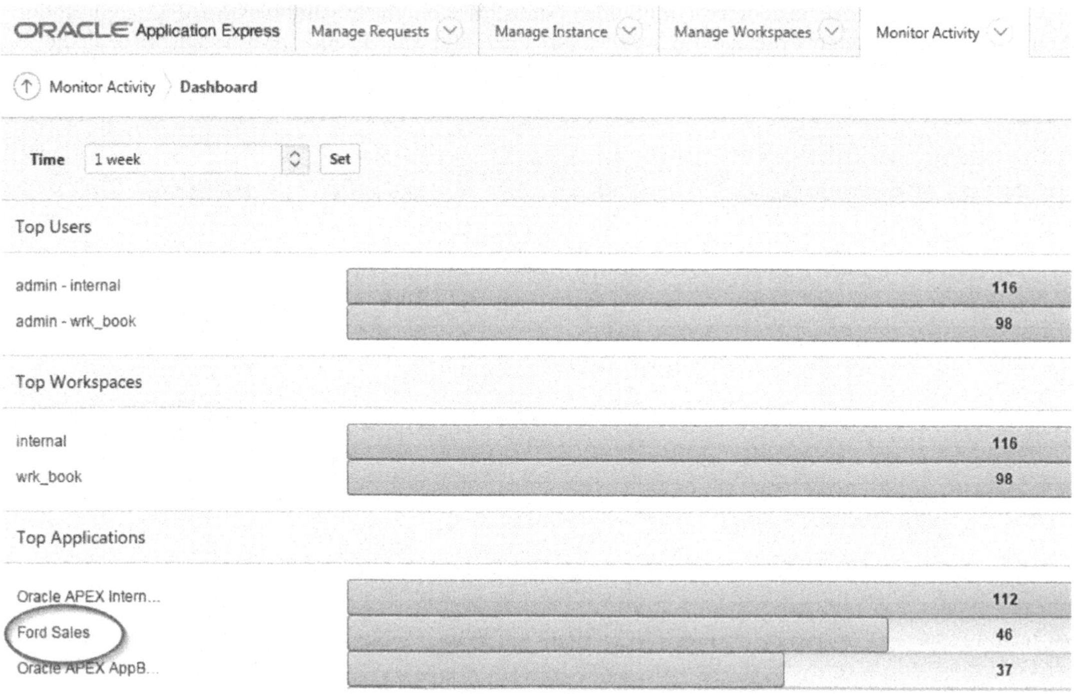

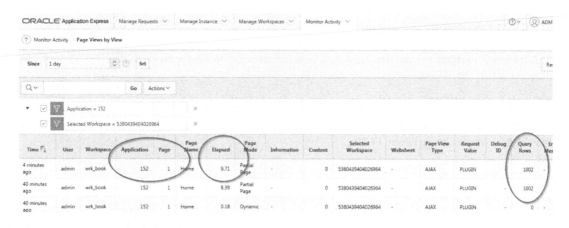

Figure 14-17. *"Top Users," "Top Workspaces," and "Top Applications"*

We are seeing now the statistics of the pages viewed for the application "Ford Sales." We can see interesting information like "Page," "Elapsed," and "Query Rows." We can quickly see which page of the application returns the biggest resultset of data and the time it took to complete. Figure 14-18 is showing the statistics of application 152.

Time	User	Workspace	Application	Page	Page Name	Elapsed	Page Mode	Information	Content	Selected Workspace	Websheet	Page View Type	Request Value	Debug ID	Query Rows
4 minutes ago	admin	wrk_book	152	1	Home	9.71	Partial Page	-	0	5380439404026964	-	AJAX	PLUGIN	-	1002
40 minutes ago	admin	wrk_book	152	1	Home	8.39	Partial Page	-	0	5380439404026964	-	AJAX	PLUGIN	-	1002
40 minutes ago	admin	wrk_book	152	1	Home	0.18	Dynamic	-	0	5380439404026964	-	AJAX	PLUGIN	-	0

Figure 14-18. *Statistics of application 152*

The page is opening the door for a multitude of statistics about the execution of the APEX applications. You can for example remove the filter on "Application = 152" and you will end up with statistics of all the applications running in that workspace. If you sort on the column "Elapsed" you can have interesting statistics, as you can see in Figure 14-19.

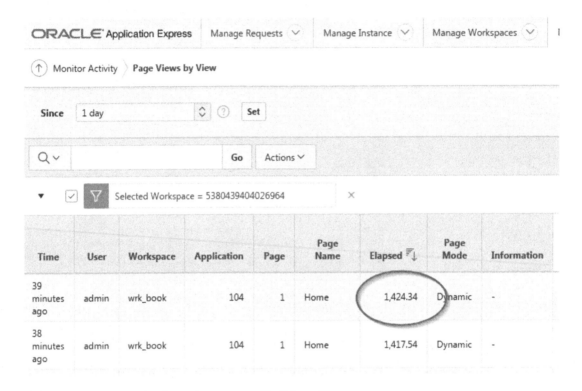

Figure 14-19. *Statistics for the workspace, sorted by "Elapsed"*

If I would be the DBA assigned to this system, I would ask the developer to have a look at application 104, page 1. We can notice that one process takes a very long time to completed, without any row returned. This is another example of a process that has to be reported to the developer for validation.

Monitoring APEX Applications at the Workspace Level

While connected to your workspace, select the "Dashboards" under the "Administration" icon (icon with the little key), as you can see in Figure 14-20.

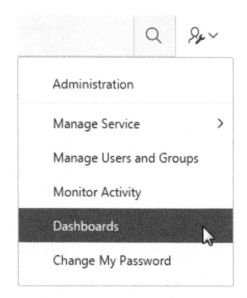

Figure 14-20. *Dashboards, under Administration menu*

From the Dashboards main page, there are two menus I prefer the most for monitoring the activities, the "Activity Dashboard" and "Performance Dashboards." Figure 14-21 shows these two menus.

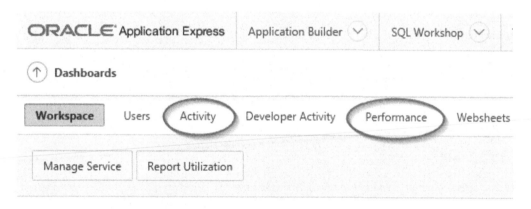

Figure 14-21. *Menu Activity and Performance*

Let's start with the Performance Dashboards. This dashboard reports the worst page performance of the workspace. This would be one of the first dashboards to analyze when you start your monitoring process. First, select the duration on which you want to have the information. You can also sort by columns and you can use filters to restrict the analysis by clicking "Actions" and "Filter." Figure 14-22 gives an example showing the last 4 weeks of information.

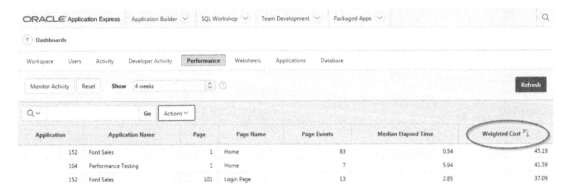

Application	Application Name	Page	Page Name	Page Events	Median Elapsed Time	Weighted Cost
152	Ford Sales	1	Home	83	0.54	45.19
104	Performance Testing	1	Home	7	5.94	41.59
152	Ford Sales	101	Login Page	13	2.85	37.09

Figure 14-22. Example of the Performance Dashboard of the Workspace

We can see page 1 of application 152 "Ford Sales" been the weighted cost page of the entire workspace. This would be a good candidate for the developer for improvements.

Let's have a look at the "Activity Dashboard" by clicking the "Activity" menu. This page is giving us the "Top users," "Top applications," "Top pages," "Recent Logins," and the "Recent errors." All this is useful information about the activity and the most popular applications. If we want to analyze the activity more deeply, I recommend going in the "Monitor Activity" page, as you can see in Figure 14-23.

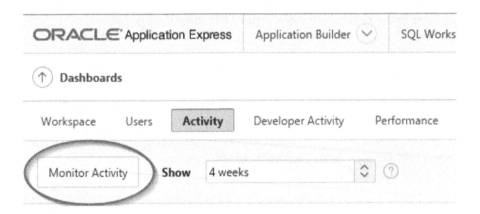

Figure 14-23. Select "Monitor Activity" from Activity Dashboard

From this page, we have a multitude of possibilities. Again, the goal here is to quickly see and monitor the popular applications. Which application is the most viewed application? Which period of the day/week has peaks of activity? Or, we can simply the list "page views" or "application views" in a specific period.

Figure 14-24 is showing the "Monitor Activity" page, and we can see different statistics of activity we can have from here.

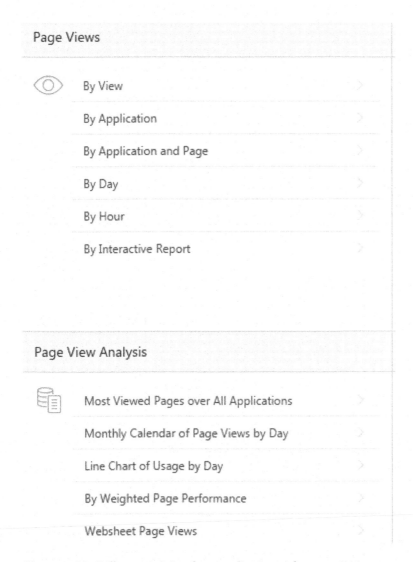

Page Views

By View

By Application

By Application and Page

By Day

By Hour

By Interactive Report

Page View Analysis

Most Viewed Pages over All Applications

Monthly Calendar of Page Views by Day

Line Chart of Usage by Day

By Weighted Page Performance

Websheet Page Views

Figure 14-24. Different statistics about application and page activities

I like to start by the "Most Viewed Pages over All Applications" view. This view is great to quickly see which application is the most popular. Another interesting view is the "Monthly Calendar of Page Views by Day," which represents the activity throughout the month. This view can help the DBA to relate on the busiest period at the database level.

Monitoring APEX Applications Using APEX and Database Views

The view APEX_ACTIVITY_LOG records all the activity including developer and runtime activities for the current workspace. We can develop SQL statements to run on this view and come up with interesting information. Figure 14-25 shows an example of a SQL statement that queries this view and gives information related to application 152, Ford Sales.

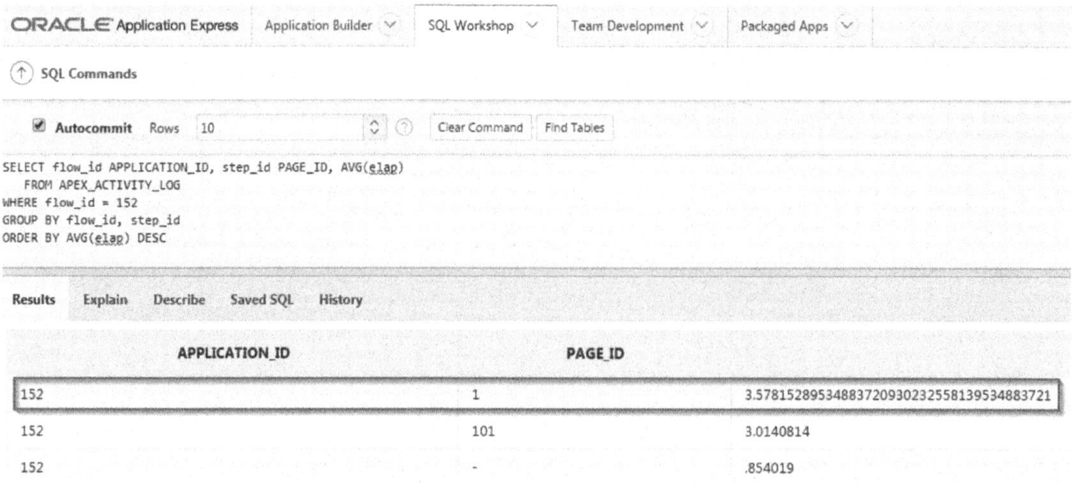

Figure 14-25. *Query on the view "APEX ACTIVITY LOG"*

The following SQL statement shows page 1 with the biggest execution average time for application 152.

```
SELECT flow_id APPLICATION_ID, step_id PAGE_ID, AVG(elap)
   FROM APEX_ACTIVITY_LOG
WHERE flow_id = 152
GROUP BY flow_id, step_id
ORDER BY AVG(elap) DESC
```

Before querying this view, we have to enable the application logging. Connected to the "internal" workspace, navigate under "Manage Instance," "Feature Configuration."

Figure 14-26 shows the "Monitoring" section of that page.

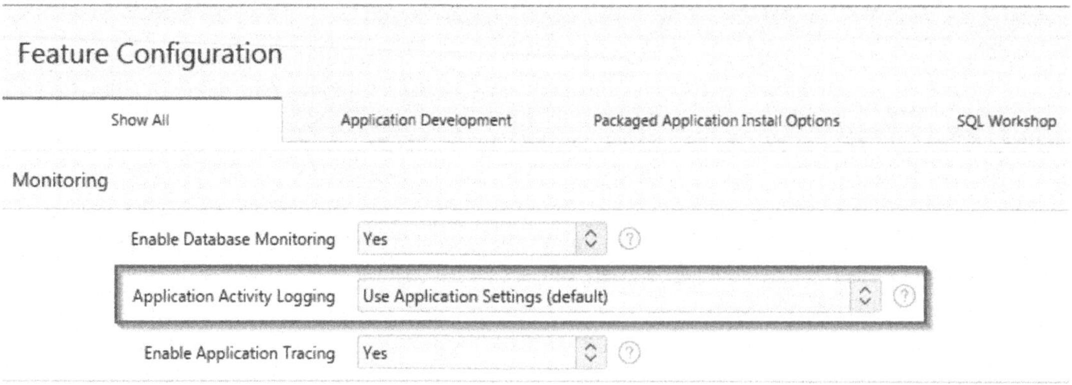

Figure 14-26. *Enabling application logging*

The different possibilities are as follows:

- Use Application Settings (default)
- Always
- Never
- Initially Disabled for New Applications and Packages Applications

Let's leave the default selection in place and verify the "Logging" property of application 152. Let's connect to the application workspace and select the "Ford Sales" application. Click "Edit Application Properties" as you can see in Figure 14-27.

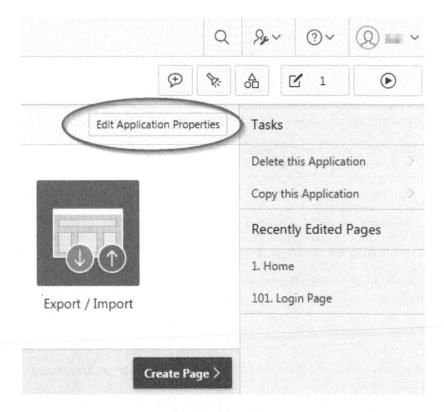

Figure 14-27. *Edit Application Properties*

Scroll down to the "Properties" section and make sure the property "Logging" is set to "Yes." From now, all the activities from application 152 are now recorded into the view APEX_ACTIVITY_LOG.

We have to know that this information in this view is not persistent as it rotates between two log tables. If you want to keep this information permanently, I suggest you copy the content of that view in a custom table in a monitoring schema of your database. From this table, you can develop an automatic monitoring procedure by querying this table and notifying if a process is reaching a specific threshold, like "Elapsed Time" or "SQL Error message."

If you decide to write a script to consolidate this information into a permanent table, here is what you should do. First of all, connected on the workspace's parsing schema, create a permanent table. Depending on the queries we will use, please create the appropriate indexes.

```
create table apex_activity_log_local as select * from apex_activity_log;
create index apex_activity_log_local_idx1 on apex_activity_log_local(flow_id);
create index apex_activity_log_local_idx2 on apex_activity_log_local(time_stamp,step_id);
```

Launch SQL*Plus and run these SQL statements. Notice the usage of the procedure "apex_util.set_security_group_id" to get the security group ID of your workspace. We will use the MERGE syntax to merge the content of the view into our table.

```
exec apex_util.set_security_group_id(apex_util.find_security_group_id('WRK_BOOK'));

merge into apex_activity_log_local a
using apex_activity_log b
on (a.time_stamp=b.time_stamp and a.step_id=b.step_id)
when not matched then
insert
values (b.time_stamp,b.component_type,b.component_name,b.component_attribute,b.
information,b.elap,
b.num_rows,b.userid,b.ip_address,b.user_agent,b.flow_id,b.step_id,b.session_id,b.sqlerrm,
b.sqlerrm_component_type,b.sqlerrm_component_name,b.page_mode,b.application_info,b.
worksheet_id,
b.ir_search,b.ir_report_id,b.websheet_id,b.webpage_id,b.datagrid_id,b.content_length);
```

Now that the logging information is in a permanent table in the parsing schema, we can develop automatic monitoring against it to notify if any process is reaching a threshold. Let's take the first example and change the FROM clause to run this query against our table.

```
SELECT flow_id APPLICATION_ID, step_id PAGE_ID, AVG(elap)
    FROM APEX_ACTIVITY_LOG_LOCAL
WHERE flow_id = 152
GROUP BY flow_id, step_id
ORDER BY AVG(elap) DESC;
```

You will have the same output as in Figure 14-25 but from the persistent table, so you can keep the logging information as long as you want.

By using this permanent table, you can more easily see the degradation or the improvement of your application response time over a long period of time.

Another way to make the relation between the Oracle session running on the database and the APEX application is by using the "v$session" view. For DBAs that prefer using this view to start the monitoring process, here is a SQL statement that gives interesting information.

```
select module, client_info, client_identifier from v$session;
```

MODULE	CLIENT_INFO	CLIENT_IDENTIFIER
SCH_BOOK/APEX:APP 152:1	5380439404026964:ADMIN	ADMIN:12002491913106

This output is very useful to distinguish or recognize which APEX application is associated to this session. The column "Module" is giving us the "Parsing DB User/APEX: Application ID: Page ID". The column "Client Info" is giving us the "Workspace ID: Authenticated User" and the column is giving us the "Authenticated User:Session ID".

We have seen in the last section how to monitor the APEX applications. We can now answer the questions about the most popular applications, such as which page is the most viewed. We can now identify the poorly performing pages and applications in the workspace or in the entire database and give the necessary information to the developer for improvements.

Summary

The objective of this chapter was to demonstrate how we could monitor the system in general. We have seen in the first section of this chapter how to monitor the database itself, by using tools like Enterprise Manager, AWR, ASH, and Database Monitor. As we know, APEX engine and applications are running entirely in the database, so one important aspect was to distinguish processes from APEX engine, APEX applications, and any other database's processes.

The second section of this chapter was about monitoring the APEX applications, either from the "INTERNAL" or application workspace point of view. If you like using SQL statements against views, we have presented two views that give interesting information about monitoring.

Being proactive and monitoring a system will, most of the time, help you identify processes that could become problematic and then involve the developer to improve them.

■ ■ ■

CHAPTER 15

Performance and Tuning

In the previous chapter, we have discussed the monitoring process and how to identify processes that are the least performing throughout the application, a specific workspace or at the database level. These are identified as "potential" processes that could be improved. The developer will analyze the information provided by the DBA, will probably perform some test by changing his APEX code, will create some indexes, will use materialized views, and so on. The objective is to optimize this process as much as possible so it will not consume excessive resources and will generally help the overall performance of the system. Even if you improve the execution of a SQL of 1 second, it might not look like a lot, but if that SQL is executed 10 times per minute, you have saved overall 10 seconds in that minute, which is a lot and will probably be visible to the end users.

In this chapter, we will see how to tune a specific process at the database level. We will give an example of how we can generate the execution plan, performing an improvement on a table, and validating our change. We will also demonstrate how to use the "Debug" feature to record a specific process. And we will see how to get reports from the data gathered during the "debug" session.

Tuning Application

The DBA is contacting you and providing you information on an APEX page that has a poor execution time. He is telling you that application ID 152, page 1 has an elapsed time of 9.71 and every execution returns 1002 rows. See in Chapter 14, Figure 14-18, for more detail on this poor execution. From a database perspective, each page is a single session, so by enabling the Oracle Tracing the execution of the page will generate Oracle trace files that will be analyzed using TKPROF.

Enabling Oracle Tracing

For enabling the tracing of the APEX application, go in the INTERNAL workspace under "Manage Instance" and "Feature Configuration." Make sure the parameter "Enable Application Tracing" is set to "Yes" as we can see in Figure 15-1.

© Francis Mignault and Luc Demanche 2016   265
F. Mignault and L. Demanche, *Oracle Application Express Administration*, DOI 10.1007/978-1-4842-1958-4_15

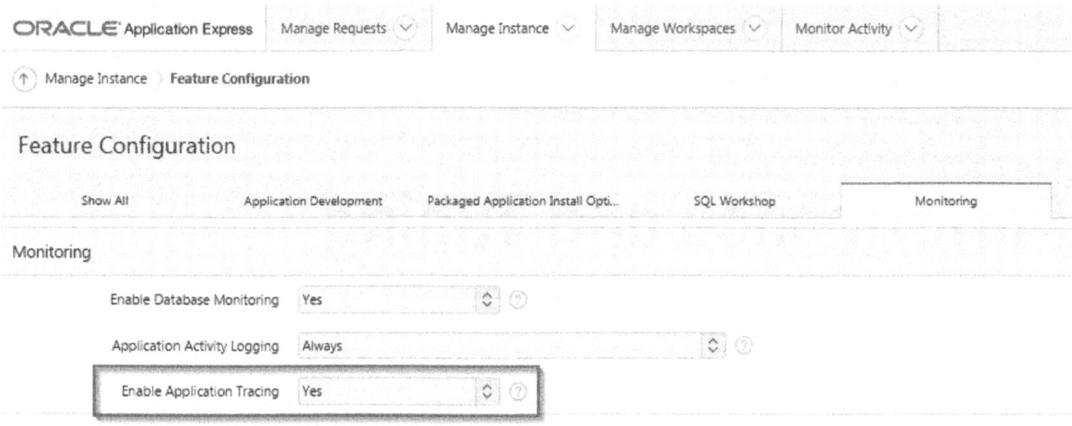

Figure 15-1. Enable Application Tracing

It is now possible for the database session to generate trace files. If we add "p_trace=YES" at the end of the URL, the database will generate tracing files from the execution of the page. With Oracle12c, the files will be generated under the DIAG folder.

Here is the example for my application 152 and page 1

```
http://server:8080/ords/f?p=152:1:11426966062954:::::&p_trace=YES
```

Using TKPROF

Once you find the right trace file, it's now time to use TKPROF and to analyze the output file. Run the utility with the following options:

```
tkprof source_file output_file [waits=yes|no] [sort=option] [print=n]
    [aggregate=yes|no] [insert=filename3] [sys=yes|no] [table=schema.table]
    [explain=user/password] [record=filename4] [width=n]
```

■ **Note** You can see more details on the different options of TKPROF at this URL:

```
http://docs.oracle.com/database/121/TGSQL/tgsql_trace.htm#GUID-9C03013B-6587-4475-8888-
16E84DAD5806
```

In the output file I can see the following regarding the execution of page 1 of application 152.

```
select
        "VENDOR_LAST_NAME",
        "VENDOR_FIRST_NAME",
        "VEHICLE",
        "STATE",
        "NB_VEHICLE",
        "VENDOR_USERNAME",
        "COMMISSION",
```

```
        sum("COMMISSION") over (),
        count(*) over () as apxws_row_cnt
 from (
select  *  from (
select * from ford_sales
) r
where ("STATE" = :APXWS_EXPR_1
and "VENDOR_LAST_NAME" = :APXWS_EXPR_2)
) r where rownum <= to_number(:APXWS_MAX_ROW_CNT)

Misses in library cache during parse: 1
Optimizer mode: ALL_ROWS
Parsing user id: 127      (recursive depth: 1)
Number of plan statistics captured: 1


Rows (1st) Rows (avg) Rows (max)  Row Source Operation
---------- ---------- ----------  ---------------------------------------------------
         1          1          1  WINDOW BUFFER (cr=207 pr=0 pw=0 time=16542 us cost=72
                                  size=95800 card=2395)
         1          1          1  COUNT STOPKEY (cr=207 pr=0 pw=0 time=16400 us)
         1          1          1  TABLE ACCESS FULL FORD_SALES (cr=207 pr=0 pw=0 time=16371
                                  us cost=72 size=95800 card=2395)
```

■ **Note**   I have truncated a section of the TKPROF output for simplicity.

In this example, we would like to work on the execution plan. We can see the "TABLE ACCESS FULL" of the table FORD_SALES in the execution plan section. This is something we might want to work on and see the results. This example is pretty simple, as the only where clause, in bold, is on the STATE and VENDOR_LAST_NAME columns.

Execution Plans

Let's use SQLDeveloper to work on the execution of this SQL. Figure 15-2 is showing the actual execution plan.

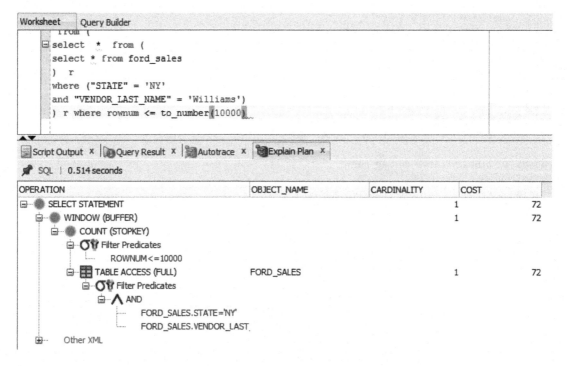

Figure 15-2. Original execution plan

We can see the "TABLE ACCESS(FULL)" and also the COST of 72.

The first test we could do is to build an index on the STATE and VENDOR_LAST_NAME columns and see if it would have an impact on the execution. Let's create the index:

```
create index ford_sales_ix_state_last_name on ford_sales(state,vendor_last_name);
```

Now that we have an index on the STATE and VENDOR_LAST_NAME columns, let's see if that index would be used by the optimizer for the next execution. Figure 15-3 is showing the new execution plan.

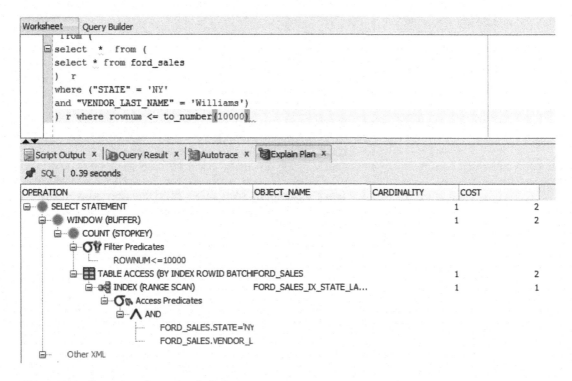

Figure 15-3. *Execution plan using the index*

As we can see, the new index has been used on the execution of the SQL statement and the COST is lower than what it was without the index. Since we have that confirmation, we would like to see how the APEX application will react by generating new trace file from the execution of the same page.

Use the same URL (that contains the &p_trace=YES) as before to generate a new Oracle trace file. When the transaction is completed, use TKPROF to generate the output. Here is the output of the execution of the same SELECT statement.

```
select
        "VENDOR_LAST_NAME",
        "VENDOR_FIRST_NAME",
        "VEHICLE",
        "STATE",
        "NB_VEHICLE",
        "VENDOR_USERNAME",
        "COMMISSION",
        sum("COMMISSION") over (),
        count(*) over () as apxws_row_cnt
 from (
select  *  from (
select * from ford_sales
)  r
where ("STATE" = :APXWS_EXPR_1
and "VENDOR_LAST_NAME" = :APXWS_EXPR_2)
) r where rownum <= to_number(:APXWS_MAX_ROW_CNT)
```

```
Misses in library cache during parse: 1
Optimizer mode: ALL_ROWS
Parsing user id: 127    (recursive depth: 1)
Number of plan statistics captured: 1

Rows (1st) Rows (avg) Rows (max)  Row Source Operation
---------- ---------- ----------  ------------------------------------------------------
        1          1          1   WINDOW BUFFER (cr=3 pr=0 pw=0 time=311 us cost=57
                                  size=247207 card=5749)
        1          1          1   COUNT STOPKEY (cr=3 pr=0 pw=0 time=167 us)
        1          1          1   TABLE ACCESS BY INDEX ROWID BATCHED FORD_SALES (cr=3
                                  pr=0 pw=0 time=128 us cost=57 size=247207 card=5749)
        1          1          1   INDEX RANGE SCAN FORD_SALES_IX_STATE_LAST_NAME (cr=2
                                  pr=0 pw=0 time=88 us cost=19 size=0 card=5749)
                                  (object id 106098)
```

■ **Note**   I have truncated a section of the TKPROF output for simplicity.

We can see in bold, the index is been used in the execution plan of the SELECT statement. The COST also decreases, as we have noticed also when we were testing the execution plan in SQLDeveloper. We can conclude that our change had an influence on the execution of the specific process and we are expecting to see an improvement of the overall performance of the application. Once the modification is deployed in production, the next monitoring process will confirm or not if that change had a positive effect on the performance.

We have seen in this section how to trace the Oracle session related to the execution of a specific page. When the monitoring process is pointing to a nonperforming page, we know now how to generate a file and use TKPROF to generate readable output. Now, the DBA and the developer can work on the optimization of this process and try to improve this page. This process of tuning the application with trace files and TKPROF can be done over and over again.

Tuning Reports

Let's imagine we have an application that contains a reporting section. Reports are usually eating a lot of resources by reading a lot of data, summarizing them so it is using I&O, CPU and memory. These processes of generating reports are usually tough to tune because of their definition, they need to read a lot of data and to process these information.

Different options exist to minimize the negative impact of generating reports on a transactional application.

1. Tune the SQL statements

   You can try to tune the SQL statements by creating indexes, using hints, using materialized views, and so on. All this might work, but will make for continual work as the volume of data grows with time.

2. Generating reports in the nonpeak period

   We can manage to have the reporting section only available in the nonpeak period. This might be difficult to manage specially for a very popular system where the nonpeak periods are rare.

3. Using Oracle Resource Manager

Oracle Resource Manager will manage the CPU demands depending on the type of workload. Chapter 17 is dedicated to Oracle Resource Manager and you will see how to deploy it so the reporting in the application will not become a performance problem. This is my recommended approach.

Using DEBUG mode

The debug mode will be used to track down the application behavior. When your application is running on debug mode, APEX writes information about how it processes each page request, step by step, into a log table. We will see how to enable and disable the debug mode as well as how to analyze the debug information.

Enabling Debug Mode

While connected to the workspace, select the application and click "Edit Application Properties" as we can see in Figure 15-4.

Figure 15-4. *Edit Application Properties*

Make sure "Debugging" is set to Yes. It means that "Debug" mode will be accessible from the browser at runtime. Figure 15-5 shows that option under the "Properties" section.

Properties

Logging	**Yes** ⑦
Debugging	Yes ⬦ ⑦
Allow Feedback	No ⬦ ⑦

Figure 15-5. *Debugging*

Running the Application in Debug Mode

Once enabled, run the application and you will notice the "Debug" icon in the Developer Toolbar. Once activated, the debug data will be recorded in the background. Once you are done with your transaction that you want to debug, simply click "No Debug" icon in the Developer Toolbar.

Viewing Debug Mode Reports

There are few ways to visualize the debug data. First, while you are running the application, you have the "View Debug" icon. This icon opens the "Debug Message Data" page with all the debugged session information.

Another way to open the "Debug Message Data" is from the Application Builder. Once you have selected the application, click the "Utilities" icon as we can see in Figure 15-6.

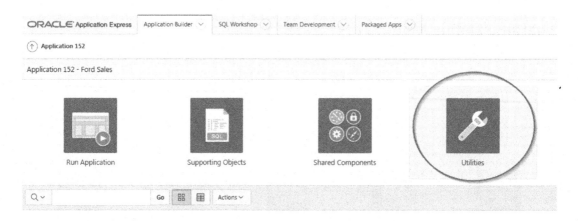

Figure 15-6. *Utilities*

From there, simply select "Debug Messages" and you will end up on the "Debug Message Data" page.

The third way you can get that page is by using the "find" button. From the Application Builder, select the application. You will have the "find" button as you can see in Figure 15-7.

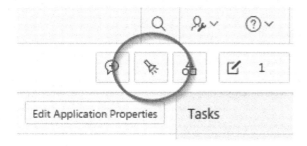

Figure 15-7. *Find button*

You will now have the "Debug Message Data" page; make sure you are on the "Debug" tab. You can then select the debugged session you want to analyze. The objective here is to see, step by step, what was processed during a transaction. If you want, you can sort and get the slowest session recorded, or you can select a specific recorded transaction, like the newest one you have just recorded. Figure 15-8 is showing the list of recorded sessions sorted by "Seconds," and we will select that session for deeper analysis.

Figure 15-8. List of recorded sessions

Once selected, you will have this page: Figure 15-9 is showing the recorded debug information of that session, and I have highlighted two very important pieces of information.

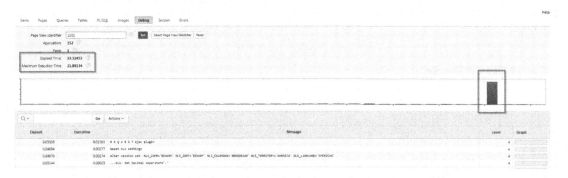

Figure 15-9. Debug data of that session

Let's first think about when the DBA called you and told you that from his monitoring process, he found out that page 1 of application 152 was one of the slowest pages. We have here the breakdown of the entire process of that page. The first red box I have highlighted give us two pieces of information.

- Elapsed Time of 23.32, which is the entire duration of that transaction.

- Maximum Execution Time of 21.89, which is the maximum execution time of one step of that transaction.

Out of the total elapsed time of 23.32 seconds, one step took 21.89 seconds. The second red box I have highlighted is that specific step. If you click that step, it will bring you directly to that step and give you more detail.

Figure 15-10 is showing the step that took 21.89 seconds to execution.

```
1.41966          0.00142    select  *  from (
                            select * from ford_sales
                            ) r
                            where ((instr(upper("VENDOR_LAST_NAME"),upper(:APXWS_SEARCH_STRING_1)) > 0
                                or instr(upper("VENDOR_FIRST_NAME"),upper(:APXWS_SEARCH_STRING_1)) > 0
                                or instr(upper("VEHICLE"),upper(:APXWS_SEARCH_STRING_1)) > 0
                                or instr(upper("STATE"),upper(:APXWS_SEARCH_STRING_1)) > 0
                                or instr(upper("NB_VEHICLE"),upper(:APXWS_SEARCH_STRING_1)) > 0
                                or instr(upper("VENDOR_USERNAME"),upper(:APXWS_SEARCH_STRING_1)) > 0
                                or instr(upper("COMMISSION"),upper(:APXWS_SEARCH_STRING_1)) > 0
                            ))
                            ) r where rownum <= to_number(:APXWS_MAX_ROW_CNT)

1.42105          0.00048    IR binding: "APXWS_SEARCH_STRING_1" value="Smith"

1.42153         21.89134    IR binding: "APXWS_MAX_ROW_CNT" value="1000000"

23.31289         0.00739    Printing rows.  Row window: 1-50.  Rows found: 51
```

Figure 15-10. *Debug data details*

From here, we can get the problematic operation, which is in this case the execution of a select statement. We also have the bind variables used during that execution. The developer can then take this information and start a tuning process to improve that specific step from that transaction. Once the tuning process is over, the developer can run another "debug" session and validate whether his improvement works or not.

Best Practices

I would like to propose some best practices when we are developing an APEX application. These are only proposals, based on experiences we've had.

- Using bind variables

  By using bind variables, we are minimizing the need for the optimizer to do hard parse. The difference between doing a hard parse and a soft parse is only milliseconds, but when we are executing queries thousands of times this adds up.

- Using stored procedures

  There are a few good reasons for using stored procedures. Stored procedure is reusable and can be deployed in other applications. It is easier to move stored procedure in production than it is to move the entire application. Today, we have more tools helping us debug a stored procedure than we do for the APEX application. Extensive data manipulation would perform better in a stored procedure.

- Tuning SQL before going into production

  Make sure the SQL are properly tuned before going into production. This proactive approach can avoid production issues.

- Doing code review

Doing code review minimizes the risk of having unexpected behavior. This is another proactive approach.

Summary

The objective of this chapter was to demonstrate how we can tune the APEX application. The usage of trace files and TKPROF is very important to gather the execution statistics. Once we get the exact picture of how the processing is done, we can start and tune the SQL statements. We have demonstrated how to use the "Debug" feature to record in detail every step that is executing during a page request. When the "Debug" session is over, we have seen how to view reports, detailed information on these steps. The developer has the necessary information to start a tuning process using trace files, TKPROF, and the "Debug" feature. Once the tuning process is over, he has the capability to rerun these gathering tools and then validate if his improvement worked or not. This process can be done over and over until the developer is satisfied with his improvements.

■ ■ ■

CHAPTER 16

Resource Manager and APEX

When the database administrator (DBA) gets a call about a potential Oracle database performance issue, most of the time, the first reaction is to verify the CPU load on the database server. Excessive CPU load can destabilize a server, and if the system becomes almost unresponsive, you would not be able to properly find the root cause and the only option in your action plan would be to reboot the server.

Oracle Resource Manager will ensure that your system's CPU load will not reach that limit and allow you to avoid any situations like having an unresponsive system. With Resource Manager, you can explicitly allocate CPU to different workloads, depending on the priority of the applications. For example, during the day, you can allocate more CPU to the OLTP type of applications, and during the night, you may have more resources for the "batch" workload. You can also allocate resources to specific Oracle users, a specific service, a specific module, and so on depending on how you want to manage the distribution of the resources.

This chapter is divided in three main sections. The first section gives an overview of Resource Manager. We will give an example of the deployment of Resource Manager Plan Directive in a multitenant architecture. The second section explains the required configuration in APEX to use the Resource Manager feature. The last section will describe two examples, one example using a client/server application and one using an APEX application, that are using Resource Manager and we will see how Resource Manager controls the resources and the impact on the system.

Overview of Resource Manager

The Oracle Resource Manager is an infrastructure that provides, since Oracle 8i, granular control of the resource distribution to the users, applications, and services. It works like the operating system scheduler by allowing one Oracle process per CPU to run at a given time. All other Oracle processes wait on an internal run queue under wait event "resmgr:cpu quantum". The Oracle process runs for a small quantum of time (100 milliseconds). At the end of the quantum of time, or when the process starts a wait (for a lock or for an I/O), Resource Manager selects another Oracle process to run.

We first create "consumer groups," which is how the sessions will be grouped together. We can imagine having consumer groups like "OLTP," "REPORTING," "CRITICAL APPS," or "NON-CRITICAL APPS." Then we will do the mapping between the Oracle sessions and the consumer groups. The mapping could be done using different methods, like Oracle users, modules, services, actions, and so on. Personally I like to distinguish sessions by using different user-defined Oracle services. When the groups and the mappings are completed, we will create a plan directive that dictates the percentage of resources available to every group.

Resource Manager with Multitenant Database

Oracle 12c brings the notion of multitenant database that is composed of the root container (CDB), a seed container (PDB$SEED), and multiple pluggable databases (PDB). If you are not using Resource Manager in the multitenant database configuration, you may encounter the following issues:

- Unequal allocation of resources among PDBs

- Unequal allocation of resources within a single PDB

- Inconsistent performance issues

Resource Manager will allow the CDB to control the amount of resources distributed to the PDBs and within the PDB itself. It might be possible that one of the PDBs is more important than others, and Resource Manager will enable you to allocate more resources to it. Resource Manager used in CDB and PDB can manage the resources on two different levels:

- CDB level: Resource Manager is managing the workload for multiple PDBs; you can specify how resources are allocated for every PDB

- PDB level: Resource Manager is distributing resources within the PDB itself

The CDB Plan directives will control the allocation of CPU and Parallel execution servers to the PDB. Each directive references one PDB only. The directive uses the notion of share to distribute the resources. A higher share value for a PDB results in more resources for that PDB. We can also specify a CPU utilization limit available to the PDB. The utilization limit restrains the system resource usage for a PDB.

Figure 16-1 shows a simple example of a configuration that distributes CPU resources between two PDBs in the same CDB. Out of the three shares (two for PDB001 and one for PDB002), 2/3 are guaranteed to PDB001 while 1/3 are guaranteed to PDB002. The "Utilization Limit" says that we are not restricting the CPU utilization for PDB001, but PDB002 can't use more than 80% of the CPU. We are also not limiting the usage of Parallel Servers between PDBs.

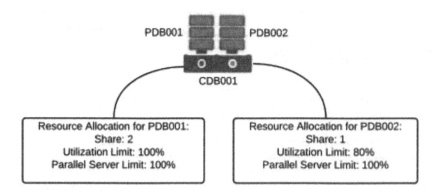

Figure 16-1. Simple configuration of resource distribution between two PDBs

Creation of the CDB Resource Plan Using Oracle Enterprise Manager

We will describe in this section how to deploy the CDB Plan directive using Oracle Enterprise Manager. From the Oracle database home page, select Administration menu and Resource Manager. Figure 16-2 shows that selection.

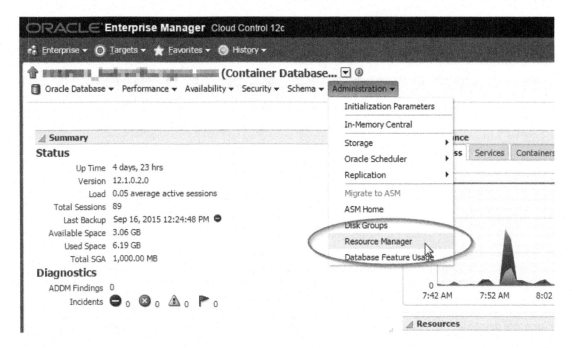

Figure 16-2. *Resource Manager selection from the Oracle Enterprise Manager Container Database home page*

We are now in the "Getting Started with Database Resource Manager" main page, and we will select "CDB Resource Plans." Figure 16-3 shows that page.

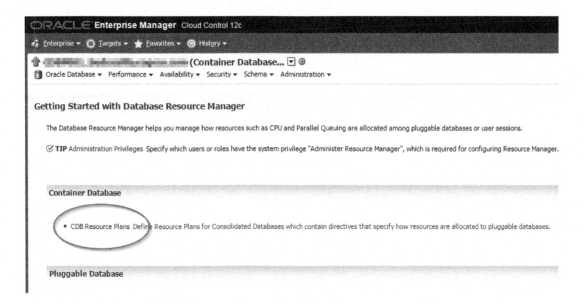

Figure 16-3. *Selection of "CDB Resource Plans"*

You will see the list of the already created CDB Resource Plans. We are now ready to create our CDB Resource Plan to control CPU and Parallel Servers between the two PDBs, PDB001 and PDB002. Figure 16-4 shows the first step of the CDB Resource Plan creation; click "Create."

Figure 16-4. *Clicking "Create"*

We now have to fill in the necessary information. First give the CDB Resource Plan a name and a description. Click "Add/Remove" to select the PDBs that will be controlled by the CDB resource plan. Make sure you are giving the proper value for "Shares," "Utilization Limit %," and "Parallel Server Limit %" associated to every PDB. Here is a table that contains the desired values:

Pluggable database	Share	Utilization Limit %	Parallel Server Limit %
PDB001	2	100	100
PDB002	1	80	100
Default Per PDB	1	100	100

Default per PDB are the values that will be automatically given to every new PDB created in this CDB.

Figure 16-5 demonstrates what you should have. When it's ready for the creation, click "Create."

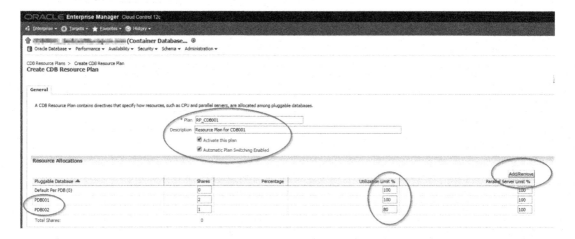

Figure 16-5. *Creation of the CDB Resource Plan*

We now have the newly activated CDB Resource Plan RP_CDB001 in place. Figure 16-6 confirms the creation and the activation of the CDB resource plan.

Figure 16-6. *Confirmation of the creation and the activation of the CDB Resource Plan*

Creation of the CDB Resource Plan Using SQL*Plus

We are recommending using Oracle Enterprise Manager for the general management of the Oracle Databases. But if for any reason, you can't use Oracle Enterprise Manager, here is the SQL statement needed to create the same CDB Resource Plan that we have created using OEM.

First you have to be connected with SQL*Plus to the CDB$ROOT container.

```
SQL> show con_name

CON_NAME
------------------------------
CDB$ROOT

SQL>
DECLARE
BEGIN
dbms_resource_manager.clear_pending_area();
dbms_resource_manager.create_pending_area();
dbms_resource_manager.create_cdb_plan( plan => 'RP_CDB001', comment => 'Resource Plan for
CDB001');
dbms_resource_manager.create_cdb_plan_directive(
    plan => 'RP_CDB001',
    pluggable_database => 'PDB001',
    comment => '',
    shares => 2,
    utilization_limit => 100,
  parallel_server_limit => 100 );
```

```
dbms_resource_manager.create_cdb_plan_directive(
    plan => 'RP_CDB001',
    pluggable_database => 'PDB002',
    comment => '',
    shares => 1,
    utilization_limit => 80,
  parallel_server_limit => 100 );
dbms_resource_manager.submit_pending_area();
END;
/
PL/SQL procedure successfully completed.

SQL> alter system set resource_manager_plan = 'RP_CDB001' scope=both;

System altered.
```

These SQL statements create and activate the CDB Resource Plan called "RP_CDB001".

■ **Note**   We recommend using Oracle Enterprise Manager to manage the Oracle Databases. But everything could be accomplished via SQL statements as well.

Creation of the PDB Resource Plan Using Oracle Enterprise Manager

Now that we have put in place the distribution of CPU resources among the PDBs, now we will see how to create the resource plan at the PDB level. The usage of Resource Manager inside the PDB is essentially unchanged compared to non-CDB databases and pre–Oracle 12c.

The PDB Resource Plan directive determines how CPU resources will be distributed among consumer groups. For our example, we will create two consumer groups.

- CRITICAL APPS, which will regroup very important applications like online ordering applications

- NON-CRITICAL APPS, which will regroup the other applications.

Here is a representation of what we will deploy to control the CPU resources at the PDB level. Figure 16-7 shows the distributions among consumer groups within PDB001.

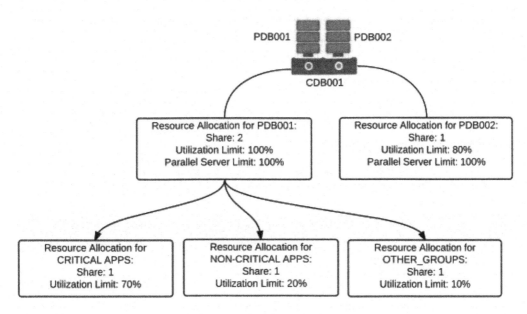

Figure 16-7. *Simple configuration of resource distribution among consumer groups*

Creation of the PDB Resource Plan Using Oracle Enterprise Manager

We will describe in this section how to deploy the PDB Plan directive using Oracle Enterprise Manager. From the Oracle PDB home page, select Administration menu and Resource Manager. Figure 16-8 shows that selection.

Figure 16-8. *Resource Manager selection from the Oracle Enterprise Manager Pluggable Database home page*

We are now in the "Getting Started with Database Resource Manager" main page. We have to perform three operations to complete the deployment of PDB Resource Plan directive.

- Creation of the consumer groups

- Definition of the consumer group mapping rules

- Creation of the plan directives

Creation of the Consumer Groups

Figure 16-9 shows the Resource Manager main page. Click "Consumer groups" for the creation of the groups. For our example, we will create two groups: CRITICAL APPS and NON-CRITICAL APPS.

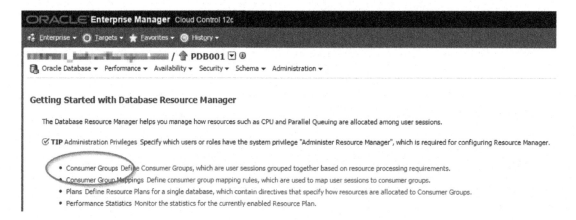

Figure 16-9. *Creation of the consumer groups*

You will have the list of the already created consumer groups. Click "Create" and you will have to provide the necessary information for the creation of the new consumer group. Figure 16-10 shows the creation page for consumer group.

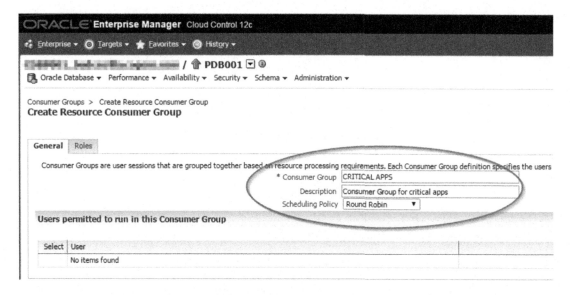

Figure 16-10. *Providing information for the consumer group creation*

We have to provide a Consumer Group and the Description only. Let's create two consumer groups like this.

Consumer Group	Description
CRITICAL_APPS	Consumer Group for critical applications
NON-CRITICAL_APPS	Consumer Group for noncritical applications

Creation of the Consumer Groups Using SQL*Plus

We are recommending using Oracle Enterprise Manager for the general management of the Oracle Databases. But if for any reason, you can't use Oracle Enterprise Manager, here is the SQL statement needed to create the same consumer groups that we have created using OEM.

First you have to be connected with SQL*Plus to the pluggable container and then you can execute these SQL statements.

```
SQL> show con_name


CON_NAME
------------------------------
PDB001

SQL>
DECLARE
BEGIN
dbms_resource_manager.clear_pending_area();
dbms_resource_manager.create_pending_area();
```

```
dbms_resource_manager.create_consumer_group(consumer_group => 'CRITICAL_APPS',comment =>
'Consumer Group for critical apps' , cpu_mth => 'ROUND-ROBIN');
dbms_resource_manager.submit_pending_area();
END;


BEGIN
dbms_resource_manager.clear_pending_area();
dbms_resource_manager.create_pending_area();
dbms_resource_manager.create_consumer_group(consumer_group => 'NON-CRITICAL_APPS',comment =>
'Consumer Group for non-critical apps' , cpu_mth => 'ROUND-ROBIN');
dbms_resource_manager.submit_pending_area();
END;
```

Define Consumer Group Mapping Rules

Now that we have two consumer groups, we have to create the mapping rules that will be used to regroup sessions together and associate them to a consumer group. As I was saying earlier in the chapter, I like to use different Oracle services to distinguish the sessions coming to the database.

Let's create two Oracle services called SRV_CRITICAL_APPS and SRV_NON-CRITICAL_APPS using SQL*Plus

```
begin
dbms_service.create_service('SRV_CRITICAL_APPS','SRV_CRITICAL_APPS');
end;
/
begin
dbms_service.start_service('SRV_CRITICAL_APPS');
end;
/

begin
dbms_service.create_service('SRV_NON-CRITICAL_APPS','SRV_NON-CRITICAL_APPS');
end;
/
begin
dbms_service.start_service('SRV_NON-CRITICAL_APPS');
end;
/
```

■ **Note**   The newly created services will be referenced in the tnsnames.ora file or connection strings using the SERVICE_NAME parameter.

As one might imagine, the service SRV_CRITICAL_APPS will be serving the critical applications and SRV_NON-CRITICAL_APPS, the noncritical applications.

From the Resource Manager main page, select "Consumer Group Mappings" shown in Figure 16-11.

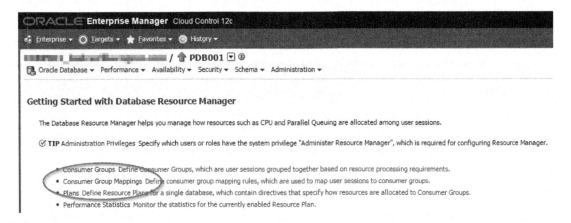

Figure 16-11. *Creation of the mapping rules*

We are now on the Consumer Group Mappings main page. Select the "Service" type (the priority number might be different) and click "Add Rule for Selected Type." Figure 16-12 shows that selection.

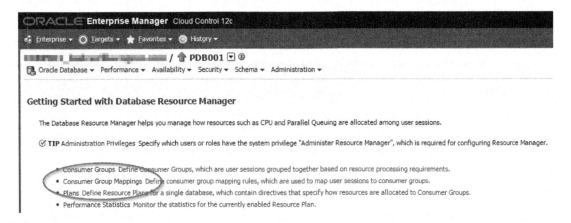

Consumer Group Mappings

General	Priorities

Create rules to enable the resource manager to automatically assign sessions to consumer groups

Attribute All ▼

Add Rule for Selected Type

Select	Priority ▲	Attribute	Value
⦿	1	Service	No Mappings Specified
○	2	Service Module and Action	No Mappings Specified

Figure 16-12. *Selection of attribute "Service"*

We have to specify which Oracle Service will be associated to the consumer group we have previously created. Figure 16-13 shows how to associate the consumer group with the service; then click "Ok."

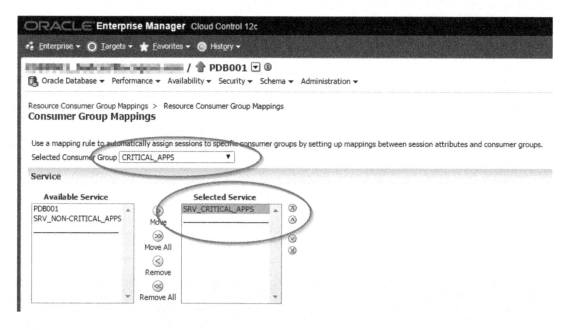

Figure 16-13. *Selection of attribute "Service"*

You should now see the association between the Oracle Service "SRV_CRITICAL_APPS" and the consumer group "CRITICAL_APPS" as we can see in Figure 16-14.

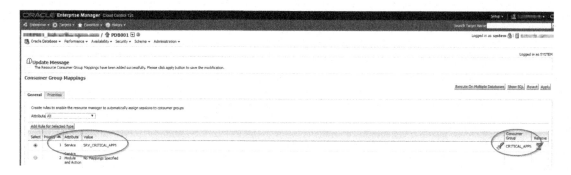

Figure 16-14. *Association between the Oracle Service and the consumer group*

Now we know that the sessions connecting to the database using the database service "SRV_CRITICAL_APPS" will be using the consumer group "CRITICAL_APPS".

Creation of the Consumer Group Mapping Rules Using SQL*Plus

We are recommending using Oracle Enterprise Manager for the general management of the Oracle Databases. But if for any reason, you can't use Oracle Enterprise Manager, here is the SQL statement needed to create the same consumer group mapping rules that we have created using OEM.

First you have to be connected with SQL*Plus to the pluggable container and then you can execute these SQL statements.

```
SQL> show con_name

CON_NAME
------------------------------
PDB001

SQL>
DECLARE
BEGIN
dbms_resource_manager.clear_pending_area();
dbms_resource_manager.create_pending_area();
dbms_resource_manager.set_consumer_group_mapping(
    dbms_resource_manager.service_name,
    'SRV_CRITICAL_APPS',
    'CRITICAL_APPS'
);
dbms_resource_manager.submit_pending_area();
END;
```

Creation of the Resource Plan Directive

The next step is to create a Resource Plan Directive that tells us the percentage of CPU resources associated to consumer groups. I will also include the notion of runaway query and automatic consumer group switching in the definition of the plan directive. Runaway query and automatic consumer group switching will allow the sessions to change the consumer group if they reach specific thresholds. This feature will help us controlling high-consuming queries on the system by switching them on consumer group with limited resources. The new plan directive will use the consumer group switching from CRITICAL_APPS to NON-CRITICAL_APPS to OTHER_GROUPS and will finish by using CANCEL_SQL if required, based on the "CPU Time Limit" argument.

Figure 16-15 shows the Resource Manager main page. Click "Plans" for the creation of the resource plan directives.

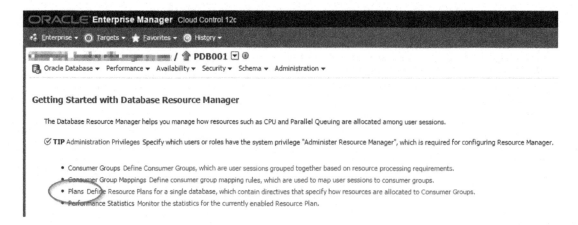

Figure 16-15. *Creation of the Resource Plan Directives*

We are now seeing the consumer plan directives already created. The next step is to create a new plan directive called "PLAN_APEX_APPS"; click "Create." Figure 16-16 shows the information that we will have to provide.

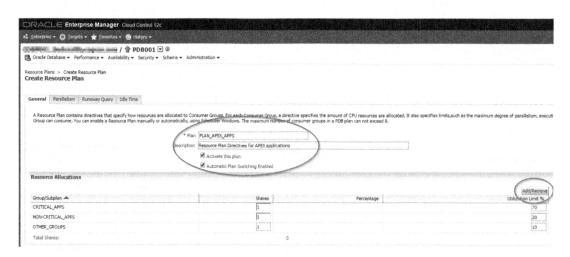

Figure 16-16. *Providing the information for the plan directive creation*

Provide the name of the plan as well as the description. Click the "Add/Remove" button and select the two consumer groups you want the new plan directive to work with. Here is a table with the desired values:

Consumer Group	Share	Utilization Limit %
CRITICAL_APPS	1	70
NON-CRITICAL_ APPS	1	20
OTHER_GROUPS	1	10

We are now ready to provide the information for the automatic consumer group switching. Click the tab "Runaway Query." We will force the session to switch from a consumer group to another by using the resource limit "CPU Time Limit(Sec)". The following table gives the necessary information:

Consumer Group	CPU Time Limit (Sec) Limit	Switch to consumer group
CRITICAL_APPS	5	NON-CRITICAL_APPS
NON-CRITICAL_APPS	10	OTHER_GROUPS
OTHER_GROUPS	15	CANCEL_SQL

Figure 16-17 shows that configuration in the tab "Runaway Query."

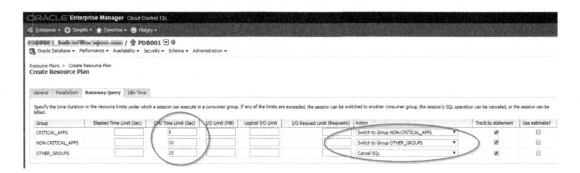

Figure 16-17. *Providing information for Runaway Query*

Click "Ok." The plan is now created and activated as we can see in Figure 16-18.

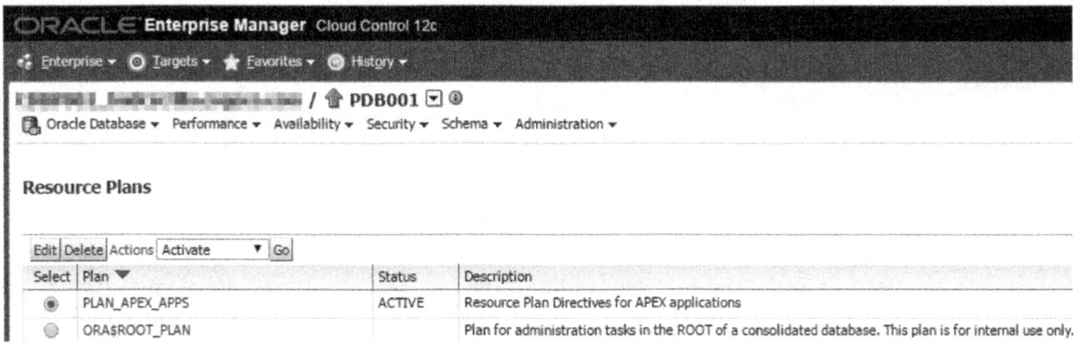

Figure 16-18. *The new plan is active*

Creation of the PDB Resource Plan Using SQL*Plus

We are recommending using Oracle Enterprise Manager for the general management of the Oracle Databases. But if for any reason you can't use Oracle Enterprise Manager, here is the SQL statement needed to create the same PDB Resource Plan that we have created using OEM.

First you have to be connected with SQL*Plus to the pluggable container and then you can execute these SQL statements.

```
SQL> show con_name

CON_NAME
------------------------------
PDB001

SQL>
DECLARE
BEGIN
dbms_resource_manager.clear_pending_area();
dbms_resource_manager.create_pending_area();
dbms_resource_manager.create_plan( plan => 'PLAN_APEX_APPS', comment => 'Resource Plan
Directives for APEX applications',max_iops => NULL,max_mbps => NULL );
dbms_resource_manager.create_plan_directive(
    plan => 'PLAN_APEX_APPS',
    group_or_subplan => 'CRITICAL_APPS',
    comment => '',
    switch_elapsed_time => NULL,
    max_utilization_limit => 70,
    mgmt_p1 => 1, mgmt_p2 => NULL, mgmt_p3 => NULL, mgmt_p4 => NULL,
    mgmt_p5 => NULL, mgmt_p6 => NULL, mgmt_p7 => NULL, mgmt_p8 => NULL ,
    parallel_degree_limit_p1 => NULL ,
    parallel_target_percentage => NULL ,
    parallel_queue_timeout => NULL ,
    parallel_stmt_critical => 'false' ,
    switch_io_logical => NULL ,
    switch_io_reqs => NULL ,
    switch_io_megabytes => NULL ,
    active_sess_pool_p1 => NULL,
    queueing_p1 => NULL,
    switch_group => 'NON-CRITICAL_APPS',
    switch_time => 5,
    switch_estimate => case 'false' when 'false' then false when 'true' then true else false
end,
    undo_pool => NULL ,
    max_idle_time => NULL,
    max_idle_blocker_time => NULL,
    switch_for_call => case 'true' when 'false' then false when 'true' then true else false
end

);
```

```
dbms_resource_manager.create_plan_directive(
    plan => 'PLAN_APEX_APPS',
    group_or_subplan => 'NON-CRITICAL_APPS',
    comment => '',
    switch_elapsed_time => NULL,
    max_utilization_limit => 20,
    mgmt_p1 => 1, mgmt_p2 => NULL, mgmt_p3 => NULL, mgmt_p4 => NULL,
    mgmt_p5 => NULL, mgmt_p6 => NULL, mgmt_p7 => NULL, mgmt_p8 => NULL ,
    parallel_degree_limit_p1 => NULL ,
    parallel_target_percentage => NULL ,
    parallel_queue_timeout => NULL ,
    parallel_stmt_critical => 'false' ,
    switch_io_logical => NULL ,
    switch_io_reqs => NULL ,
    switch_io_megabytes => NULL ,
    active_sess_pool_p1 => NULL,
    queueing_p1 => NULL,
    switch_group => 'OTHER_GROUPS',
    switch_time => 10,
    switch_estimate => case 'false' when 'false' then false when 'true' then true else false
end,
    undo_pool => NULL ,
    max_idle_time => NULL,
    max_idle_blocker_time => NULL,
    switch_for_call => case 'true' when 'false' then false when 'true' then true else false
end

);
dbms_resource_manager.create_plan_directive(
    plan => 'PLAN_APEX_APPS',
    group_or_subplan => 'OTHER_GROUPS',
    comment => '',
    switch_elapsed_time => NULL,
    max_utilization_limit => 10,
    mgmt_p1 => 1, mgmt_p2 => NULL, mgmt_p3 => NULL, mgmt_p4 => NULL,
    mgmt_p5 => NULL, mgmt_p6 => NULL, mgmt_p7 => NULL, mgmt_p8 => NULL ,
    parallel_degree_limit_p1 => NULL ,
    parallel_target_percentage => NULL ,
    parallel_queue_timeout => NULL ,
    parallel_stmt_critical => 'false' ,
    switch_io_logical => NULL ,
    switch_io_reqs => NULL ,
    switch_io_megabytes => NULL ,
    active_sess_pool_p1 => NULL,
    queueing_p1 => NULL,
    switch_group => 'CANCEL_SQL',
    switch_time => 15,
    switch_estimate => case 'false' when 'false' then false when 'true' then true else false
end,
```

```
    undo_pool => NULL ,
    max_idle_time => NULL,
    max_idle_blocker_time => NULL,
    switch_for_call => case 'true' when 'false' then false when 'true' then true else false
end

);
dbms_resource_manager.submit_pending_area();
END;
/

PL/SQL procedure successfully completed.

SQL> alter system set resource_manager_plan='PLAN_APEX_APPS' scope=both;

System altered.
```

■ **Note**   We recommend using Oracle Enterprise Manager to manage the Oracle Databases. But everything can be accomplished by SQL statement as well.

Configuring APEX Workspace to Use Resource Manager

There is a new feature with Oracle Application Express 5.0 where you can associate a Resource Manager consumer group to an APEX workspace. You are guaranteed that all of the applications within this workspace will be using the consumer group associated. So we can imagine having workspaces for different criticality levels for various application(s).

Workspace Name	Consumer Group	Description
WRK_HIGH_CRITICAL_APPS	CRITICAL_APPS	Applications that need as many resources as possible
WRK_MEDIUM_CRITICAL_APPS	MEDIUM_APPS	Applications that are not critical, but need a good amount of resources
WRK_LOW_CRITICAL_APPS	LOW_APPS	Noncritical applications

■ **Note**   A strategy for consumer group switching should always be considered when you are using Resource Manager.

Before associating the consumer group to the APEX workspace, we have to grant the privilege to switch to this consumer group. Here is an example of a grant for the three consumer groups mentioned in the example.

First you have to be connected with SQL*Plus to the pluggable container and then you can execute these SQL statements.

```
SQL> show con_name

CON_NAME
------------------------------
PDB001

SQL> exec DBMS_RESOURCE_MANAGER_PRIVS.GRANT_SWITCH_CONSUMER_GROUP('PUBLIC','CRITICAL_
APPS',false);
SQL> exec DBMS_RESOURCE_MANAGER_PRIVS.GRANT_SWITCH_CONSUMER_GROUP('PUBLIC','MEDIUM_
APPS',false);
SQL> exec DBMS_RESOURCE_MANAGER_PRIVS.GRANT_SWITCH_CONSUMER_GROUP('PUBLIC','LOW_
APPS',false);
```

■ **Note** Before associating a consumer group to a workspace, you have to grant the switch privilege.

Now we will see how to associate a consumer group to an APEX workspace. First login to the Application Express INTERNAL workspace. From the main menu, click "Manage Workspaces." Figure 16-19 shows that page.

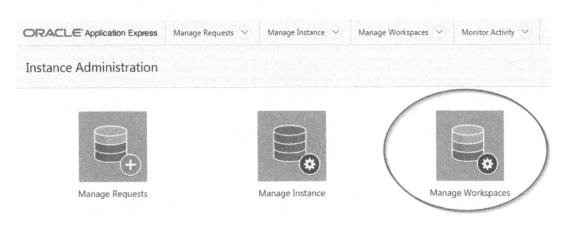

Figure 16-19. *Select Manage Workspaces*

Under "Workspace Reports," click "Existing Workspaces." We will have the list of the existing workspaces. Click the workspace to which you want to modify by associating a consumer group. Figure 16-20 shows how to select the workspace.

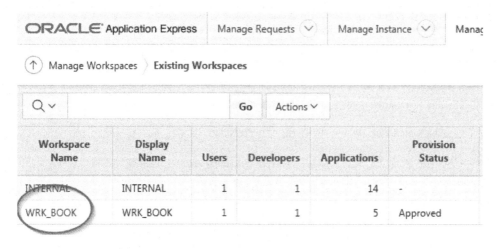

Figure 16-20. *Selecting the workspace to be modified*

We are at the page where we can associate the consumer group. Click "Workspace Isolation" and you will see the drop-down list called "Resource Consumer Group." Select the consumer group that you would like to associate to this workspace. Figure 16-21 shows the required selection.

Figure 16-21. *How to select the required consumer group*

Starting now, every application that runs from this workspace will run in the consumer group "CRITICAL_APPS".

If you get that error saying "Resource Manager consumer group has not been granted..." it means that you forget to grant the switch privilege. Figure 16-22 shows that error.

Resource Manager consumer group NON-CRITICAL_APPS has not been granted to APEX_050000

APEX.AUTHENTICATION.RM_INFO_TO_GRANT

Return to application.

Figure 16-22. *You didn't grant the proper privilege for the consumer group switching*

Resource Manager Demonstrations

The objective of this section is to demonstrate the impact and importance of Resource Manager to control the resource utilizations. We will focus on two different features of Resource Manager;

- CPU utilization limits at the CDB level

- Runaway and consumer group switching at the PDB level

I will use two different applications to perform the demonstration. The first application is a free GUI load generator tool called Swingbeach. This free stress-test tool is designed to generate load on Oracle database. The second application I will use is a simple APEX application I have built especially to show the consumer group switching.

CPU Utilization Limits at the CDB Level

The load generator tool Swingbeach will be connecting to the database using the service SRV_CRITICAL_APPS. Figure 16-23 shows the connection information.

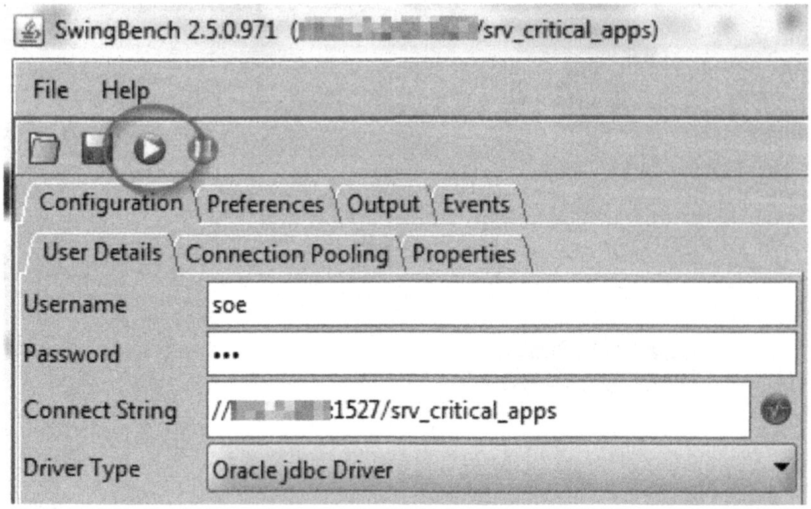

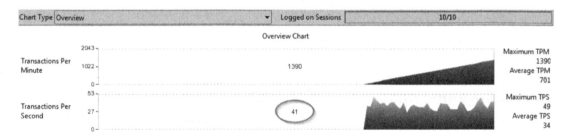

Figure 16-23. *Connection information using service*

I have configured Swingbeach to generate a load of 10 users with a mix of update, select, insert, and delete operations. To start the load generation, click the play symbol. That will start the generation of the activity with the database. Figure 16-24 shows the activity happening on the database. The average number of transactions per second (TPS) is 41.

Figure 16-24. *Transactions occurring on the database; average TPS at 41*

The objective of this demonstration is to see the impact of the CPU Utilization Limit% at the CDB level on the overall activity on the system. Let's modify the CPU Utilization Limit% using Oracle Enterprise Manager. We will change that value to 0. In theory, the activity on the system should stop. Figure 16-25 shows the modification at the CDB resource plan level.

Edit CDB Resource Plan: RP_CDB001

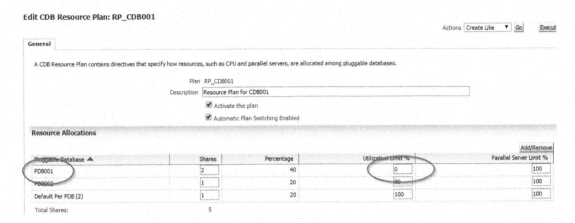

Actions [Create Like ▼] [Go]   Execute

Pluggable Database ▲	Shares	Percentage	Utilization Limit %	Parallel Server Limit %
PDB001	2	40	0	100
PDB002	1	20	80	100
Default Per PDB (2)	1	20	100	100
Total Shares:	5			

Figure 16-25. *Change the value of CPU Utilization Limit% to 0*

The CDB resource plan is not giving any CPU resources to PDB001. It means that no activity is allowed in that database. After a few seconds, I will reallocate the CPU resources. Figure 16-26 shows the direct impact on the application.

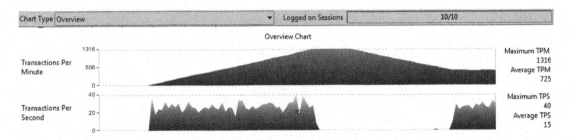

Figure 16-26. *CPU attribution changes and the impact on the application*

By allocation of 0% of CPU resource to PDB001, all of the Oracle processes were waiting on an internal run queue under wait event "resmgr:cpu quantum". The system was waiting to get CPU cycles, but the CDB Resource Plan was not giving any. When I reallocate CPU resources to PDB001, Oracle was getting CPU cycles and the system went back to normal.

Runaway and Consumer Group Switching at the PDB Level

To demonstrate the consumer group switching, we will use an APEX application that does a long cartesian join SQL statement. The objective is to show the consumer group switching that is triggered using the CPU Time Limit. Using SQLDeveloper I will show the sessions starting using the consumer group CRITICAL_APPS and automatically switching to the consumer group NON-CRITICAL_APPS after 5 seconds. Ten seconds after, the same session will be running using the consumer group OTHER_GROUPS and will be canceled by Oracle after 15 seconds of being in the consumer group. Here is the table summarizing that configuration.

Consumer Group	CPU Time Limit (Sec) Limit	Switch to consumer group
CRITICAL_APPS	5	NON-CRITICAL_APPS
NON-CRITICAL_APPS	10	OTHER_GROUPS
OTHER_GROUPS	15	CANCEL_SQL

Let's start the process using the APEX application. Figure 16-27 shows that APEX application and the launch of the process.

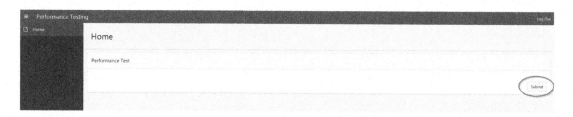

***Figure 16-27.** Launching the process*

Connected to the PDB, I will use this SQL statement to follow the progression of the session. The objective is to validate the automatic consumer group switching. Here is the SQL statement:

```
SELECT se.sid sess_id, ses.username, co.name consumer_group, ses.module, metric.cpu_
utilization_limit,se.state
 FROM v$rsrc_session_info se, v$rsrc_consumer_group co, v$session ses, v$rsrcmgrmetric
metric
 WHERE se.current_consumer_group_id = co.id
   AND se.sid = ses.sid
   AND se.current_consumer_group_id = metric.consumer_group_id
   AND module like 'SCH_BOOK%';
```

Figure 16-28 shows the status of the session when we just launched the process.

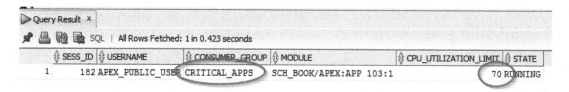

***Figure 16-28.** Status of the session*

We can confirm that the session is using the CRITICAL_APPS consumer group as we have associated this consumer group to the workspace where this application is running from. We can also confirm the CPU utilization limit (70%) that was set for this consumer group.

Now, let's see a new status of the session. Figure 16-29 shows a new status.

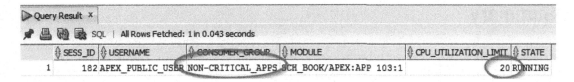

Figure 16-29. *Status of the session*

We can confirm now that the session switched consumer group and now it is running using NON-CRITICAL_APPS with the appropriate CPU utilization limit of 20%.

Let see another status of the session. Figure 16-30 shows the new status.

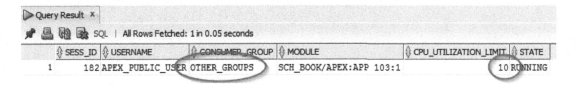

Figure 16-30. *Status of the session*

We can confirm now the session running using OTHER_GROUPS, using the appropriate CPU utilization limit of 10%.

Then, we get the following message in the APEX application: "ORA-00040: active time limit exceeded - call aborted". Figure 16-31 shows the message from the application.

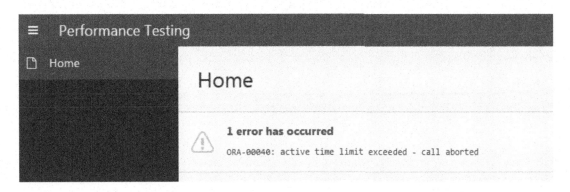

Figure 16-31. *Message from the application*

The message is coming from the last consumer group switching where it says that the SQL would be canceled. That shows the automatic consumer group switching feature of the Resource Manager.

Summary

In this chapter, we have seen how Resource Manager could help us to manage resource availability. In the multitenant context, we can create rules that control the amount of resources (CPU and Parallel Servers) allocated among the different PDBs.

We have seen how to create rules at the CDB as well as at the PDB level using either Oracle Enterprise Manager or SQL*Plus. We have demonstrated, using Swingbeach, how Resource Manager (from a CDB point of view) can be used to allocate resources among the PDBs. We have also demonstrated using a simple APEX application how the automatic consumer group switching works. We can see now how Resource Manager is a great tool to manage the system resources and to avoid any situations where the system becomes unresponsive.